KU-548-595

PERFECT®

Complete
Italian Grammar

WITHDRAWN

BOLTON COLLEGE

042978

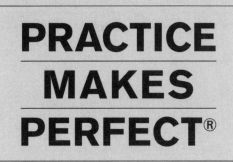

PRACTICE MAKES PERFECT®

Complete Italian Grammar

PREMIUM SECOND EDITION

Marcel Danesi, PhD

New York Chicago San Francisco Athens London Madrid
Mexico City Milan New Delhi Singapore Sydney Toronto

Copyright © 2016 by McGraw-Hill Education, Inc. All rights reserved. Printed in the United States of America. Except as permitted under the United States Copyright Act of 1976, no part of this publication may be reproduced or distributed in any form or by any means, or stored in a database or retrieval system, without the prior written permission of the publisher.

1 2 3 4 5 6 7 8 9 10   RHR/RHR   1 2 1 0 9 8 7 6

ISBN   978-1-259-58772-6
MHID   1-259-58772-X

e-ISBN   978-1-259-58773-3
e-MHID   1-259-58773-8

Interior design by Village Bookworks, Inc.

McGraw-Hill Education products are available at special quantity discounts to use as premiums and sales promotions or for use in corporate training programs. To contact a representative, please visit the Contact Us pages at www.mhprofessional.com.

McGraw-Hill Education Language Lab App

Audio recordings of the Answer Key, flash cards, and a digital glossary are all available to support your study of this book. Go to www.mhlanguagelab.com to access the online version of this application, or to locate links to the mobile app for iOS and Android devices. More details about the features of the app are available on the inside front cover.

Other titles by Marcel Danesi
Practice Makes Perfect: Italian Conversation
Italian Demystified, 2nd edition

BOLTON COLLEGE LIBRARY

Acc. No.	042978
Class No.	458·2421 DAN
Sup.	DAWSON £14·99
Date	10/16
Site	DR SF LRC

Contents

Preface

Practice Makes Perfect: Complete Italian Grammar focuses on topics of importance to intermediate- to advanced-level learners. By concentrating on areas of grammar for making more complex, meaningful sentences and conversations, the book is designed to improve the ability to communicate effectively in Italian at higher levels.

Practice Makes Perfect is, thus, geared toward those who have already learned the basics of grammar, focusing on topics that consistently need to be practiced in an in-depth manner by non-beginning learners. The book covers topics that often prove difficult for English speakers when they learn Italian, such as the correct use of object pronouns. Numerous practical exercises give students the opportunity to test what they have learned.

There are twenty chapters covering everything from the formation and use of nouns to the structure of sentences and clauses. Each chapter is designed to deal with a topic of grammar as completely as possible.

Each chapter presents the main points related to a topic. Each point is followed by an **Esercizio**. Along the way, information boxes provide further detail on some topics, offer tips, or introduce related vocabulary. At the back of the book, there are Italian-English and English-Italian glossaries (containing all the words and expressions used in the book), irregular verb charts, and the answers to all the exercises.

This handbook is designed as a reference grammar for intermediate or advanced learners with a large practice component—there are over 300 distinct exercise questions consisting of various types and parts. As they say, practice makes perfect. It can also be used as a textbook in intermediate courses of Italian, since it contains the same kinds of information and exercises that are normally found in such courses and in more elaborate formal textbooks. The difference is that this book takes nothing for granted. As mentioned, it contains many sidebars throughout to clarify, supplement, or complement a topic. This feature will allow you to stay within the confines of this single book. You will not need to resort to other materials. Although it is review grammar, very little has been taken for granted!

This Premium Second Edition presents several new features. At the end of each chapter is a **Grammar in culture** section that links a grammar topic to culture or usage, with a related exercise. This section underscores the relevance of grammar to the study of culture.

In addition, extensive support materials are available in the McGraw-Hill Education Language Lab app:

- ◆ Flash cards comprising all vocabulary used in this book

- ◆ An auto-fill glossary (a digital version of the glossaries at the back of this book)

- ◆ Audio recordings of the Answer key for exercises with complete-sentence answers in Italian. With the mobile version of this app, you can record your own answers, then replay them alongside the native-speaker recordings.

Buon divertimento!

Acknowledgments

I wish to express my sincere gratitude to Garret Lemoi of McGraw-Hill for his superb editing and encouragement, not to mention his wonderful advice. I also thank Grace Freedson for her support and help. I am truly grateful to her.

Complete
Italian Grammar

Nouns and titles

Simple Italian sentences, like English sentences, are composed of a subject, a verb, and an object. The subject consists of a noun or noun phrase. It is what the sentence is about and around which the rest of the sentence revolves. The subject is, more generally, the performer of some action. Many types of objects also consist of a noun (or noun phrase). In this case the noun is the person, concept, thing, etc., toward which the action of the verb is directed or to which a preposition expresses some relation. This unit and the next one describe nouns.

Mio nipote studia la matematica.	*My grandson studies math.* (subject noun phrase)
L'**amore** esiste dappertutto.	*Love exists everywhere.* (subject noun)
Ieri sera io ho chiamato **mia nipote.**	*Last night I called my granddaughter.* (object noun phrase)
Lui è un **amico caro**.	*He's a dear friend.* (object noun phrase)
Lei vive **in periferia**.	*She lives in the suburbs.* (object noun phrase)
Abbiamo comprato un **televisore plasma**.	*We bought a plasma TV.* (object noun phrase)

Nouns can be regular or irregular. Regular ones have predictable endings in the singular and plural. Nouns are also classified as either common or proper. The former refer to persons, objects, places, concepts, and all the other things that make up the world. Proper nouns are the actual names and surnames given to people, geographical places and formations, brands, and the like.

Common nouns

A common noun can generally be recognized by its vowel ending, which indicates if it is masculine or feminine. This is called grammatical gender. Gender is important because it determines the form of both the articles and adjectives that accompany nouns in sentences and phrases. Generally, nouns ending in -**o** are masculine. They are made plural by changing the -**o** to -**i**.

MASCULINE SINGULAR		MASCULINE PLURAL	
figlio	son	**figli**	sons
gatto	cat	**gatti**	cats
libro	book	**libri**	books
ragazzo	boy	**ragazzi**	boys
zio	uncle	**zii**	uncles

Nouns ending in -**a** are generally feminine. They are made plural by changing the -**a** to -**e**.

FEMININE SINGULAR		FEMININE PLURAL	
casa	house	**case**	houses
figlia	daughter	**figlie**	daughters
penna	pen	**penne**	pens
ragazza	girl	**ragazze**	girls
zia	aunt	**zie**	aunts

Lastly, nouns ending in -**e** are either masculine or feminine. This is not an option; gender is fixed by the grammar of Italian. To find out if a noun ending in -**e** is masculine or feminine you will have to consult a dictionary, or else you will have to infer it by observing the form (article, adjective, etc.) that accompanies it. Such nouns are made plural by changing the -**e** to -**i**, no matter what their gender is.

MASCULINE SINGULAR		MASCULINE PLURAL	
(il) cane	(the) dog	**(i) cani**	(the) dogs
(il) cellulare	(the) cell phone	**(i) cellulari**	(the) cell phones
(il) padre	(the) father	**(i) padri**	(the) fathers
(il) portatile	(the) laptop	**(i) portatili**	(the) laptops

FEMININE SINGULAR		FEMININE PLURAL	
(la) madre	(the) mother	**(le) madri**	(the) mothers
(la) nazione	(the) nation	**(le) nazioni**	(the) nations
(la) notte	(the) night	**(le) notti**	(the) nights
(la) parete	(the) wall (partition)	**(le) pareti**	(the) walls (partitions)

Here's a tip. Most nouns ending in -**ione**, especially in -**zione** and -**sione,** are feminine.

la stazione	the (train) station
la regione	the region
la riunione	the meeting

Useful common nouns

anno	*year*	**gonna**	*skirt*
giorno	*day*	**macchina**	*car*
vestito	*dress, suit*		
casa	*house*	**chiave** *(f.)*	*key*
cosa	*thing*	**cognome** *(m.)*	*surname, family name*
cravatta	*necktie*	**giornale** *(m.)*	*newspaper*
donna	*woman*	**nome** *(m.)*	*name*

(m. = masculine, f. = feminine)

Common nouns are not capitalized unless they occur at the beginning of a sentence. Unlike English, nouns referring to languages, speakers of a language, or inhabitants of an area are not normally capitalized.

L'italiano è una bellissima lingua.	*Italian is a very beautiful language.*
Lui è italiano, ma lei non è italiana.	*He is Italian, but she is not Italian.*
Lui invece è americano, e anche lei è americana.	*He, instead, is American, and she, too, is American.*
Ci sono tanti siciliani in questo posto.	*There are a lot of Sicilians in this place.*

Note: The noun **gente** (*people*) is singular in Italian.

La gente parla troppo.	*People talk too much.*
Lui conosce tanta gente.	*He knows a lot of people.*

Note: The plural of **l'uomo** (*the man*) is irregular; it is **gli uomini** (*the men*).

Lui è un bravo uomo.	*He is a good man.*
Chi sono quegli uomini?	*Who are those men?*

Also, note that some nouns ending in **-ione** are masculine. Those ending in **-one** are all masculine.

il copione	*the script*
il cordone	*the rope*
il mattone	*the brick*

ESERCIZIO
1·1

A. *Provide the singular or plural form of each noun, as required.*

SINGULAR	PLURAL
1. zio	_____
2. _____	ragazzi
3. libro	_____
4. _____	gatti
5. figlio	_____

6. _____ zie

7. ragazza _____

8. _____ penne

9. figlia _____

10. _____ case

11. cane _____

12. _____ cellulari

13. padre _____

14. _____ pareti

15. madre _____

16. _____ nazioni

17. notte _____

18. _____ cose

19. casa _____

20. _____ anni

21. giorno _____

22. _____ vestiti

23. cravatta _____

24. _____ donne

25. gonna _____

26. _____ macchine

27. chiave _____

28. _____ cognomi

29. giornale _____

30. _____ nomi

31. copione _____

32. _____ riunioni

33. cordone _____

34. _____ mattoni

B. *Provide the missing endings to the common nouns in the following sentences.*

1. A suo nipot_____ piace la matematic_____.

2. L'amor_____ conquista *(conquers)* tutto.

3. Quella donn_____ ha chiamato mia nipot_____.

4. Marco è un caro amic_____.

5. La mia amic_____ vive in periferi_____.

6. I miei amic_____ hanno comprato un televisor_____ plasma.

7. L'italian_____ è una lingu_____ facile.

8. Lui è italian_____, ma lei è american_____.

9. Dov'è quella region_____?

10. A che ora c'è la riunion_____?

C. *There is an error in each sentence. Spot it and rewrite the sentence to correct it. You might have to make adjustments to the other words as well.*

1. Quei due uomi sono italiani.

   _____

2. La gente parlano troppo.

   _____

3. Sara è Siciliana.

   _____

4. Alessandro parla Francese.

   _____

Gender patterns

Every noun in Italian is marked for gender—that is to say, it is classified as either masculine or feminine. In the case of nouns referring to people (or animals), the grammatical gender of the noun usually matches the biological sex of the person (or animal).

   With few exceptions, nouns that refer to males (people or animals) are masculine, and those that refer to females (people or animals) are feminine.

MASCULINE (MALES)		FEMININE (FEMALES)	
l'americano	*the male American*	**l'americana**	*the female American*
l'amico	*the male friend*	**l'amica**	*the female friend*
l'italiano	*the male Italian*	**l'italiana**	*the female Italian*
il gatto	*the male cat*	**la gatta**	*the female cat*

There are exceptions. For example, **il soprano** (*soprano*) is a masculine noun but it refers to a female person and **la guardia** (*guard*) is a feminine noun but can refer to either a male or female person.

Nouns ending in -a and referring to both males and females

la persona	*person (male or female)*
la spia	*spy (male or female)*
la stella	*star (male or female)*

Some nouns ending in **-e** refer to males or females. Note that with these nouns any other forms (articles, adjectives, etc.) that accompany the nouns must indicate the correct grammatical gender.

MASCULINE (MALES)		FEMININE (FEMALES)	
il cantante	*the male singer*	**la cantante**	*the female singer*
il francese	*the French man*	**la francese**	*the French woman*
il nipote	*the grandson; nephew*	**la nipote**	*the granddaughter; niece*
il padre	*the father*	**la madre**	*the mother*
l'inglese	*the English man*	**l'inglese**	*the English woman*

Some masculine nouns ending in **-e** correspond to feminine nouns ending in **-a**.

MASCULINE (MALES)		FEMININE (FEMALES)	
il cameriere	*the waiter*	**la cameriera**	*the waitress*
il signore	*the gentleman*	**la signora**	*the lady*
l'infermiere	*the male nurse*	**l'infermiera**	*the female nurse*

Note: The plural ending **-i** is used when the noun refers to both male *and* female beings taken together as a group, whereas the plural ending **-e** refers only to a group of females.

SINGULAR		PLURAL	
l'italiano	*the (male) Italian*	**gli italiani**	*the Italians (males only or males and females together)*
l'italiana	*the (female) Italian*	**le italiane**	*the Italians (females only)*
l'americano	*the (male) American*	**gli americani**	*the Americans (males only or males and females together)*
l'americana	*the (female) American*	**le americane**	*the Americans (females only)*

ESERCIZIO

1·2

A. *Provide the corresponding nouns referring to males and females. The first one is done for you.*

	MALE	FEMALE
1. American	*americano*	*americana*
2. Italian		
3. friend		
4. soprano		
5. guard		
6. star		
7. spy		
8. person		
9. English		
10. French		
11. singer		
12. nurse		

B. *How do you say the following in Italian?*

1. grandson or nephew   il _____

2. Americans (in general)   gli _____

3. female Italians   le _____

4. granddaughter or niece   la _____

5. waiters (in general)   i _____

6. waitresses   le _____

7. gentleman   il _____

8. lady   la _____

Spelling adjustments in the plural

The consonants in the noun endings **-co**, **-go**, **-ca**, and **-ga** represent hard sounds. There are two possibilities for changing the **-co** and **-go** endings to the plural.

If the hard sounds are to be retained, the masculine plural endings are spelled respectively **-chi** and **-ghi**. To remember that **ch** and **gh** represent hard sounds in Italian, think of English words that use them in the same way: *chemistry, ache, school, charisma, ghost.*

Nouns and titles   **7**

SINGULAR		PLURAL	
gioco	*game*	**giochi**	*games*
tedesco	*German*	**tedeschi**	*Germans*
lago	*lake*	**laghi**	*lakes*
luogo	*place*	**luoghi**	*places*

If the corresponding soft sounds are required instead, the masculine plural endings are spelled respectively **-ci** and **-gi**.

SINGULAR		PLURAL	
amico	*friend*	**amici**	*friends*
greco	*Greek*	**greci**	*Greeks*
biologo	*biologist*	**biologi**	*biologists*
antropologo	*anthropologist*	**antropologi**	*anthropologists*

So, when do you use one or the other plural form? In general, if **-co** is preceded by **e** or **i** (as in **amico** and **greco**), the noun is pluralized to **-ci** (**amici**, **greci**). Otherwise the hard sound is retained (**-chi**). In the case of **-go**, the tendency is to retain the hard sound. However, when the noun ends in the suffix **-logo** and refers to a profession, career, or activity, then the appropriate plural suffix is **-logi**.

il teologo	*the theologian*	**i teologi**	*the theologians*

These rules should be considered "rules of thumb" rather than strict grammatical rules (covering a large number of cases, however).

Exceptions to the rules of thumb

il porco	*the pig*	**i porci**	*the pigs*
il fico	*the fig*	**i fichi**	*the figs*
il sindaco	*the mayor*	**i sindaci**	*the mayors*
il monaco	*the monk*	**i monaci**	*the monks*

The endings **-ca** and **-ga** are always changed to **-che** and **-ghe**, which represent hard sounds.

SINGULAR		PLURAL	
banca	*bank*	**banche**	*banks*
greca	*female Greek*	**greche**	*female Greeks*
riga	*straight ruler*	**righe**	*straight rulers*

The consonants in the endings **-cio** and **-gio** represent soft sounds. Note that the **i** is not pronounced. It is put there simply to indicate that the consonants are to be pronounced softly. There is only one way to change such nouns to the plural, which is to retain the soft sounds with the endings: **-ci** and **-gi**.

SINGULAR		PLURAL	
bacio	*kiss*	**baci**	*kisses*
orologio	*watch*	**orologi**	*watches*

If the **i** in **-io** is stressed, it is retained in the plural, otherwise it is not retained. To be sure if it is stressed or not, consult a dictionary.

SINGULAR		PLURAL	
zio (stressed)	uncle	**zii**	uncles
occhio (unstressed)	eye	**occhi**	eyes

There are two possibilities for changing nouns ending in **-cia** and **-gia** to the plural. If the **i** in the ending is stressed, it is pronounced in the plural and, thus, retained in spelling.

SINGULAR		PLURAL	
farmacia	pharmacy	**farmacie**	pharmacies
bugia	lie	**bugie**	lies

If the **i** indicates that the preceding consonant represents a soft sound in the singular but is not stressed in the pronunciation, it is not retained in the plural spelling.

SINGULAR		PLURAL	
valigia	suitcase	**valige**	suitcases
faccia	face	**facce**	faces

To know if the **i** is stressed or not, consult a dictionary. The only exception to these rules applies to the word for *shirt*.

SINGULAR		PLURAL	
camicia	shirt	**camicie**	shirts

ESERCIZIO

1·3

A. *Provide the plural forms of the following nouns.*

1. luogo _____

2. tedesco _____

3. antropologo _____

4. greco _____

5. amico _____

6. gioco _____

7. biologo _____

8. lago _____

9. monaco _____

10. fico _____

11. sindaco _____

12. porco _____

13. riga _____

14. greca _____

15. banca _____

16. camicia _____

B. *Now, do the reverse. Provide the singular forms of the given plural nouns.*

1. baci _____

2. occhi _____

3. zii _____

4. orologi _____

5. farmacie _____

6. bugie _____

7. facce _____

8. valige _____

Mass nouns

There are two types of common nouns: count and mass. Count nouns refer to persons, things, etc., that can be counted (as their designation suggests). They have both singular and plural forms. The nouns you have been using so far are count nouns.

Mass nouns refer instead to things that cannot be counted, and therefore generally have only a singular form.

l'acqua	*water*
la fame	*hunger*
la sete	*thirst*
lo zucchero	*sugar*

Mass nouns can, of course, be used in a figurative or poetic way. In such cases they can be put in the plural.

le acque del mare	*the waters of the sea*

Common mass nouns

la carne	*meat*	**il riso**	*rice*
il latte	*milk*	**il sale**	*salt*
il pane	*bread*	**l'uva**	*grapes*
il pepe	*pepper*		

A few nouns have only a plural form. They refer to things made up of more than one part.

i baffi	mustache
le forbici	scissors
gli occhiali	(eye)glasses
le mutande	underwear
i pantaloni	pants

ESERCIZIO
1·4

A. *Can you figure out what each clue refers to?*

1. È dolce. (*It is sweet.*) _____

2. Si usano per vedere. (*They are used for seeing.*) _____

3. Crescono sopra le labbra. (*They grow above the lips.*) _____

4. È un liquido bianco. (*It's a white liquid.*) _____

5. Si usa per fare il vino. (*It is used to make wine.*) _____

B. *How do you say the following in Italian?*

1. salt and pepper _____

2. meat, bread, and rice _____

3. hunger and thirst _____

4. water _____

5. the waters of the sea _____

6. pants and underwear _____

7. scissors and eyeglasses _____

Proper nouns and titles

The same gender patterns described above apply to proper nouns. However, such nouns generally have only a singular form, with some exceptions. For example, *the United States*, as in English, is plural in Italian, even though it is a proper noun: **gli Stati Uniti**. Note that a proper noun is capitalized.

MASCULINE		FEMININE	
Alessandro	*Alexander*	**Alessandra**	*Alexandra*
Franco	*Frank*	**Franca**	*Franca*
Giovanni	*John*	**Maria**	*Mary*
Paolo	*Paul*	**Paola**	*Paula*
Pasquale	*Pat*	**l'Italia**	*Italy*
il Natale	*Christmas*	**la Pasqua**	*Easter*
il Tevere	*the Tiber*	**Giovanna**	*Joanne*

Italians use more titles than Americans do to address people. Here are a few common ones.

MALE TITLE	FEMALE TITLE	MEANING
signore	**signora, signorina**	*Mr.; Mrs./Ms., Miss*
dottore	**dottoressa**	*Doctor*
professore	**professoressa**	*Professor*
avvocato	**avvocato**	*Lawyer*
geometra	**geometra**	*Draftsperson*
ragioniere	**ragioniera**	*Accountant (Bookkeeper)*
architetto	**architetto**	*Architect*

Title peculiarities

The title of **dottore/dottoressa** is used to address both a medical doctor and any university graduate.

The title of **professore/professoressa** is used to address both a university professor and any junior high and high school teacher.

Capitalizing titles is optional.

Note: The final **-e** of a masculine title is dropped before a name. This rule does not apply to feminine titles. This is a rule of style, rather than strict grammar. So, it is not technically wrong to keep the **-e**, but very few Italians do so.

MASCULINE TITLE		USED BEFORE A NAME	
il signore	*the gentleman*	**il signor Verdi**	*Mr. Verdi*
il professore	*the professor*	**il professor Rossi**	*Professor Rossi*
il dottore	*the doctor*	**il dottor Bianchi**	*Dr. Bianchi*

FEMININE TITLE		USED BEFORE A NAME	
la signora	*the lady*	**la signora Verdi**	*Mrs. Verdi*
la professoressa	*the professor*	**la professoressa Rossi**	*Professor Rossi*
la dottoressa	*the doctor*	**la dottoressa Bianchi**	*Dr. Bianchi*

Note as well that the title is preceded by the definite article. The article is dropped in direct speech (talking to someone and using the title):

TITLE	DIRECT SPEECH	
il dottor Giusti	«Buongiorno, **dottor Giusti**.»	*"Good morning, Dr. Giusti."*
la professoressa Dini	«Salve, **professoressa Dini**.»	*"Hello, Prof. Dini."*

A. *Provide the corresponding male or female form.*

MALE	FEMALE
1. Paolo	_____
2. _____	Franca
3. Alessandro	_____
4. _____	Giovanna
5. nipote	_____
6. _____	signora
7. professore	_____
8. _____	dottoressa
9. geometra	_____
10. _____	ragioniera
11. il dottor Totti	_____
12. _____	la professoressa Nardini
13. architetto	_____
14. _____	avvocato

B. *How do you say the following in Italian?*

1. Luke, Andrew, and Nicholas are friends.

_____

2. I love Christmas and Easter in Italy.

_____

3. Mr. Rossi is a friend of the family (*famiglia*).

_____

4. "Hello, Mr. Rossi."

_____

5. Mrs. Rossi is a friend of the family.

_____

6. "Good morning, Mrs. Rossi."

_____

C. *Use check marks to indicate the categories to which each given noun belongs.*

NOUN	COMMON	PROPER	COUNT	MASS	MASC.	FEM.	SING.	PL.
1. ragazzo	——	——	——	——	——	——	——	——
2. Giovanna	——	——	——	——	——	——	——	——
3. libri	——	——	——	——	——	——	——	——
4. camicie	——	——	——	——	——	——	——	——
5. Tevere	——	——	——	——	——	——	——	——
6. casa	——	——	——	——	——	——	——	——
7. pane	——	——	——	——	——	——	——	——
8. antropologi	——	——	——	——	——	——	——	——

D. *Rewrite each sentence by changing it from the masculine to the feminine, or vice versa, as required by the noun(s) in parentheses.*

EXAMPLE   Maria è un'amica. (Giovanni)

___*Giovanni è un amico.*___

1. Il signor Rossini è italiano. (la signora Binni)

_____

2. Giovanni e Luca sono due uomini. (Maria e Paola)

_____

3. I ragazzi sono francesi. (le ragazze)

_____

4. La professoressa Smith è americana. (il professor Jones)

_____

5. Maria è mia zia. (Pasquale)

_____

Grammar in culture

Many nouns have cultural and social naming functions. Among these are the names of the 20 Italian regions (**le regioni**) and their capital cities (**i capoluoghi**). Locate these regions and cities on a map of Italy, and try to commit the names and relative geographical locations to memory.

REGIONE	CAPOLUOGO
Abruzzo	L'Aquila
Basilicata	Potenza
Calabria	Catanzaro
Campania	Napoli
Emilia-Romagna	Bologna
Friuli-Venezia Giulia	Trieste
Lazio	Roma
Liguria	Genova
Lombardia	Milano
Marche	Ancona
Molise	Campobasso
Piemonte	Torino
Puglia	Bari
Sardegna	Cagliari
Sicilia	Palermo
Toscana	Firenze
Trentino-Alto Adige	Trento
Umbria	Perugia
Valle d'Aosta	Aosta
Veneto	Venezia

ESERCIZIO

1·6

There is incorrect information in each sentence. Rewrite the sentence with the correct information.

1. Trento è il capoluogo della Lombardia.

   _____

2. La Sardegna, l'Umbria e la Valle d'Aosta sono capoluoghi.

   _____

3. Venezia è il capoluogo del Piemonte.

   _____

4. Firenze e Aosta sono regioni.

   _____

5. La Basilicata è il capoluogo del Friuli-Venezia Giulia.

   _____

More about nouns

·2·

In the languages of the world, nouns make up from 70 to 80 percent of all words. In Italian it is almost 85 percent. Obviously, knowing as much as possible about nouns is an important aspect of learning Italian grammar. So, a second unit is devoted to this topic.

In the previous unit, we dealt with basic noun forms and gender patterns. In this unit we will go a little more in depth, completing the "grammatical story" of Italian nouns.

More gender patterns

Let's start with a few more gender patterns.

Nouns ending in **-ista** refer to both male and female persons, and are thus both masculine and feminine. Many of these nouns are used to indicate occupations, professions, etc.

MASCULINE (MALES)		FEMININE (FEMALES)	
il musicista	*the male musician*	**la musicista**	*the female musician*
il dentista	*the male dentist*	**la dentista**	*the female dentist*
il pianista	*the male pianist*	**la pianista**	*the female pianist*
il farmacista	*the male pharmacist*	**la farmacista**	*the female pharmacist*

Their plural forms vary according to gender. If the noun is used to indicate a group of males or a mixed group of males and females, then the masculine plural is formed by changing the final vowel to **-i**. If it is used to indicate a group of females, then the feminine plural is formed by changing the final vowel to **-e**.

MASCULINE SINGULAR		MASCULINE PLURAL	
il musicista	*the male musician*	**i musicisti**	*the male musicians / the musicians (in general)*
il dentista	*the male dentist*	**i dentisti**	*the male dentists / the dentists (in general)*

FEMININE SINGULAR		FEMININE PLURAL	
la musicista	*the female musician*	**le musiciste**	*the female musicians*
la dentista	*the female dentist*	**le dentiste**	*the female dentists*

Masculine nouns ending in **-tore** often correspond to feminine nouns ending in **-trice**.

16

MASCULINE (MALES)		FEMININE (FEMALES)	
l'attore	the male actor	l'attrice	the female actor
il pittore	the male painter	la pittrice	the female painter
l'autore	the male author	l'autrice	the female author
lo scultore	the male sculptor	la scultrice	the female sculptor

Some masculine nouns, generally ending in -**e**, correspond to feminine nouns ending in -**essa**.

MASCULINE (MALES)		FEMININE (FEMALES)	
il dottore	the male doctor	la dottoressa	the female doctor
l'elefante	the male elephant	l'elefantessa	the female elephant
il leone	the lion	la leonessa	the lioness
il professore	the male professor	la professoressa	the female professor
lo studente	the male student	la studentessa	the female student

Some feminine forms have been eliminated in Italy, especially in the area of the professions.

l'architetto	male or female architect
l'avvocato	male or female lawyer
lo scultore	male or female sculptor

The names of trees are generally masculine, whereas the names of the fruits they bear are usually feminine.

TREE = MASCULINE		FRUIT = FEMININE	
l'arancio	the orange tree	l'arancia	the orange
il ciliegio	the cherry tree	la ciliegia	the cherry
il melo	the apple tree	la mela	the apple
il pero	the pear tree	la pera	the pear
il pesco	the peach tree	la pesca	the peach

Exceptions

Il limone (*the lemon*), **il fico** (*the fig*), and **il mandarino** (*the mandarin*) refer to both the tree and the fruit.

ESERCIZIO
2·1

A. *Provide the singular form of each noun.*

SINGULAR	PLURAL
1. _____	pianiste
2. _____	dentisti
3. _____	farmacisti
4. _____	musiciste

B. *Provide the corresponding male or female form of each noun.*

	MALE	FEMALE
1.	attore	_____
2.	_____	scultrice
3.	autore	_____
4.	_____	pittrice
5.	farmacista	_____
6.	_____	dottoressa
7.	leone	_____
8.	_____	professoressa
9.	elefante	_____
10.	_____	avvocato
11.	studente	_____

C. *You are given the name of either a tree or a fruit. Provide the other as required.*

	TREE	FRUIT
1.	ciliegio	_____
2.	_____	pera
3.	melo	_____
4.	_____	arancia
5.	pesco	_____
6.	_____	limone
7.	mandarino	_____
8.	_____	fico

Nouns of Greek origin

Some Italian nouns are of Greek origin. Some end in -**ema** and -**amma**, which correspond to English nouns ending in *-em* and *-am*. They are all masculine.

il diagramma	*the diagram*
il dramma	*the drama*
il problema	*the problem*
il programma	*the program*
il sistema	*the system*
il teorema	*the theorem*

As masculine nouns, the final **-a** changes to **-i** in the plural.

SINGULAR		PLURAL	
il diagramma	*the diagram*	**i diagrammi**	*the diagrams*
il problema	*the problem*	**i problemi**	*the problems*
il programma	*the program*	**i programmi**	*the programs*

Nouns ending in **-si** in the singular are also of Greek origin. They correspond to English nouns ending in *-sis*. They are all feminine.

l'analisi	*the analysis*
la crisi	*the crisis*
l'ipotesi	*the hypothesis*
la tesi	*the thesis*

Note: There is an exception to this rule; **il brindisi** (*drinking toast*) is masculine and is of Germanic origin.

The singular **-si** ending for all these words is not changed in the plural.

SINGULAR		PLURAL	
il brindisi	*the toast*	**i brindisi**	*the toasts*
la crisi	*the crisis*	**le crisi**	*the crises*
l'ipotesi	*the hypothesis*	**le ipotesi**	*the hypotheses*
la tesi	*the thesis*	**le tesi**	*the theses*

ESERCIZIO
2·2

A. *Provide the plural forms of the following nouns.*

SINGULAR	PLURAL
1. ipotesi	_____
2. tesi	_____
3. programma	_____
4. problema	_____
5. sistema	_____

B. *Now, provide the singular forms.*

1. _____	brindisi
2. _____	crisi
3. _____	diagrammi
4. _____	teoremi
5. _____	drammi
6. _____	analisi

Other types of nouns

Nouns ending in an accented -**à** or -**ù** are feminine; those ending in other accented vowels are masculine.

MASCULINE		FEMININE	
il caffè	the coffee	la città	the city
il lunedì	Monday	la gioventù	youth
il tassì	the taxi	l'università	the university
il tè	the tea	la virtù	virtue

Exceptions

Il papà (*dad*), **il menù** (*menu*), and **il ragù** (*meat sauce*) are masculine.

These endings are not changed in the plural.

SINGULAR		PLURAL	
il caffè	the coffee	i caffè	the coffees
la città	the city	le città	the cities
il tassì	the taxi	i tassì	the taxis
il tè	the tea	i tè	the teas
l'università	the university	le università	the universities

A few nouns ending in -**o** are feminine, because they are shortened forms and thus retain their original feminine gender.

FEMININE NOUN		SHORTENED FORM	
la fotografia	the photograph	la foto	the photo
la motocicletta	the motorcycle	la moto	the motorcycle
la radiofonia	the radio transmission	la radio	the radio

A few nouns ending in -**a** are masculine because they are, analogously, shortened forms and thus retain their original masculine gender.

MASCULINE NOUN		SHORTENED FORM	
il cinematografo	the movie theater	il cinema	the movies

Shortened nouns are not changed in the plural.

SINGULAR		PLURAL	
il cinema	the movie theater	i cinema	the movie theaters
la foto	the photo	le foto	the photos
la moto	the motorcycle	le moto	the motorcycles
la radio	the radio	le radio	the radios

Nouns that have been borrowed from other languages, primarily English, are generally masculine. These typically end in a consonant.

l'autobus	*the bus*
il clacson	*the car horn*
il computer	*the computer*
lo sport	*the sport*
il tennis	*tennis*
il tram	*the streetcar, trolley*

Exceptions

The following are feminine.

la chat	*chatroom*
la mail (l'e-mail)	*e-mail, e-mail message*

Such nouns are invariable—that is, they are not changed in the plural.

SINGULAR		PLURAL	
il clacson	*the car horn*	**i clacson**	*the car horns*
il computer	*the computer*	**i computer**	*the computers*
la mail	*the e-mail*	**le mail**	*the e-mails*
lo sport	*the sports*	**gli sport**	*the sports*

Like the English nouns *memorandum* and *compendium*, which have the plural forms *memoranda* and *compendia*, Italian also has a few nouns whose plural forms end in **-a**. These derive from Latin words that were pluralized in this way. In Italian, these nouns are masculine in the singular but feminine in the plural.

SINGULAR		PLURAL	
il braccio	*arm*	**le braccia**	*arms*
il dito	*the finger*	**le dita**	*the fingers*
il ginocchio	*the knee*	**le ginocchia**	*the knees*
il labbro	*the lip*	**le labbra**	*the lips*
il paio	*the pair*	**le paia**	*the pairs*

There are not too many of these nouns, and most refer to parts of the human body. In some cases, the regular plural form is used when the noun is used with an extended or figurative meaning.

i bracci della croce	*the arms of a cross*
i labbri della ferita	*the lips of a wound*

Note: There are also some nouns which are simply irregular and don't follow a rule or pattern.

il bue	*the ox*
la mano	*the hand*
il pianeta	*the planet*
il vaglia	*the money order*

They are also irregular in the plural.

SINGULAR		PLURAL	
il bue	*the ox*	**i buoi**	*the oxen*
la mano	*the hand*	**le mani**	*the hands*
il pianeta	*the planet*	**i pianeti**	*the planets*
il vaglia	*the money order*	**i vaglia**	*the money orders*

ESERCIZIO 2·3

A. *Indicate if the noun is masculine or feminine.*

NOUN	MASCULINE	FEMININE
1. città	_____	_____
2. lunedì	_____	_____
3. papà	_____	_____
4. tè	_____	_____
5. menù	_____	_____
6. ragù	_____	_____
7. caffè	_____	_____
8. gioventù	_____	_____
9. virtù	_____	_____
10. università	_____	_____
11. tassì	_____	_____
12. tram	_____	_____
13. autobus	_____	_____

B. *Provide the singular or plural form of each noun, as required.*

SINGULAR	PLURAL
1. caffè	_____
2. _____	città
3. foto	_____
4. _____	cinema
5. moto	_____
6. _____	computer
7. vaglia	_____

8. _____   mail

9. dito   _____

10. _____   braccia

11. paio   _____

12. _____   ginocchia

13. il braccio della croce   _____

14. _____   i labbri della ferita

15. bue   _____

16. _____   radio

17. mano   _____

18. _____   pianeti

19. clacson   _____

20. _____   sport

Altered nouns

Suffixes are forms with set meanings that are attached after a noun (or other part of speech), altering its meaning in some specific way. Such nouns are called, logically enough, altered nouns. Common suffixes are as follows.

The suffixes **-ino**, **-etto**, and **-ello**, with corresponding feminine forms **-ina**, **-etta**, and **-ella**, are often used to add a nuance of "littleness" or "smallness" to the meaning of the noun.

NOUN		ALTERED NOUN	
ragazzo	*boy*	**ragazzino**	*small boy*
ragazza	*girl*	**ragazzina**	*little girl*
gallo	*rooster*	**galletto**	*little rooster*
asino	*donkey*	**asinello**	*small donkey*

Be careful!

There are a number of exceptions. For example: **il libretto** does not mean *small book* but *opera libretto* or *bankbook*. The appropriate suffix is **il libricino** (*the little book*). Also **la manina** means *little hand* but **la manetta** means *handcuff*.

The suffix **-one/-ona** is sometimes used to add a nuance of "bigness" or "largeness" to the meaning of the noun.

NOUN		ALTERED NOUN	
libro	*book*	**librone**	*big book*
ragazza	*girl*	**ragazzona**	*big girl*
ragazzo	*boy*	**ragazzone**	*big boy*

The suffix **-uccio/-uccia** (also **-uzzo/-uzza**) is sometimes used to add a nuance of "smallness" with a tinge of criticism or, on the contrary, "dearness" to the meaning of the noun. The suffix **-accio/-accia** is used instead to add a nuance of "badness" or "ugliness" to the meaning of the noun.

NOUN		ALTERED NOUN	
affare	*business transaction*	**affaraccio**	*hollow business transaction*
corpo	*body*	**corpaccio**	*ugly body*
Sara	*Sarah*	**Saruccia**	*dear little Sarah*

There is no steadfast rule as to when such suffixes can be used and with which nouns they can be used. Their use is more a matter of style than it is of grammar. Only through exposure and practice will you develop facility with them.

ESERCIZIO
2·4

A. *Add a suffix to each noun as indicated, altering its meaning accordingly.*

NOUN	SMALLNESS SUFFIX	LARGENESS SUFFIX
1. asino	_____	_____
2. ragazza	_____	_____
3. libro	_____	_____
4. mano	_____	_____

B. *How would you say the following, using appropriate suffixes?*

1. a big arm   un _____

2. an ugly body   un _____

3. a handcuff   una _____

4. a small problem   un _____

5. a big problem   un _____

6. un ugly, bad problem   un _____

7. a hollow business transaction un _____

8. a big business transaction   un _____

9. cute little Mary   _____

Compound nouns

Compound nouns are nouns made of two parts of speech. For example, in English, the compound noun *handkerchief* is made up of two nouns *hand* + *kerchief*. Here are some common Italian compound nouns.

CONSTITUENT PARTS	COMPOUND NOUN	
arco + baleno	l'arcobaleno	*rainbow*
caccia + vite	il cacciavite	*screwdriver*
capo + luogo	il capoluogo	*capital of a region*
capo + reparto	il caporeparto	*head of a department*
cassa + forte	la cassaforte	*safe (for valuables)*
ferro + via	la ferrovia	*railroad*
franco + bollo	il francobollo	*postage stamp*
piano + forte	il pianoforte	*piano*
salva + gente	il salvagente	*life jacket*

To form the plural of such nouns, observe the following guidelines.

Most compound nouns are pluralized in the normal fashion, by changing the final vowel.

SINGULAR		PLURAL	
l'arcobaleno	*the rainbow*	gli arcobaleni	*the rainbows*
la ferrovia	*the railroad*	le ferrovie	*the railroads*

But there are exceptions. In some cases, the final vowels of both parts of the word are changed.

SINGULAR		PLURAL	
la cassaforte	*safe (for valuables)*	le casseforti	*safes (for valuables)*

If the compound noun has a verb as one of its parts, it does not change at all in traditional grammar. Today, however, there is a tendency to pluralize such a noun in the normal fashion. The following examples conform to tradition.

SINGULAR		PLURAL	
il cacciavite	*the screwdriver*	i cacciavite	*the screwdrivers*
il salvagente	*the life jacket*	i salvagente	*the life jackets*

To be certain of the correct plural form, you will need to look up such nouns in a good dictionary (as do most native speakers, by the way).

ESERCIZIO
2·5

A. *Provide the singular or plural form of each noun, as required.*

SINGULAR	PLURAL
1. arcobaleno	_____
2. _____	salvagente
3. ferrovia	_____

4. _____ casseforti

5. pianoforte _____

B. *Can you figure out what compound noun corresponds to each clue?*

EXAMPLE Ci passa sopra il treno. (*The train goes over it.*)

___*la ferrovia*___

1. Si chiama anche «manager» oggi. (*He/She is also called "manager" today.*)

   _____

2. È un utensile. (*It's a utensil/tool.*)

   _____

3. Si mette sulla busta. (*It's put on an envelope.*)

   _____

4. È lo strumento di Chopin. (*It's Chopin's instrument.*)

   _____

5. È la città principale di una regione. (*It's the main city of a region.*)

   _____

C. *Choose the appropriate form that corresponds to each phrase.* (*Note:* **piccolo** = *little, small;* **caro** = *dear;* **grande** = *big;* **plurale** = *plural;* **frutta** = *fruit.*)

1. il piccolo Marcello

   a. Marcellino b. Marcellone

2. la piccola e cara Teresa

   a. Teresina b. Teresuccia

3. il grande Alessandro

   a. Alessandrone b. Alessandruccio

4. un piccolo gallo

   a. una gallina b. un galletto

5. il plurale di **problema**

   a. problemi b. problema

6. la frutta del pesco

   a. la pesca b. il pesco

7. la frutta del limone

   a. la limonata b. il limone

8. il plurale di **ipotesi**

   a. ipotesi b. ipotesina

D. *Complete the chart with the missing noun forms.*

MASC. SING.	MASC. PL.	FEM. SING.	FEM. PL.
1. pianista	_____	_____	_____
2. _____	farmacisti	_____	_____
3. _____	_____	attrice	_____
4. _____	_____	_____	scultrici
5. elefante	_____	_____	_____
6. _____	studenti	_____	_____

E. *You are given eight nouns in their singular form. However, the sentences provided require that they be inserted in their plural form. So, complete each sentence with the appropriate noun in its plural form (which, of course, might be the same form as the singular).*

autobus	sport	caffè	tennis
foto	città	paio	dito

1. Bevo sempre troppi _____. (*I always drink too many . . . .*)

2. Voglio vedere tante _____ in Italia. (*I want to see many . . . in Italy.*)

3. Dove sono le _____ delle vacanze? (*Where are the . . . from vacation?*)

4. Mio nipote pratica tanti _____. (*My grandson plays a lot of . . . .*)

5. Il mio sport preferito è il _____. (*My favorite sport is . . . .*)

6. Iero ho preso l'_____ per andare a scuola. (*Yesterday I took the . . . to go to school.*)

7. Lui ha le _____ lunghe. (*He has long . . . .*)

8. Ieri lei ha comprato due _____ di scarpe. (*Yesterday she bought two . . . of shoes.*)

Grammar in culture

Many Italian nouns associated with the Internet, social media, and mobile devices are borrowed from English.

l'app	*app*
il blog	*blog*
Facebook	*Facebook*
il file	*file*
Instagram	*Instagram*
Internet	*Internet*
Twitter	*Twitter*
il wiki	*wiki*
YouTube	*YouTube*

Other computer-related terms are not English borrowings.

il caricamento	*uploading*
la navigazione	*navigation (of the Web)*
la piattaforma	*platform*
la rete sociale (social network)	*social network*
lo scaricamento	*downloading*
il sito web	*website*

ESERCIZIO
2·6

Choose the appropriate word.

1. È una piattaforma web.

   a. app   b. YouTube

2. È un servizio di rete sociale (*social network*).

   a. Facebook   b. scaricamento

3. È un servizio di rete sociale che permette di scattare (*to take*) foto.

   a. Instagram   b. caricamento

4. È un particolare tipo di sito.

   a. sito web   b. blog

5. È un servizio gratuito (*free*) di rete sociale e microblogging.

   a. Twitter   b. navigazione

Articles

Articles are "function words" which mark nouns as specific or nonspecific, that is, as referring to something in particular or in general. A function word is a form that has grammatical meaning or value.

SPECIFIC REFERENCE		NONSPECIFIC REFERENCE	
il bambino	*the child*	**un bambino**	*a child*
la porta	*the door*	**una porta**	*a door*

The indefinite article

The indefinite article, **un** (the form listed in the dictionary), corresponds to both English indefinite article forms *a* and *an*. It has only singular forms that vary according to the gender and initial letter of the noun they precede.

The form **uno** is used before a masculine singular noun beginning with **z**, **s + consonant**, **gn**, or **ps**.

uno zio	*an uncle*
uno studente	*a student*
uno gnocco	*a dumpling*
uno psicologo	*a psychologist*

The form **un** is used before a masculine singular noun beginning with any other letters (consonants or vowels).

un amico	*a friend*
un orologio	*a watch*
un portatile	*a laptop*
un ragazzo	*a boy*

The form **una** is used before a feminine singular noun beginning with any consonant (including **z**, **s + consonant**, **gn**, or **ps**).

una porta	*a door*
una zia	*an aunt*
una studentessa	*a student*
una psicologa	*a psychologist*

Lastly, the form **un'** is used before a feminine singular noun beginning with any vowel.

un'americana	*an American*
un'amica	*a friend*
un'isola	*an island*
un'ora	*an hour*

Be careful!

When an adjective precedes the noun, it is necessary to adjust the indefinite article according to the beginning letters of the adjective.

un'amica	*a friend*	**una cara amica**	*a dear friend*
uno zio	*an uncle*	**un caro zio**	*a dear uncle*

ESERCIZIO
3·1

A. *You are given some nouns taken from the above lists and from previous units. Provide the appropriate form of the indefinite article for each one.*

1. _____ americano
2. _____ americana
3. _____ studente
4. _____ zia
5. _____ studentessa
6. _____ ora
7. _____ gnocco
8. _____ portatile
9. _____ tesi
10. _____ brindisi
11. _____ problema
12. _____ programma

13. _____ caffè
14. _____ foto
15. _____ computer
16. _____ mano
17. _____ radio
18. _____ pianoforte
19. _____ isola
20. _____ porta
21. _____ psicologo
22. _____ psicologa
23. _____ orologio

B. *Now you are given some noun phrases consisting of the indefinite article, an adjective, and a noun. Provide the corresponding masculine or feminine noun phrase as required. Again, the words are taken from this and previous units. (Note:* **bravo** *= good;* **grande** *= big, important.)*

MASCULINE	FEMININE
1. un caro amico	_____
2. _____	una piccola zia
3. un bravo figlio	_____
4. _____	una brava cantante

5. un grande professore   _____

6. _____   una brava signora

7. un bravo musicista   _____

8. _____   una grande scultrice

The definite article

The definite article has both singular and plural forms. The singular forms are as follows.

The form **lo** is used before a masculine singular noun beginning with **z**, **s + consonant**, **gn**, or **ps**. It corresponds to the previously described uses of **uno**.

lo zio	*the uncle*
lo studente	*the student*
lo gnocco	*the dumpling*
lo psicologo	*the psychologist*

The form **il** is used before a masculine singular noun beginning with any other consonant. It corresponds to the previously described uses of **un**.

il bambino	*the child*
il cellulare	*the cell phone*
il portatile	*the laptop*
il ragazzo	*the boy*

The form **la** is used before a feminine singular noun beginning with any consonant. It corresponds to the previously described uses of **una**.

la porta	*the door*
la zia	*the aunt*
la studentessa	*the student*
la psicologa	*the psychologist*

The form **l'** is used before a masculine or feminine singular noun beginning with any vowel. It corresponds in the feminine to the previously described uses of **un'** and in the masculine to the previously described uses of **un**.

l'amico	*the (male) friend*
l'isola	*the island*
l'ora	*the hour*
l'orologio	*the watch*

The corresponding plural forms of the definite article are as follows.

The form **gli** is used before a masculine plural noun beginning with **z**, **s + consonant**, **gn**, **ps**, or any vowel. It is the plural of both **lo** and **l'**.

SINGULAR		PLURAL	
lo zio	*the uncle*	**gli zii**	*the uncles*
lo studente	*the student*	**gli studenti**	*the students*
lo gnocco	*the dumpling*	**gli gnocchi**	*the dumplings*
lo psicologo	*the psychologist*	**gli psicologi**	*the psychologists*
l'amico	*the friend*	**gli amici**	*the friends*
l'orologio	*the watch*	**gli orologi**	*the watches*

The form **i** is used before a masculine plural noun beginning with any other consonant. It is the plural of **il**.

SINGULAR		PLURAL	
il bambino	*the child*	**i bambini**	*the children*
il cellulare	*the cell phone*	**i cellulari**	*the cell phones*
il portatile	*the laptop*	**i portatili**	*the laptops*
il ragazzo	*the boy*	**i ragazzi**	*the boys*

The form **le** is used before a feminine plural noun beginning with any sound (consonant or vowel). It is the plural of both **la** and **l'**.

SINGULAR		PLURAL	
l'isola	*the island*	**le isole**	*the islands*
l'ora	*the hour*	**le ore**	*the hours*
la porta	*the door*	**le porte**	*the doors*
la zia	*the aunt*	**le zie**	*the aunts*

Once again, be careful!

When an adjective precedes the noun, it is necessary to adjust the definite article according to the beginning letters of the adjective.

l'amica	*the friend*	**la cara amica**	*the dear friend*
gli amici	*the friends*	**i cari amici**	*the dear friends*
lo zio	*the uncle*	**il caro zio**	*the dear uncle*

ESERCIZIO
3·2

A. *You are given some noun phrases composed of the indefinite article and a noun. Provide the corresponding noun phrase with the definite article for each one. Then, make the new phrase plural.*

EXAMPLE   un ragazzo

_____*il ragazzo*_____   _____*i ragazzi*_____

	SINGULAR	PLURAL
1. un vestito	_____	_____
2. una studentessa	_____	_____
3. uno psicologo	_____	_____
4. una psicologa	_____	_____
5. una tesi	_____	_____
6. un tedesco	_____	_____
7. uno sport	_____	_____

8. un problema _____ _____

9. un orologio _____ _____

10. un'ora _____ _____

11. un amico _____ _____

12. un'amica _____ _____

13. uno zio _____ _____

14. una zia _____ _____

15. un bambino _____ _____

16. una bambina _____ _____

17. uno gnocco _____ _____

18. uno studente _____ _____

B. *Now you are given a phrase that is either in the singular or the plural. Provide its corresponding form as required.*

SINGULAR	PLURAL
1. lo zio	_____
2. _____	i vaglia
3. la valigia	_____
4. _____	le virtù
5. l'uomo	_____
6. _____	i tè
7. lo gnocco	_____
8. _____	i sistemi
9. lo scultore	_____
10. _____	i programmi
11. la radio	_____
12. _____	le università
13. il paio	_____
14. _____	gli orologi
15. il musicista	_____
16. _____	le infermiere

Uses of the indefinite article

English and Italian use the articles in similar ways. However, there are differences. They are described in this and the remaining sections of this unit.

The indefinite article is omitted in exclamations of the type shown below.

Che buon caffè!	*What a good coffee!*
Che macchina bella!	*What a beautiful car!*

It is also omitted in the expression **mal di…** .

mal di denti	*a toothache*
mal di gola	*a sore throat*
mal di stomaco	*a stomachache*
mal di testa	*a headache*

In Italian, the indefinite article must be repeated before every noun, while the article is often used only before the first noun in English.

un amico e uno studente	*a friend and (a) student*
un ragazzo e una ragazza	*a boy and (a) girl*
una zia e uno zio	*an aunt and (an) uncle*

ESERCIZIO

3·3

A. *Provide the appropriate indefinite article forms for the following sentences. If no article is required, leave the space blank. (Note:* **anche** *= also, too;* **e** *= and;* **film** *= movie;* **grande** *= great;* **o** *= or;* **sempre** *= always;* **simpatico** *= nice;* **solo** *= only;* **studiare** *= to study.)*

1. Mia madre aveva (*had*) _____ mal di denti ieri.

2. Anch'io ho _____ mal di gola.

3. Che _____ bella musica!

4. Mio padre ha _____ mal di testa o _____ mal di stomaco.

5. Che _____ bella macchina!

6. In questa classe conosco (*I know*) solo _____ studente

   e _____ studentessa.

7. Lui è _____ persona simpatica; e anche lei è _____ persona simpatica.

8. Io studio sempre _____ ora ogni giorno (*every day*).

B. *How do you say the following in Italian?*

1. I have only an aunt and uncle.

   _____

2. I bought (**ho comprato**) a car.

   _____

3. What a nice house!

   _____

4. What a great movie!

   _____

Uses of the definite article

The definite article is normally used in front of a mass noun, especially if it is the subject of a sentence.

L'acqua è un liquido.	*Water is a liquid.*
Lui beve solo **il caffè**.	*He drinks only coffee.*
La pazienza è una virtù.	*Patience is a virtue.*

It is also used with nouns in the plural that express generalizations.

Gli americani sono simpatici.	*Americans are nice.*
Oggi tutti hanno **i cellulari.**	*Today everybody has cell phones.*

The definite article is used in front of geographical names (continents, countries, states, rivers, islands, mountains, etc.), except the names of cities.

le Alpi	*the Alps*
il Belgio	*Belgium*
la California	*California*
l'Italia	*Italy*
il Mediterraneo	*the Mediterranean*
il Piemonte	*Piedmont*
la Sicilia	*Sicily*
gli Stati Uniti	*the United States*
il Tevere	*the Tiber*

But:

Firenze	*Florence*
Napoli	*Naples*
Roma	*Rome*
Venezia	*Venice*

It is usually dropped after the preposition **in** plus an unmodified geographical noun.

Vado **in** Italia.	*I'm going to Italy.*
Vivo **in** Francia.	*I live in France.*

But when the noun is modified, the definite article must be restored. (Note, if you have forgotten: **nell'** = in + l'; **nella** = in + la; **nel** = in + il; **nei** = in + i; **negli** = in + gli; **nelle** = in + le.)

Vado **nell'Italia centrale**.	*I'm going to central Italy.*
Vivo **nella Francia meridionale**.	*I live in southern France.*

Like the indefinite article, the definite article must be repeated before each noun.

l'amico e lo studente	*the friend and the student*
il ragazzo e la ragazza	*the boy and the girl*

Useful expressions

settentrionale	*northern*
centrale	*central*
meridionale	*southern*
orientale	*eastern*
occidentale	*western*

The definite article is commonly used in place of possessive adjectives if referring to family members, parts of the body, and clothing.

Oggi vado in centro con **la zia**.	*Today I'm going downtown with my aunt.*
Mi fa male **la testa**.	*My head hurts.*
Lui non si mette mai **la giacca**.	*He never puts his jacket on.*

The definite article is used with the days of the week to indicate a habitual action.

Il lunedì gioco sempre a tennis.	*On Mondays I always play tennis.*
La domenica vado regolarmente in chiesa.	*On Sundays I go regularly to church.*

Days of the week

lunedì (*m.*)	*Monday*
martedì (*m.*)	*Tuesday*
mercoledì (*m.*)	*Wednesday*
giovedì (*m.*)	*Thursday*
venerdì (*m.*)	*Friday*
sabato (*m.*)	*Saturday*
domenica (*f.*)	*Sunday*

Note that **domenica** is the only day of the week that is feminine.

The definite article is used with titles, unless the person bearing the title is being spoken to directly.

Il dottor Rossi è italiano.	*Dr. Rossi is Italian.*
La professoressa Bianchi è molto brava.	*Professor Bianchi is very good.*

But:

«**Dottor Rossi**, come va?»	*"Dr. Rossi, how is it going?"*
«**Professoressa Bianchi**, come sta?»	*"Professor Bianchi, how are you?"*

The definite article is used before the names of languages and nouns referring to school subjects.

Amo **lo spagnolo**.	*I love Spanish.*
Mi piace solo **la matematica**.	*I only like mathematics.*

School subjects

la biologia	*biology*	**la lingua**	*language*
la chimica	*chemistry*	**la matematica**	*math*
la fisica	*physics*	**la musica**	*music*
il francese	*French*	**la scienza**	*science*
la geografia	*geography*	**lo spagnolo**	*Spanish*
l'italiano	*Italian*	**la storia**	*history*

However, it is dropped when the prepositions **di** and **in** precede the school subject.

Ecco il mio libro **di spagnolo**.	*Here is the Spanish book.*
Lui è molto bravo **in matematica**.	*He is very good in math.*

But the definite article is restored if the noun is plural or modified.

Lei è molto brava **nelle lingue moderne**.	*She is very good in modern languages.*

The definite article is used with **scorso** (*last*) and **prossimo** (*next*) in time expressions.

la settimana scorsa	*last week*
il mese prossimo	*next month*

Time vocabulary

oggi	*today*
ieri	*yesterday*
domani	*tomorrow*
la settimana	*week*
il mese	*month*
l'anno	*year*

But, it is not used in some other common expressions.

a destra	*to/on the right*
a sinistra	*to/on the left*
a casa	*at home*

A. *Complete each sentence with the appropriate form of the definite article (if required).*

1. _____ acqua è necessaria per vivere (*to live*).

2. _____ caffè è buono.

3. _____ italiani sono simpatici.

4. _____ pazienza è la virtù più importante.

5. Anche _____ americani sono simpatici.

6. Mi piacciono (*I like*) _____ lingue e _____ storia.

7. _____ Sicilia è una bella regione.

8. _____ anno prossimo vado in _____ Piemonte.

9. Forse vado (in) _____ Italia settentrionale.

10. Mia zia vive (a) _____ Roma.

11. Lei si mette sempre _____ giacca per andare (*to go*) in centro.

12. _____ venerdì, io gioco sempre a tennis.

13. _____ domenica vado regolarmente in chiesa.

14. _____ martedì o _____ mercoledì guardo (*I watch*) la televisione.

15. _____ giovedì o _____ sabato vado in centro.

16. Come si chiama (*What is the name of*) _____ professoressa d'italiano?

17. Come sta, _____ professoressa Bianchi?

18. Mi fa male _____ testa.

B. *How do you say the following in Italian?*

1. I drink only tea.

   _____

2. I love (**amo**) spaghetti.

   _____

3. I have only an aunt and uncle in Italy.

   _____

4. He lives in southern Italy.

   _____

5. She lives in the eastern United States.

   _____

6. I instead (**invece**) live in the western United States.

   _____

7. I like (**Mi piacciono**) biology, chemistry, science, geography, math, and physics.

   _____

8. She is very good in music and in languages.

   _____

9. Last month I bought (**ho comprato**) a car.

   _____

10. Next year I am going (**vado**) to Italy.

    _____

11. Next week I am going downtown.

    _____

12. He lives to the left and she lives to the right.

    _____

C. *Provide the corresponding indefinite or definite article, as required.*

INDEFINITE ARTICLE	DEFINITE ARTICLE
1. un ragazzo	_____
2. _____	l'anno
3. una settimana	_____
4. _____	il mese
5. un caffè	_____
6. _____	lo psicologo

D. *Rewrite each phrase in the plural.*

SINGULAR	PLURAL
1. il ragazzo	_____
2. lo spagnolo	_____
3. la scienza	_____
4. la giacca	_____
5. l'amico	_____
6. l'amica	_____
7. il cellulare	_____
8. la virtù	_____

E. *Complete each sentence with the article or word required, if one is necessary.*

1. Che _____ bel film! (*What a nice movie!*)

2. Ho _____ mal di stomaco. (*I have a stomachache.*)

3. Loro hanno un cane e _____ gatto. (*They have a dog and cat.*)

4. Sono la zia e _____ zio dall'Italia. (*They're the aunt and uncle from Italy.*)

5. Io amo _____ carne. (*I love meat.*)

6. _____ italiani sanno vivere. (*Italians know how to live.*)

7. Loro vanno spesso _____ Italia. (*They go often to Italy.*)

8. _____ Francia è un bel paese. (*France is a beautiful country.*)

9. Oggi vado in centro con _____ zio. (*Today I am going downtown with my uncle.*)

10. _____ venerdì vanno spesso al cinema. (*On Fridays they often go to the movies.*)

11. Conosci _____ professor Martini? (*Do you know Professor Martini?*)

12. Mio fratello ama _____ matematica. (*My brother loves math.*)

13. Lei è andata al cinema _____ settimana scorsa. (*She went to the movies last week.*)

14. Loro vivono _____ destra. (*They live on the right.*)

F. *Match the words and expressions in the left column with those in the right column to make complete logical sentences.*

1. Lui è _____   a. dottoressa Rossi, come va?

2. Lui va spesso _____   b. il mio libro.

3. Buongiorno, _____   c. i miei libri.

4. Mio fratello è bravo _____   d. le mie amiche.

5. Questo è _____   e. nell'Italia settentrionale.

6. Quelli sono _____   f. un caro zio.

7. Quelle sono _____   g. in matematica.

Grammar in culture

In the changing world of technology, grammar follows suit. Today, the Italian article is rarely used with a noun that refers to the Internet or to a specific social media site.

Vado spesso su Internet.	*not*	Vado spesso su**l** Internet.
Non sono su Facebook.	*not*	Non sono su**l** Facebook.
Amo Twitter.	*not*	Amo **il** Twitter.
Mi piace molto Instagram.	*not*	Mi piace molto **l'**Instagram.

Otherwise, the article is used.

Mi piace molto **il** sito del tuo amico.	*not*	Mi piace molto sito del tuo amico.

ESERCIZIO
3·5

Complete each sentence with the appropriate article, if one is needed.

1. Non leggo mai _____ blog di quel giornalista.

2. Non mi piace _____ Facebook; preferisco _____ Twitter.

3. Anche tu usi spesso _____ Instagram?

4. Questo è _____ sito della mia professoressa.

5. Oggi _____ Internet ha cambiato (*changed*) tutto.

Adjectives

Adjectives are words that modify or describe nouns and other parts of speech.

È una macchina **nuova**.	*It's a new car.*
Mi piacciono solo le macchine **italiane**.	*I only like Italian cars.*

In general, adjectives are identifiable by changes in the vowel endings, which show agreement with the nouns they modify.

lo studente americano	*the (male) American student*
gli studenti americani	*the American students*
la studentessa italiana	*the (female) Italian student*
le studentesse italiane	*the (female) Italian students*

Descriptive adjectives

The most common type of adjective is called descriptive. As its name implies, it is a word that describes the noun it modifies—that is, it indicates whether someone is tall or short, something is good or bad, and so on. What does modifying a noun mean grammatically? For most intents and purposes, it means that the final vowel of an adjective must change to match the gender and number of the noun.

There are two main types of descriptive adjectives, as listed in the dictionary:

1. the type that ends in **-o**

alto	*tall*

2. the type that ends in **-e**

intelligente	*intelligent*

As with masculine singular nouns which end in **-o** or **-e**, the masculine plural forms of both of these types of adjectives end in **-i**.

SINGULAR		PLURAL	
l'uomo alto	*the tall man*	**gli uomini alti**	*the tall men*
l'uomo intelligente	*the intelligent man*	**gli uomini intelligenti**	*the intelligent men*
il cantante alto	*the tall singer*	**i cantanti alti**	*the tall singers*
il cantante intelligente	*the intelligent singer*	**i cantanti intelligenti**	*the intelligent singers*

The corresponding feminine singular forms of these two types of adjectives end, as you may expect, in **-a** and **-e**, respectively. The feminine plural forms of type (1) adjectives end in **-e**; the feminine plural forms of type (2) adjectives end in **-i**.

SINGULAR		PLURAL	
la donna alta	*the tall woman*	**le donne alte**	*the tall women*
la donna intelligente	*the intelligent woman*	**le donne intelligenti**	*the intelligent women*
la scultrice alta	*the tall (female) sculptor*	**le scultrici alte**	*the tall sculptors*
la scultrice intelligente	*the intelligent sculptor*	**le scultrici intelligenti**	*the intelligent sculptors*

Common descriptive adjectives

alto	*tall*	**basso**	*short*
bello	*beautiful*	**brutto**	*ugly*
grande	*big*	**piccolo**	*small*
magro	*skinny*	**grasso**	*fat*
nuovo	*new*	**vecchio**	*old*
ricco	*rich*	**povero**	*poor*

Invariable adjectives

A few adjectives are invariable; that is, their ending does not change. The most common are the color adjectives: **arancione** (*orange*), **blu** (*dark blue*), **marrone** (*brown*), **rosa** (*pink*), and **viola** (*violet, purple*).

SINGULAR		PLURAL	
la giacca arancione	*the orange jacket*	**le giacche arancione**	*the orange jackets*
il vestito blu	*the blue dress*	**i vestiti blu**	*the blue dresses*
la camicia marrone	*the brown shirt*	**le camicie marrone**	*the brown shirts*
la sciarpa rosa	*the pink scarf*	**le sciarpe rosa**	*the pink scarves*
lo zaino viola	*the purple backpack*	**gli zaini viola**	*the purple backpacks*

Other color adjectives

These are regular color adjectives, that is, their endings change according to the normal rules for adjectives.

azzurro	*blue*
bianco	*white*
celeste	*sky blue*
giallo	*yellow*
grigio	*gray*
nero	*black*
rosso	*red*
verde	*green*

Note: Adjectives ending in **-co**, **-go**, **-cio**, and **-gio** undergo the same spelling changes when pluralized that the nouns with these endings do (see Unit 1).

SINGULAR		PLURAL	
l'uomo simpatico	*the nice man*	**gli uomini simpatici**	*the nice men*
la camicia bianca	*the white shirt*	**le camicie bianche**	*the white shirts*
il bambino stanco	*the tired child*	**i bambini stanchi**	*the tired children*
la gonna lunga	*the long skirt*	**le gonne lunghe**	*the long skirts*
il vestito grigio	*the gray suit*	**i vestiti grigi**	*the gray suits*

When two nouns are modified by an adjective, the adjective must be in the plural. If the two nouns are feminine, then the appropriate feminine plural ending is used; if the two nouns are both masculine, or of mixed gender, then the appropriate masculine plural ending is used.

Two feminine nouns

La camicia e la gonna sono rosse.   *The shirt and (the) skirt are red.*

Two masculine nouns

Il cappotto e l'impermeabile sono rossi.   *The coat and (the) raincoat are red.*

Mixed gender nouns

La camicia e il cappotto sono rossi.   *The shirt and (the) coat are red.*

ESERCIZIO
4·1

A. *Provide the missing ending for each adjective.*

1. la bambina ricc_____

2. i ragazzi alt_____

3. la casa grand_____

4. le case grand_____

5. gli uomini stanc_____

6. le donne pover_____

7. la bambina bell_____

8. i cantanti brutt_____

9. le cantanti magr_____

10. la giacca ross_____

11. le giacche bl_____

12. le sciarpe verd_____

13. le sciarpe viol_____

14. la camicia bianc_____

15. le camicie marron_____

16. gli zaini celest_____

17. le gonne grig_____

18. i vestiti ros_____

19. l'impermeabile azzurr_____

20. gli impermeabili giall_____

21. i cappotti arancion_____

22. la camicia e la sciarpa bianc_____

23. la gonna e il cappotto ross_____

B. *Provide the corresponding singular or plural phrase, as required.*

SINGULAR	PLURAL
1. lo zio vecchio	_____
2. _____	le studentesse intelligenti
3. la valigia grande	_____
4. _____	le città piccole
5. l'uomo ricco	_____
6. _____	le donne stanche
7. il ragazzo simpatico	_____
8. _____	le cantanti simpatiche
9. il vestito lungo	_____
10. _____	le sciarpe lunghe

C. *Rewrite each phrase with the opposite adjective.*

EXAMPLE   l'uomo alto

      l'uomo basso

1. la macchina nuova   _____
2. gli uomini alti   _____
3. le donne povere   _____
4. il cane grande   _____
5. i cantanti grassi   _____
6. i professori belli   _____
7. le ragazze povere   _____
8. il vestito nero   _____

Position

Descriptive adjectives generally come after the noun or nouns they modify.

una camicia bianca	*a white shirt*
un libro interessante	*an interesting book*

Some adjectives, however, can come either before or after.

È una **bella camicia**.	(or)	È una **camicia bella**.	*It's a beautiful shirt.*
Giulia è una **ragazza simpatica**.	(or)	Giulia è una **simpatica ragazza**.	*Julie is a nice girl.*

Be careful!

As discussed in Unit 3, you will have to adjust the form of the article to the adjective that is put before a noun.

lo zio simpatico	but	il simpatico zio
l'amico povero	but	il povero amico
un'amica simpatica	but	una simpatica amica
gli studenti nuovi	but	i nuovi studenti

You will have to learn which descriptive adjectives can come before through practice and use. As you listen to someone speak or as you read something, make a mental note of the position of the adjective. Some common adjectives that can come before or after a noun are the following.

bello	*beautiful*
brutto	*ugly*
buono	*good*
caro	*dear; expensive*
cattivo	*bad*
giovane	*young*
grande	*big, large; great*
nuovo	*new*
povero	*poor*
simpatico	*nice, charming*
vecchio	*old*

A few of these adjectives change in meaning depending on their position. Needless to say, when you are unsure of the meaning and use of an adjective, check a dictionary. Here are the four most common adjectives whose meaning changes depending on their position before or after the noun.

	BEFORE THE NOUN	AFTER THE NOUN
caro	*dear*	*expensive*
	Lui è un **caro amico**.	È una **giacca cara**.
	He's a dear friend.	*It's an expensive jacket.*
grande	*great*	*big*
	È un **grande libro**.	È un **libro grande**.
	It's a great book.	*It's a big book.*
povero	*poor (deserving of pity)*	*poor (not wealthy)*
	Lui è un **povero uomo**.	Lui è un **uomo povero**.
	He is a poor man (pitiable).	*He is a poor man (not wealthy).*
vecchio	*old (known for many years)*	*old (in age)*
	Lei è una **vecchia amica**.	Lei è una **donna vecchia**.
	She is an old friend.	*She is an old woman.*

Note: Descriptive adjectives can also be separated from the nouns they modify by a linking verb. The most common linking verbs are: **essere** (*to be*), **sembrare** (*to seem*), and **diventare** (*to become*).

Quella giacca **è** nuova.	*That jacket is new.*
Quell'uomo **sembra** intelligente.	*That man seems intelligent.*
Questa macchina **sta diventando** vecchia.	*This car is becoming old.*

Adjectives used in this way are known as predicate adjectives, because they occur in the predicate slot, after the verb that links them to the noun or nouns they modify.

One final word about the position of descriptive adjectives. When these adjectives are accompanied by an adverb, another adjective, or some other part of speech, they must follow the noun.

| Lui è un **simpatico uomo**. | *He is a nice man.* |

But:

| Lui è un **uomo molto simpatico**. | *He is a very nice man.* |
| Lui è un **uomo simpatico e bravo**. | *He is a nice and good man.* |

ESERCIZIO

4·2

A. *Rewrite each sentence by changing the position of the adjective—if it is before the noun move it after and vice versa—and by making any other changes that are then required.*

1. Lui è uno studente simpatico.

   _____

2. È un nuovo zaino.

   _____

3. Ho comprato un orologio nuovo.

   _____

4. Marco e Maria sono amici simpatici.

   _____

5. Lei è un'amica ricca.

   _____

B. *Match each sentence to its correct English equivalent.*

1. Lei è una donna vecchia.

   a. *She's an elderly woman.*   b. *She is a woman whom I have known for a while.*

2. Loro sono vecchi amici.

   a. *They are elderly friends.*   b. *They are friends whom we have known for ages.*

3. Noi siamo persone povere.

   a. *We are impoverished people.*   b. *We are unfortunate people.*

4. Lui è un povero cantante.

   a. *He is an impoverished singer.*   b. *He is a pitiable singer.*

5. La Ferrari è una macchina cara.

   a. *The Ferrari is an expensive car.*   b. *The Ferrari is a dear car.*

6. Giulio è un caro amico.

   a. *Giulio is an expensive friend.*   b. *Giulio is a dear friend.*

7. Quello è un grande film.

   a. *That is a big movie (long in length).*   b. *That is a great movie.*

8. Alessandro è un ragazzo grande.

   a. *Alexander is a big boy.*   b. *Alexander is a great boy.*

Form-changing adjectives

The adjectives **buono** (*good, kind*), **bello** (*beautiful, nice, handsome*), **grande** (*big, large, great*), and **santo** (*saint*) undergo changes in form when they are placed before a noun.

Let's start with **buono**. Before masculine nouns beginning with **z**, **s + consonant**, **gn**, and **ps**, its forms are as follows (remember that the partitive **dei** = *some*).

SINGULAR		PLURAL	
buono		**buoni**	
un buono zio	*a kind uncle*	**dei buoni zii**	(*some*) *kind uncles*
un buono studente	*a kind student*	**dei buoni studenti**	(*some*) *kind students*

Before masculine nouns beginning with any other consonant or any vowel, its forms are as follows.

SINGULAR		PLURAL	
buon		**buoni**	
un buon ragazzo	*a good boy*	**dei buoni ragazzi**	(*some*) *good boys*
un buon amico	*a good friend*	**dei buoni amici**	(*some*) *good friends*

Before feminine nouns beginning with any consonant, its forms are as follows (remember that the partitive **delle** = *some*).

SINGULAR		PLURAL	
buona		**buone**	
una buona bambina	*a good child*	**delle buone bambine**	(*some*) *good children*
una buona pizza	*a good pizza*	**delle buone pizze**	(*some*) *good pizzas*

Before feminine nouns beginning with any vowel, the forms are as follows.

SINGULAR		PLURAL	
buon'		**buone**	
una buon'amica	*a good friend*	**delle buone amiche**	(*some*) *good friends*
una buon'infermiera	*a good nurse*	**delle buone infermiere**	(*some*) *good nurses*

Tips!

Note that the singular forms undergo the same kinds of form changes as the indefinite article (see Unit 3).

uno	→	**buono**
un	→	**buon**
una	→	**buona**
un'	→	**buon'**

Note also that the apostrophe is used only with the feminine form (**buon'**), as is the case with the indefinite article.

When referring to people, **buono** means *good* in the sense of *good in nature, kind*. If *good at doing something* is intended, then the adjective **bravo** is more appropriate.

È un **buon ragazzo**.	*He is a good (natured) boy.*
È un **bravo studente**.	*He is a good student. (He is good at being a student.)*

When **buono** is placed after the noun, it is treated as a normal type (1) descriptive adjective ending in **-o** (remember the forms of the partitive: **di + i = dei, di + gli = degli, di + le = delle**).

BEFORE THE NOUN		AFTER THE NOUN	
un buon amico	*a good friend (m.)*	**un amico buono**	*a good friend (m.)*
una buon'amica	*a good friend (f.)*	**un'amica buona**	*a good friend (f.)*
un buono zio	*a kind uncle*	**uno zio buono**	*a kind uncle*
dei buoni amici	*good friends (m.)*	**degli amici buoni**	*good friends (m.)*
delle buone amiche	*good friends (f.)*	**delle amiche buone**	*good friends (f.)*
dei buoni zii	*kind uncles*	**degli zii buoni**	*kind uncles*

Be careful!

As discussed above and in Unit 3, you will have to adjust the form of the article (or partitive) to the adjective that is put before a noun.

uno zio buono	but	un buono zio
l'amico buono	but	il buon amico
un'amica buona	but	una buon'amica
degli studenti buoni	but	dei buoni studenti

Now, let's consider **bello**. Before masculine nouns beginning with **z, s + consonant, gn**, and **ps**, its forms are as follows.

SINGULAR		PLURAL	
bello		**begli**	
un bello zaino	*a nice backpack*	**dei begli zaini**	*(some) nice backpacks*
un bello sport	*a nice sport*	**dei begli sport**	*(some) nice sports*

Before masculine nouns beginning with any other consonant, its forms are as follows.

SINGULAR		PLURAL	
bel		**bei**	
un bel cane	*a beautiful dog*	**dei bei cani**	*(some) beautiful dogs*
un bel gatto	*a beautiful cat*	**dei bei gatti**	*(some) beautiful cats*

Before masculine nouns beginning with any vowel, its forms are as follows.

SINGULAR		PLURAL	
bell'		**begli**	
un bell'uomo	*a handsome man*	**dei begli uomini**	*(some) handsome men*
un bell'orologio	*a beautiful watch*	**dei begli orologi**	*(some) beautiful watches*

Before feminine nouns beginning with any consonant, its forms are as follows.

SINGULAR		PLURAL	
bella		**belle**	
una bella donna	*a beautiful woman*	**delle belle donne**	*(some) beautiful women*
una bella camicia	*a nice shirt*	**delle belle camicie**	*(some) nice shirts*

Before feminine nouns beginning with any vowel, the forms are as follows.

SINGULAR		PLURAL	
bell'		**belle**	
una bell'amica	*a beautiful friend*	**delle belle amiche**	*(some) beautiful friends*
una bell'attrice	*a beautiful actress*	**delle belle attrici**	*(some) beautiful actresses*

Tip!

Note that **bello** undergoes the same kinds of form changes as the definite article (see Unit 3).

lo	→	bello
l'	→	bell'
gli	→	begli
il	→	bel
i	→	bei
la	→	bella
le	→	belle

If placed after the noun, **bello** is treated like a normal type (1) descriptive adjective ending in **-o**.

BEFORE		AFTER	
un bell'uomo	*a handsome man*	**un uomo bello**	*a handsome man*
una bell'attrice	*a beautiful actress*	**un'attrice bella**	*a beautiful actress*
un bello zaino	*a nice backpack*	**uno zaino bello**	*a nice backpack*
dei begli uomini	*handsome men*	**degli uomini belli**	*handsome men*
delle belle attrici	*beautiful actresses*	**delle attrici belle**	*beautiful actresses*
dei begli zaini	*nice backpacks*	**degli zaini belli**	*nice backpacks*

Once again, be careful!

As discussed above and in Unit 3, you will have to adapt the form of the article (or partitive) to the adjective that is put before a noun.

uno zaino bello	but	un bello zaino
l'amico bello	but	il bell'amico
l'amica bella	but	la bell'amica
degli studenti belli	but	dei begli studenti

Grande has the optional forms **gran** (before a masculine singular noun beginning with any consonant except **z**, **s + consonant**, **ps**, and **gn**), and **grand'** (before any singular noun beginning with a vowel). Otherwise, it is treated as a normal type (2) adjective ending in **-e**.

un gran film	(or)	un grande film	*a great movie*
un grand'amico	(or)	un grande amico	*a great friend*
una grand'attrice	(or)	una grande attrice	*a great actress*

But in all other cases only **grande** is allowed. And there is only one plural form: **grandi**.

un grande scrittore	*a great writer*
una grande donna	*a great woman*
dei grandi amici	*great friends*
delle grandi attrici	*great actresses*

Finally, consider **santo**. It undergoes changes only before proper names. Before masculine singular proper names beginning with **z**, **s + consonant**, **gn**, and **ps**, the form used is **Santo**.

Santo Stefano	*St. Stephen*
Santo Spirito	*Holy Spirit*

Before masculine singular proper names beginning with any other consonant, the form used is **San**.

San Paolo	*St. Paul*
San Giovanni	*St. John*

Before masculine and feminine proper names beginning with any vowel, the form used is **Sant'**.

Sant'Anna	*St. Ann*
Sant'Antonio	*St. Anthony*
Sant'Elisabetta	*St. Elizabeth*
Sant'Eugenio	*St. Eugene (Eugenius)*

Before feminine proper names beginning with any consonant, the form used is **Santa**.

Santa Maria	*St. Mary*
Santa Caterina	*St. Catherine*

With common nouns, **santo** is treated like a normal type (1) adjective ending in **-o**.

un santo bambino	*a saintly child*
una santa donna	*a saintly woman*

A. *Rewrite each phrase by putting the adjective before the noun and by making any other necessary changes.*

EXAMPLE   amico buono
_____*buon amico*_____

1. zio buono _____

2. zia buona _____

3. amico buono _____

4. amica buona _____

5. padre buono _____

6. ragazzi buoni _____

7. amiche buone _____

8. zaino bello _____

9. libro bello _____

10. orologio bello _____

11. zaini belli _____

12. libri belli _____

13. orologi belli _____

14. donna bella _____

15. donne belle _____

16. attrice bella _____

17. attrici belle _____

B. *Rewrite each phrase by putting the adjective after the noun. Don't forget to make any necessary changes to the article or partitive.*

BEFORE   AFTER

1. un bello zaino _____

2. dei grandi scultori _____

3. un buon caffè _____

4. dei buoni ragionieri _____

5. un bell'uomo _____

6. un buon portatile _____

7. dei bei programmi _____

8. un buono psicologo _____

9. una buona psicologa _____

10. un gran problema _____

11. una buona pesca _____

12. delle grandi autrici _____

13. un buon orologio _____

14. un gran musicista _____

15. una bella donna _____

16. un buon affare _____

C. *Each of the following is the name of a saint. Add the appropriate form of* **santo** *to each name.*

1. _____ Marco

2. _____ Isabella

3. _____ Bernardo

4. _____ Francesco

5. _____ Agnese (*f.*)

6. _____ Alessio

Comparison of adjectives

Someone or something can have a comparatively equal, greater, or lesser degree of some quality (as specified by some adjective). These degrees are called: positive, comparative, and superlative.

For the positive degree either **così... come** or **tanto... quanto** are used. (Note: **felice** = *happy.*)

Alessandro è **così** felice **come** sua sorella.	*Alexander is as happy as his sister.*
Loro sono **tanto** simpatici **quanto** intelligenti.	*They are as nice as they are intelligent.*

The first words in these constructions are optional in colloquial or informal speech.

Alessandro è felice **come** sua sorella.
Loro sono simpatici **quanto** intelligenti.

For the comparative degree **più** (*more*) or **meno** (*less*) is used, as the case may be.

Marco è **intelligente**.	*Mark is intelligent.*	Maria è **più intelligente**.	*Mary is more intelligent.*
Lui è **simpatico**.	*He's nice.*	Lei è **meno simpatica**.	*She is less nice.*
Sara è **alta**.	*Sarah is tall.*	Alessandro è **più alto**.	*Alexander is taller.*

For the superlative degree the definite article is used (in its proper form, of course!) followed by **più** or **meno**, as the case may be. The English preposition *in* is rendered by **di** in this case. (Note: **costoso** = *costly, expensive.* Recall that **di** + **il** = **del**; **di** + **la** = **della**, etc.)

Maria è **la più alta della** sua classe.	*Mary is the tallest in her class.*
Lui è **il più simpatico della** famiglia.	*He is the nicest in the family.*
Quelle macchine sono **le meno costose**.	*Those cars are the least expensive.*

In superlative constructions, the definite article is not repeated if it is already in front of a noun.

Maria è **la** ragazza **più alta** della classe.	*Mary is the tallest girl in the class.*
Bruno è **il** ragazzo **meno intelligente** della classe.	*Bruno is the least intelligent boy in the class.*

Note the following

In comparative constructions, the word *than* is rendered in one of two ways.

◆ If two forms (nouns or noun phrases) are compared by one adjective, the preposition **di** is used.

Giovanni è più alto **di** Marco.	*John is taller than Mark.*
Maria è meno ricca **di** sua sorella.	*Mary is less rich than her sister.*

◆ If two adjectives are used to compare the same form, **che** is used instead.

Lui è più simpatico **che** intelligente.	*He is nicer than he is intelligent.*
Maria è meno elegante **che** simpatica.	*Mary is less elegant than she is nice.*

The construction **di quello che** (also **di quel che** or **di ciò che**) corresponds to the English form *than* before a dependent clause (a clause that generally follows the main one).

Marco è più intelligente **di quel che** crede.	*Mark is more intelligent than what he believes.*
Maria è meno elegante **di quello che** pensa.	*Mary is less elegant than what she thinks.*

Some adjectives have both regular and irregular comparative and superlative forms.

buono	*good*	**più buono** (or) **migliore**	*better*
cattivo	*bad*	**più cattivo** (or) **peggiore**	*worse*
grande	*big*	**più grande** (or) **maggiore**	*bigger (older)*
piccolo	*small*	**più piccolo** (or) **minore**	*smaller (younger)*

Questo pane è **buono**, ma quello è **migliore**.	*This bread is good, but that one is better.*
Questo caffè è **cattivo**, ma quello è **peggiore**.	*This coffee is bad, but that one is worse.*
Lui è **il** fratello **maggiore**.	*He is the oldest brother.*
Lei è **la** sorella **minore**.	*She is the youngest sister.*

To express *very* as part of the adjective, just drop the final vowel of the adjective and add **-issimo**. These adjectives are then treated like normal type (1) adjectives ending in **-o**.

alto → alt- + -issimo = **altissimo**	*very tall*
buono → buon- + -issimo = **buonissimo**	*very good*
facile → facil- + -issimo = **facilissimo**	*very easy*
grande → grand- + -issimo = **grandissimo**	*very big*

Marco è **intelligentissimo**.	*Mark is very intelligent.*
Anche Claudia è **intelligentissima**.	*Claudia is also very intelligent.*
Quelle ragazze sono **bravissime**.	*Those girls are very good.*
Quelle lezioni sono **facilissime**.	*Those classes are very easy.*

A. *Say the following things using complete sentences.*

EXAMPLE   Mark is _____ than Claudia.

taller →   *Marco è più alto di Claudia.*

1. John is as _____ as Mary.

   a. tall _____

   b. intelligent _____

   c. nice _____

   d. happy _____

2. Mr. Sabatini is _____ than the students.

   a. happier _____

   b. richer _____

   c. nicer _____

   d. more tired _____

3. Mrs. Sabatini is less _____ than the students.

   a. happy _____

   b. rich _____

   c. nice _____

   d. tired _____

4. The jackets are _____ than the coats.

   a. more expensive _____

   b. longer _____

   c. more beautiful _____

   d. newer _____

5. The raincoats are _____ than the dresses.

   a. less expensive _____

   b. longer _____

   c. less beautiful _____

   d. older _____

B. *Complete each sentence with the appropriate form. If no form is necessary, leave the space blank.*

1. Lui è _____ professore più bravo _____ università.

2. Lei è _____ più intelligente _____ tutti *(everyone)*.

3. Giovanni è più bravo _____ intelligente.

4. Giovanni è più bravo _____ Pasquale.

5. Gli studenti sono più simpatici _____ intelligenti.

6. Maria è più intelligente _____ crede.

C. *Provide an equivalent form.*

1. più buoni   _____

2. più grande   _____

3. più cattiva   _____

4. più piccole   _____

5. più grandi   _____

6. molto ricco   _____

7. molto rossi   _____

8. molto facile   _____

9. molto belle   _____

10. molto simpatici   _____

11. molto simpatiche _____

12. molto buona   _____

D. *Provide the corresponding masculine or feminine form of each noun phrase, as required.*

MASCULINE	FEMININE
1. l'uomo intelligente	_____
2. _____	l'amica elegante
3. lo zio alto	_____
4. _____	la bella studentessa
5. il fratello simpaticissimo	_____
6. _____	la buon'amica
7. il ragazzo francese	_____
8. _____	una bravissima professoressa
9. un buono zio	_____
10. _____	una bella ragazza

11. un bell'amico   _____

12. _____   Santa Maria

E. *Choose the correct response.*

1. To refer to a man who is not wealthy, you would say _____.

   a. un povero uomo   b. un uomo povero

2. To refer to a friend who is old in age, you would say _____.

   a. un vecchio amico   b. un amico vecchio

3. Sara è così brava _____ il fratello.

   a. tanto   b. come

4. Alessandro è più simpatico _____ Maria.

   a. di   b. che

5. Marco è più simpatico _____ intelligente.

   a. di   b. che

6. Maria è più intelligente _____ quel che crede.

   a. di   b. che

Grammar in culture

Adjectives have many social functions. One of these is talking about the weather (**il tempo**). The following sentences use weather-related adjectives.

Il tempo è bello. / Fa bel tempo.	*The weather is nice.*
Il tempo è brutto. / Fa brutto tempo.	*The weather is bad.*
Il tempo è cattivo. / Fa cattivo tempo.	*The weather is awful.*
È sereno.	*It's clear.*
È nuvoloso.	*It's cloudy.*
È umido.	*It's humid.*
È piovoso.	*It's rainy.*
È burrascoso.	*It's stormy.*
È ventoso.	*It's windy.*

Some weather-related expressions require nouns rather than adjectives in Italian, even though the nouns are treated like adjectives in English.

Fa caldo.	*It is hot.*
Fa fresco.	*It is cool.*
Fa freddo.	*It is cold.*

How do you say the following in Italian?

1. It's hot and it's rainy.

   _____

2. It's always cold here (**qui**) and it's always cloudy.

   _____

3. The weather is nice today. It's clear and cool.

   _____

4. It's rainy today. The weather is awful.

   _____

Pronouns

·5·

Pronouns are words used in place of nouns, substantives (words taking on the function of nouns), or noun phrases (nouns accompanied by articles, demonstratives, adjectives, etc.).

Giovanni è italiano.	*John is Italian.*
Lui è italiano.	*He is Italian.*

We will deal with several types of pronouns in other units, including demonstrative, possessive, interrogative, indefinite, and relative pronouns. The discussion in this and the next unit will thus focus on personal pronouns (*I, me, you, us, them,* etc.).

Subject pronouns

Personal pronouns are classified as subject, object, or reflexive pronouns. They are also classified according to the person(s) speaking (first person), the person(s) spoken to (second person), or the person(s) spoken about (third person). The pronoun can, of course, be in the singular (referring to one person) or in the plural (referring to more than one person).

Subject pronouns are used as the subjects of verbs.

Io parlo italiano e **lui** parla francese.	*I speak Italian and he speaks French.*
Anche **loro** andranno in Italia.	*They, too, will be going to Italy.*

The Italian subject pronouns are (*fam.* = *familiar*; *pol.* = *polite*):

	SINGULAR		PLURAL	
FIRST PERSON	**io**	*I*	**noi**	*we*
SECOND PERSON	**tu**	*you (fam.)*	**voi**	*you (fam.)*
THIRD PERSON	**lui**	*he*	**loro**	*they*
	lei	*she*	**Loro**	*you (pol.)*
	Lei	*you (pol.)*		

Note that **io** is not capitalized unless it is the first word of a sentence.

Pronouns are optional in simple affirmative sentences, because it is easy to tell from the verb which person is the subject.

Io non capisco.	(or)	Non **capisco**.	*I do not understand.*
Loro vanno in Italia.	(or)	**Vanno** in Italia.	*They are going to Italy.*

However, they must be used for emphasis, to avoid ambiguity, or if more than one subject pronoun is required.

Devi parlare **tu**, non **io**!	*You have to speak, not I!*
Non è possibile che l'abbiano fatto **loro**.	*It's not possible that they did it.*
Mentre **lui** guarda la TV, **lei** ascolta la radio.	*While he watches TV, she listens to the radio.*
Lui e **io** vogliamo che **tu** dica la verità.	*He and I want you to tell the truth.*

Note

Subject pronouns must also be used after the following words.

anche	*also, too*
neanche	*neither, not even* (synonyms are **neppure** and **nemmeno**)
proprio	*really*

Anche **tu** devi venire alla festa.	*You, too, must come to the party.*
Non è venuto neanche **lui**.	*He didn't come either.*
Signor Rossini, è proprio **Lei**?	*Mr. Rossini, is it really you?*

The subject pronoun *it* is not usually stated in Italian.

È vero.	*It is true.*
Sembra che sia vero.	*It appears to be true.*

However, if this subject is required, then the following can be used.

esso (*m., sing.*)	**essi** (*m., pl.*)
essa (*f., sing.*)	**esse** (*f., pl.*)

È una buona ragione, ma neanche **essa** sarà creduta.	*It's a good reason, but not even it will be believed.*
Sono buone ragioni, ma neanche **esse** saranno credute.	*They are good reasons, but not even they will be believed.*

You has both familiar and polite forms.

Maria, anche **tu** studi l'italiano?	*Mary, are you also studying Italian?*
Signora Giusti, anche **Lei** studia l'italiano?	*Mrs. Giusti, are you also studying Italian?*

In writing, the polite forms (**Lei**, **Loro**) are capitalized in order to distinguish them from **lei** meaning *she* and **loro** meaning *they*, but this is not obligatory. In the plural, there is a strong tendency in current Italian to use **voi** as the plural of both **tu** and **Lei**. **Loro** is restricted to very formal situations.

The forms **lui** and **lei** are used in ordinary conversation and for most purposes. However, there are two more formal pronouns: **egli** and **ella**, respectively. These are used especially in reference to famous people.

Dante scrisse la *Divina Commedia*. **Egli** era fiorentino.	*Dante wrote the* Divine Comedy. *He was Florentine.*
Chi era Natalia Ginzburg? **Ella** era una grande scrittrice.	*Who was Natalia Ginzburg? She was a great writer.*

A. *Provide the missing pronouns.*

1. Anch'_____ voglio andare in Italia.

2. Devi chiamare _____, non io!

3. Non è possibile che siano stati _____.

4. Mio fratello guarda sempre la TV. _____ guarda sempre programmi interessanti.

5. Mia sorella legge molto. _____ vuole diventare professoressa d'università.

6. Anche _____ siamo andati in centro ieri.

7. Siete proprio _____?

8. Galileo era un grande scienziato (*scientist*). _____ era toscano.

9. Elsa Morante è una grande scrittrice. _____ è molto famosa.

10. Maria, vai anche _____ alla festa?

11. Signora Marchi, va anche _____ al cinema?

12. Signore e signori, anche _____ siete/sono felici?

B. *Rewrite each sentence by making each verb plural and adjusting the rest of the sentence accordingly. (Note:* **importante** = *important;* **interessante** = *interesting.)*

1. Anche esso è un problema importante.

_____

2. Anche essa è una tesi interessante.

_____

3. Io andrò in Italia quest'anno.

_____

4. Lui è italiano.

_____

5. Lei è italiana.

_____

Object pronouns

Object pronouns are used as objects of verbs and other structures. Their main use is to replace direct or indirect objects.

Direct object

Marco sta leggendo **quel libro** adesso.	*Marco is reading that book now.*
Marco **lo** sta leggendo.	*Marco is reading it.*

Indirect object

Marco darà quel libro **a sua sorella**.	*Marco will give that book to his sister.*
Marco **le** darà quel libro domani.	*Marco will give her that book tomorrow.*

Italian object pronouns generally come right before the verb. There are some exceptions, however, as will be discussed later on. The direct and indirect object pronouns are as follows.

DIRECT		INDIRECT	
mi	*me*	**mi**	*to me*
ti	*you (fam., sing.)*	**ti**	*to you (fam., sing.)*
La	*you (pol., sing.)*	**Le**	*to you (pol., sing.)*
lo	*him; it*	**gli**	*to him*
la	*her; it*	**le**	*to her*
ci	*us*	**ci**	*to us*
vi	*you (fam., pl.)*	**vi**	*to you (fam., pl.)*
li	*them (m.)*	**gli**	*to them (m.)*
le	*them (f.)*	**gli**	*to them (f.)*

Notice that the plural of the indirect object pronouns **gli** (*to him*) and **le** (*to her*) is **gli** (*to them*). This means that you will have to be very careful when determining which meaning is intended by the context of the sentence.

Dove sono i tuoi amici?	*Where are your (male) friends?*
Gli voglio parlare.	*I want to speak to them.*
Dove sono le tue amiche?	*Where are your (female) friends?*
Gli voglio parlare.	*I want to speak to them.*

Third-person forms

The English direct object pronouns *it* and *them* are expressed by the third-person direct object pronouns. Be careful! Choose the pronoun according to the gender and number of the noun it replaces. And, again, these go before the verb.

Masculine singular

Il ragazzo comprerà **il gelato** domani.	*The boy will buy the ice cream tomorrow.*
Il ragazzo **lo** comprerà domani.	*The boy will buy it tomorrow.*

Masculine plural

Quella donna comprerà **i biglietti** domani.	*That woman will buy the tickets tomorrow.*
Quella donna **li** comprerà domani.	*That woman will buy them tomorrow.*

Feminine singular

Mio fratello comprerà **la rivista** domani.	*My brother will buy the magazine tomorrow.*
Mio fratello **la** comprerà domani.	*My brother will buy it tomorrow.*

Feminine plural

Sua sorella comprerà **le riviste** domani.	*His sister will buy the magazines tomorrow.*
Sua sorella **le** comprerà domani.	*His sister will buy them tomorrow.*

A. *Complete each sentence with the appropriate direct or indirect pronoun, as required. Use the English pronouns given as a guide. (Note:* **va bene** *= OK;* **indirizzo** *= address.)*

1. *(to) me*

   a. Giovanni _____ chiama ogni sera.

   b. Giovanni _____ ha dato la sua penna.

2. *(to) you (fam., sing.)*

   a. La sua amica _____ ha telefonato, non è vero?

   b. Lui vuole che io _____ chiami stasera.

3. *(to) you (pol., sing.)*

   a. Professoressa, _____ chiamo domani, va bene?

   b. Professoressa, _____ do il mio compito domani, va bene?

4. *(to) him*

   a. Conosci Marco? Mia sorella _____ telefona spesso.

   b. Sì, io _____ conosco molto bene.

5. *(to) her*

   a. Ieri ho visto Maria e _____ ho dato il tuo indirizzo.

   b. Anche tu hai visto Maria, no? No, ma forse _____ chiamo stasera.

6. *(to) us*

   a. Marco e Maria, quando _____ venite a visitare?

   b. Signor Verdi e signora Verdi, quando _____ telefonerete?

7. *(to) you (fam., pl.)*

   a. Claudia e Franca, _____ devo dire qualcosa.

   b. Claudia e Franca, non _____ ho dato niente ieri.

8. *(to) them (m.)*

   a. Conosci quegli studenti? No, non _____ conosco.

   b. Scrivi mai a quegli studenti? No, non _____ scrivo mai.

9. *(to) them (f.)*

   a. Conosci quelle studentesse? No, non _____ conosco.

   b. Scrivi mai a quelle studentesse? No, non _____ scrivo mai.

B. *Rewrite each sentence by replacing the italicized object with the appropriate pronoun. (Note:* **volentieri** *= gladly;* **stivale** *[m.] = boots.)*

EXAMPLE   Io comprerò *quella camicia* domani.

Io la comprerò domani.

1. Marco guarda sempre *la televisione* ogni sera.

   _____

2. Anche lei preferisce *quel programma*.

   _____

3. Mangeremo *gli spaghetti* volentieri in quel ristorante.

   _____

4. Anche Maria vuole *le patate*.

   _____

5. Compreremo *le scarpe* domani.

   _____

6. Loro compreranno *gli stivali* in centro.

   _____

7. Anch'io prendo *l'espresso*, va bene?

   _____

8. Vuoi *la carne* anche tu?

   _____

Stressed pronouns

There is a second type of personal object pronoun that goes after the verb. It is known as a stressed or tonic pronoun.

DIRECT OBJECT PRONOUNS			
BEFORE, UNSTRESSED		AFTER, STRESSED	
mi	*me*	**me**	*me*
ti	*you (fam.)*	**te**	*you (fam.)*
La	*you (pol.)*	**Lei**	*you (pol.)*
lo	*him*	**lui**	*him*
la	*her*	**lei**	*her*
ci	*us*	**noi**	*us*
vi	*you (fam., pl.)*	**voi**	*you (fam., pl.)*
li	*them (m.)*	**loro**	*them*
le	*them (f.)*	**loro**	*them*

INDIRECT OBJECT PRONOUNS

BEFORE, UNSTRESSED		AFTER, STRESSED	
mi	*to me*	**a me**	*to me*
ti	*to you (fam., sing.)*	**a te**	*to you (fam., sing.)*
Le	*to you (pol., sing.)*	**a Lei**	*to you (pol., sing.)*
gli	*to him*	**a lui**	*to him*
le	*to her*	**a lei**	*to her*
ci	*to us*	**a noi**	*to us*
vi	*to you (fam., pl.)*	**a voi**	*to you (fam., pl.)*
gli	*to them (m.)*	**a loro**	*to them*
gli	*to them (f.)*	**a loro**	*to them*

For most purposes, the two types can be used alternatively, although the unstressed pronouns are more common in most types of discourse. The stressed pronouns are more appropriate when emphasis is required or in order to avoid ambiguity.

Marco lo darà **a me**, non **a te**!	*Mark will give it to me, not to you!*
Ieri ho scritto **a te**, e solo **a te**!	*Yesterday I wrote to you, and only you!*

These are the only object pronouns you can use after a preposition.

Maria viene **con noi**.	*Mary is coming with us.*
Il professore parla **di te**.	*The professor is speaking about you.*
L'ha fatto **per me**.	*He did it for me.*

ESERCIZIO

5·3

A. *Complete each sentence with the appropriate stressed direct or indirect object pronoun, as required. Use the English pronouns given as a guide.*

1. *(to) me*

   a. Claudia chiama solo _____ ogni sera, non la sua amica.

   b. Giovanni ha dato la sua penna _____, non al suo amico.

2. *(to) you (fam., sing.)*

   a. Claudia ha telefonato _____, non è vero?

   b. Lui vuole che io chiami anche _____ stasera.

3. *(to) you (pol., sing.)*

   a. Dottor Marchi, chiamo _____, non l'altro medico, domani, va bene?

   b. Professoressa Verdi, do il mio compito _____ domani, va bene?

4. *(to) him*

   a. Conosci il professor Giusti? Mia sorella telefona solo _____ per studiare per gli esami.

   b. Sì, io conosco proprio _____ molto bene.

5. *(to) her*

   a. Ieri ho visto la tua amica e ho dato il tuo indirizzo anche _____.

   b. Anche tu hai visto Paola, no? No, ma forse esco con _____ stasera.

6. *(to) us*

   a. Marco e Maria, quando uscirete con _____?

   b. Signor Verdi e signora Verdi, quando telefonerete _____?

7. *(to) you* (*fam., pl.*)

   a. Marco e Maria, parlerò di _____ alla professoressa.

   b. Claudia e Franca, non ho dato niente _____ ieri.

8. *(to) them* (*m.*)

   a. Conosci quegli studenti? Sì, e domani parlerò di _____ al professore.

   b. Scrivi mai a quegli studenti? No, non scrivo mai _____.

9. *(to) them* (*f.*)

   a. Conosci quelle studentesse? Sì, e domani parlerò di _____ al professore.

   b. Scrivi mai a quelle studentesse? No, non scrivo mai _____.

B. *How do you say the following in Italian?*

1. Mark will give your address to me, not to him!

   _____

2. Yesterday I wrote to you (*fam., sing.*), and only you!

   _____

3. Mary is coming with us, not with them, to the movies tomorrow.

   _____

4. The professor is always speaking about you (*fam., pl.*), not about us!

   _____

5. Mary, I did it for you!

   _____

6. Mrs. Verdi, I did it for you!

   _____

Other pronouns

Words such as **molto**, **tanto**, etc., can also function as pronouns.

Lui mangia **assai**.	*He eats quite a lot.*
Tuo fratello dorme **molto**, no?	*Your brother sleeps a lot, doesn't he?*
Ieri ho mangiato **troppo**.	*Yesterday I ate too much.*

When referring to people in general, use the plural forms **alcuni**, **molti**, **parecchi**, **pochi**, **tanti**, **tutti**, etc.

Molti vanno in Italia quest'anno.	*Many (people) are going to Italy this year.*
Tutti sanno quello.	*Everyone knows that.*

Use the corresponding feminine forms (**molte**, **alcune**, etc.) when referring to females.

Di quelle ragazze, **molte** sono italiane.	*Of those girls, many are Italian.*
Di tutte quelle donne, **alcune** sono americane.	*Of all those women, some are American.*

The pronoun **ne** has four main functions. It is placed before the verb when used to replace the following structures:

◆ partitives

Comprerai anche **delle patate**?	*Will you also buy some potatoes?*
Sì, **ne** comprerò.	*Yes, I'll buy some.*

◆ numbers and quantitative expressions

Quanti **libri** devi leggere?	*How many books do you have to read?*
Ne devo leggere tre.	*I have to read three (of them).*

◆ indefinite expressions

Leggi molti **libri** di solito, non è vero?	*You usually read a lot of books, don't you?*
Sì, **ne** leggo molti di solito.	*Yes, I usually read a lot (of them).*

◆ topic phrases introduced by **di**

Ha parlato **di matematica**, vero?	*He spoke about mathematics, didn't he?*
Sì, **ne** ha parlato.	*Yes, he spoke about it.*

The locative (place) pronoun **ci** means *there*. It also is placed before the verb.

Andate **in Italia**, non è vero?	*You are going to Italy, aren't you?*
Sì, **ci** andiamo domani.	*Yes, we are going there tomorrow.*
Marco vive **a Perugia**, non è vero?	*Marco lives in Perugia, doesn't he?*
Sì, **ci** vive da molti anni.	*Yes, he has been living there for many years.*

Ne is used instead to express *from there*.

Sei arrivato **dall'Italia** ieri, non è vero?	*You arrived from Italy yesterday, didn't you?*
Sì, **ne** sono arrivato proprio ieri.	*Yes, I came from there just yesterday.*

A. *Rewrite each sentence by replacing the italicized word or phrase with either* **ne** *or* **ci**.

1. Sì, comprerò *delle matite*.

   _____

2. Mio fratello comprerà *degli zaini* domani.

   _____

3. Devo guardare due *programmi* stasera.

   _____

4. Di solito leggo molte *riviste* ogni settimana.

   _____

5. Anche lei ha parlato *di Dante*.

   _____

6. Andiamo *in Italia* domani.

   _____

7. Mia sorella vive *a Chicago* da molti anni.

   _____

8. Loro arrivano *dalla Francia* tra poco.

   _____

B. *How do you say the following in Italian?*

1. My brother eats quite a lot.

   _____

2. Does your sister sleep a lot?

   _____

3. Yesterday we ate too much.

   _____

4. Only a few are going to Italy this year. But many went last year.

   _____

5. Of those women, many are Italian and a few are American.

   _____

C. *Choose the appropriate pronoun to complete each sentence.*

1. Giovanni è andato anche _____ in Italia.

    a. lui   b. egli

2. Petrarca era anche _____ un fiorentino.

    a. lui   b. egli

3. Claudia, quando _____ hai chiamato?

    a. mi   b. me

4. Marco, è vero che _____ hai parlato già?

    a. gli   b. lui

5. Noi abbiamo parlato a tuo fratello ieri. Non _____ abbiamo detto proprio niente.

    a. gli   b. le

6. Noi abbiamo parlato a quella donna ieri. Non _____ abbiamo detto proprio niente.

    a. gli   b. le

7. Vieni con _____ in centro!

    a. mi   b. me

D. *Rewrite each sentence by replacing the italicized object pronoun words or phrases with the appropriate unstressed pronouns and by making all necessary changes.*

1. Claudia darà *il libro* a me domani.

    _____

2. Io darò *le matite* a te dopo.

    _____

3. Io ho dato le scarpe *alla loro amica*.

    _____

4. Voglio *gli gnocchi* anch'io.

    _____

5. Lui chiama spesso *il fratello e sua sorella*.

    _____

6. Lui vuole *delle scarpe*.

    _____

7. Non voglio *la carne*.

    _____

8. Prendo due *matite*.

    _____

9. Marco andrà *in Italia* domani.

_____

10. Lei comprerà molte *cose* per la festa.

_____

11. Prendo quattro *tazze di caffè* di solito.

_____

Grammar in culture

Familiar vs. polite address in Italian is an important social distinction. Grammatically, this involves using appropriate pronouns and verb forms. Use the third-person plural polite forms with strangers and those with whom you are on a formal social basis; otherwise use the second-person familiar forms (with family, friends, children, colleagues, and animals).

FAMILIAR	POLITE
tu	**Lei**
Anche **tu** sei italiana, Maria, vero? *Maria, you're Italian as well, right?*	Anche **Lei** è italiana, dottoressa Verdi, vero? *Dr. Verdi, you're Italian as well, right?*
voi	**Loro**
Venite anche **voi**, Marco e Maria? *You're coming too, Marco and Maria?*	Vengono anche **Loro**, signor e signora Rossi? *You're coming too, Mr. and Mrs. Rossi?*
ti	**La**
Maria, **ti** chiamo domani. *Maria, I'll call you tomorrow.*	Professore, **La** chiamo domani. *Professor, I'll call you tomorrow.*
ti / a te	**Le / a Lei**
Maria, **ti** ho detto tutto. *Mary, I told you everything.*	Signore, **Le** ho detto tutto. *Sir, I told you everything.*
Maria, ho dato il mio cellulare **a te**. *Maria, I gave my cell phone to you.*	Signore, ho dato il mio cellulare **a Lei**. *Sir, I gave my cell phone to you.*

Rewrite each sentence, using the addressee in parentheses and making all necessary changes.

EXAMPLE   Maria, vieni anche tu? (Signora Verdi)

Signora Verdi, viene anche Lei?

1. Professore, La chiamo domani, va bene? (Gina)

_____

2. Mamma, ti ho dato il regalo (*gift*) per Natale. (Professore)

_____

3. Signor e signora Marchi, partono anche Loro domani? (Gina e Claudia)

_____

4. Ragazzino (*little boy*), chi sei tu? (Signore)

_____

5. Marco, ho dato quella cosa a te ieri. (Professoressa)

_____

More pronouns

As you saw in the previous unit, pronouns constitute a fairly complex part of Italian grammar. And there is more to know about them, as you may recall from previous study. In this unit, we will conclude the treatment of these pesky pronouns.

Object pronouns with compound tenses

The past participle of verbs in compound tenses agrees with the object pronouns **lo**, **la**, **li**, **le**, and **ne**.

Agreement with lo

Hanno visto **il nuovo film**?	*Did they see the new movie?*
Sì, **lo** hanno vist**o** (**l'**hanno vist**o**).	*Yes, they saw it.*

Agreement with la

Hai comprato **la camicia**?	*Did you buy the shirt?*
Sì, **la** ho comprat**a** (**l'**ho comprat**a**) ieri.	*Yes, I bought it yesterday.*

Agreement with li

Avete finito **gli spaghetti**?	*Did you finish the spaghetti?*
Sì, **li** abbiamo finit**i**.	*Yes, we finished them.*

Agreement with le

Hai mangiato **le mele**?	*Did you eat the apples?*
Sì, **le** ho mangiat**e**.	*Yes, I ate them.*

Agreement with ne (when used to replace quantitative expressions only)

Quante **mele** hai mangiato?	*How many apples did you eat?*
Ne ho mangiat**e** quattro.	*I ate four of them.*
Quanti **panini** hai mangiato?	*How many sandwiches did you eat?*
Ne ho mangiat**i** tanti.	*I ate a lot.*

Note: Only the singular forms **lo** and **la** can be elided with the auxiliary forms of **avere**.

Agreement with the other direct object pronouns—**mi**, **ti**, **ci**, **vi**—is optional.

Claudia **ci** ha chiamato. (or)	*Claudia called us.*
Claudia **ci** ha chiamat**i**.	

There is no agreement with indirect object pronouns.

Giovanni **gli** ha scritto.   *John wrote to him (to them).*
Giovanni **le** ha scritto.   *John wrote to her.*

So, be careful!

Direct object pronoun: agreement

Lui ha già mangiato **le patate**.   *He already ate the potatoes.*
Lui **le** ha già mangiate.   *He already ate them.*

Indirect object pronoun: no agreement

Lui ha scritto **a sua sorella**.   *He wrote to his sister.*
Lui **le** ha scritto.   *He wrote to her.*

ESERCIZIO
6·1

A. *Rewrite each sentence by replacing each italicized object word or phrase with the appropriate unstressed object pronoun and by making all other necessary changes.*

1. Mio fratello ha comprato *quello zaino* ieri.

   _____

2. Abbiamo dato quello zaino *a mio fratello*.

   _____

3. Loro hanno preso *quegli stivali* ieri.

   _____

4. Ho dato quegli stivali *ai miei amici* ieri.

   _____

5. Mia sorella ha comprato *quella borsa* ieri.

   _____

6. Mia madre ha dato quella borsa *a mia sorella*.

   _____

7. Abbiamo visto *quelle scarpe* in centro.

   _____

8. Abbiamo dato quelle scarpe *alle nostre amiche* ieri.

   _____

9. Ho mangiato tre *patate*.

   _____

10. Abbiamo comprato molte *cose* in centro ieri.

    _____

B. *Answer each question affirmatively using the appropriate unstressed pronoun and making any necessary adjustment to the past participle.*

EXAMPLE   Hai preso quella matita?

_____*Sì, l'ho presa.*_____

1. Hai preso quello zaino?

_____

2. Hai comprato quelle scarpe?

_____

3. Hai visto la tua amica?

_____

4. Hai chiamato i tuoi amici?

_____

5. Hai mangiato delle patate?

_____

Double pronouns

When both direct and indirect object pronouns are used, the following rules apply:

- The indirect object pronoun always precedes the direct object pronoun (the only possible forms are **lo**, **la**, **li**, **le**) and the pronoun **ne**.

Claudia **mi** darà **il libro** domani.	*Claudia will give the book to me tomorrow.*
Claudia **me lo** darà domani.	*Claudia will give it to me tomorrow.*
Giovanni **mi** comprerà **delle matite**.	*John will buy me some pencils.*
Giovanni **me ne** comprerà.	*John will buy me some.*

- The indirect pronouns **mi**, **ti**, **ci**, and **vi** are changed to **me**, **te**, **ce**, and **ve**, respectively.

Lei **mi** darà **il libro** domani.	*She is giving me the book tomorrow.*
Lei **me lo** darà domani.	*She is giving it to me tomorrow.*
Maria **vi** darà **quelle scarpe** per Natale.	*Mary will give you those shoes for Christmas.*
Maria **ve le** darà per Natale.	*Mary will give you them for Christmas.*

Note that the rule regarding agreement between the direct object pronoun and the past participle still applies.

Lui **ci** ha dato **la sua bella penna** ieri.	*He gave his beautiful pen to us yesterday.*
Lui **ce l'**ha dat**a** ieri.	*He gave it to us yesterday.*
Giovanni **ti** ha dato **i suoi libri** già.	*John has already given his books to you.*
Giovanni **te li** ha dat**i** già.	*John has already given them to you.*

◆ The indirect pronouns **gli** and **le** are both changed to **glie** and combined with **lo**, **la**, **li**, **le**, or **ne** to form one word: **glielo, gliela, glieli, gliele, gliene**.

Claudia dà **il libro a Paolo** domani.	*Claudia will give the book to Paul tomorrow.*
Claudia **glielo** dà domani.	*Claudia will give it to him tomorrow.*
Maria darà **quella borsa a sua sorella**.	*Mary will give her sister that purse.*
Maria **gliela** darà.	*Mary will give it to her it.*

Note again the agreement between the past participle and the direct object pronoun, even though it is part of the combined word.

Io ho dato **i miei orologi ad Alessandro**.	*I gave my watches to Alexander.*
Io **glieli** ho dat**i**.	*I gave them to him.*
Io ho dato **le mie chiavi a Marco**.	*I gave my keys to Mark.*
Io **gliele** ho dat**e**.	*I gave them to him.*
Io ho comprato **due matite a mio zio**.	*I bought my uncle two pencils.*
Io **gliene** ho comprat**e** due.	*I bought him two (of them).*

ESERCIZIO
6·2

A. *Rewrite each sentence by replacing the italicized object words or phrases with the appropriate double object pronouns and by making all other necessary changes.*

1. Mia sorella *mi* ha comprato *quello zaino* ieri.

   _____

2. *Gli* ho dato *quello zaino* ieri.

   _____

3. Loro ti hanno preso *quegli stivali* ieri.

   _____

4. *Le* ho dato *quegli stivali* ieri.

   _____

5. Nostra madre *ci* ha comprato *quella macchina* qualche anno fa.

   _____

6. Mia madre *le* ha dato *quella borsa*.

   _____

7. *Vi* abbiamo comprato *quelle scarpe* in centro.

   _____

8. *Gli* abbiamo dato *quelle scarpe* ieri.

   _____

9. *Gli* ho dato tre *patate*.

   _____

10. *Le* abbiamo comprato molte *cose* in centro ieri.

   _____

B. *Answer each question affirmatively using the appropriate double pronoun and making any necessary adjustment to the past participle.*

EXAMPLE   Mi hai preso quella matita?

_____Sì, te l'ho presa._____

1. Ci hai preso quello zaino?

   _____

2. Gli hai comprato quelle scarpe?

   _____

3. Ti ho dato le mie matite?

   _____

4. Le hai detto quelle cose?

   _____

5. Mi hai preso delle patate?

   _____

Attached pronouns

Object pronouns are attached to an infinitive or gerund. Double pronouns are both attached. Note that the final **-e** of the infinitive is dropped when a single or double pronoun is attached.

Prima di mangiare **il gelato**, voglio i ravioli.	*Before eating the ice cream, I want ravioli.*
Prima di mangiar**lo**, voglio i ravioli.	*Before eating it, I want ravioli.*
Vedendo **Maria**, l'ho chiamata.	*Seeing Mary, I called her.*
Vedendo**la**, l'ho chiamata.	*Seeing her, I called her.*

They are also attached to the form **ecco** (see Unit 7).

Ecco **la matita**.	*Here is the pencil.*
Ecco**la**.	*Here it is.*
Ecco **Giovanni e Claudia**.	*Here are John and Claudia.*
Ecco**li**.	*Here they are.*
Ecco **le chiavi per te**.	*Here are the keys for you.*
Ecco**tele**.	*Here they are for you.*

All double pronouns are written as one unit when attached to a verb.

With the modal verbs (**potere, dovere, volere**) you can either attach the object pronouns to the infinitive, or put them before the modal verb.

Non posso mangiare **la carne**.	*I cannot eat meat.*
Non posso mangiar**la**. (or) Non **la** posso mangiare.	*I cannot eat it.*
Lei **gli** vuole dare **il suo portatile**.	*She wants to give him her laptop.*
Lei vuole dar**glielo**. (or) Lei **glielo** vuole dare.	*She wants to give it to him.*

Object pronouns with imperative verbs

The object pronouns (single and double) are also attached to the familiar forms of the imperative (**tu, noi, voi**). They are not attached to the polite **Lei** and **Loro** forms.

Familiar

Giovanni, mangia **la mela**!	*John, eat the apple!*
Giovanni, mangia**la**!	*John, eat it!*
Sara, scrivi **l'e-mail a tuo fratello**!	*Sarah, write the e-mail to your brother!*
Sara, scrivi**gliela**!	*Sarah, write it to him!*
Marco e Maria, date **la vostra penna a me**!	*Mark and Mary, give your pen to me!*
Marco e Maria, date**mela**!	*Mark and Maria, give it to me!*

Polite

Signor Marchi, mangi **la mela**!	*Mr. Marchi, eat the apple!*
Signor Marchi, **la** mangi!	*Mr. Marchi, eat it!*
Signor Dini, scriva **l'e-mail a Suo fratello**!	*Mr. Dini, write the e-mail to your brother!*
Signor Dini, **gliela** scriva!	*Mr. Dini, write it to him!*

When attaching pronouns to familiar forms ending with an apostrophe—**da', di', fa', sta',** and **va'** (see Unit 15)—you must double the first letter of the pronoun. There is, of course, no double **gl**.

Da' la penna a me!	*Give the pen to me!*
Dammi la penna!	*Give me the pen!*
Dammela!	*Give it to me!*
Di' la verità a lui!	*Tell him the truth!*
Dilla a lui!	*Tell it to him!*
Digliela!	*Tell it to him!*
Fa' quel compito per lui!	*Do that task for him!*
Fallo per lui!	*Do it for him!*
Faglielo!	*Do it for him!*
Da' due matite a me!	*Give me two pencils!*
Danne due a me!	*Give me two (of them)!*
Dammene due!	*Give me two (of them)!*
Va' in Italia!	*Go to Italy!*
Vacci!	*Go there!*

With the second-person singular negative infinitive form, you can either attach the pronouns to the infinitive or else put them before.

AFFIRMATIVE		NEGATIVE			
Mangia**lo**!	*Eat it!*	Non mangiar**lo**!	(or)	Non **lo** mangiare!	*Don't eat it!*
Manda**mela**!	*Send it to me!*	Non mandar**mela**!	(or)	Non **me la** mandare!	*Don't send it to me!*

A. *Rewrite each sentence by replacing the italicized words with single or double object pronouns, as necessary, and by making all necessary changes. (Note: **favore** [m.] = favor.)*

1. Prima di bere *la bibita*, voglio mangiare.

   _____

2. Vedendo *i miei amici*, li ho chiamati.

   _____

3. Ecco *le tue amiche*.

   _____

4. Ecco *gli stivali nuovi per te*.

   _____

5. Non voglio mangiare *gli spaghetti*.

   _____

6. Potremo andare *in Italia* tra poco.

   _____

7. Vogliamo scrivere molte *cose a lui*.

   _____

8. Giovanni, bevi *il caffè*!

   _____

9. Alessandro da' *la tua penna a me*!

   _____

10. Maria, fa' *questo favore a tua madre*!

    _____

11. Signora Marchi, dica *la verità a me*!

    _____

12. Franco, di' *la verità a me*!

    _____

B. *How do you say the following in Italian?*

1. John, give the pen to me! Don't give it to her!

   _____

2. Doctor Verdi, tell him the truth! But don't tell it to them (f.)!

   _____

3. Mom, do that task for me! But don't do it for him!

_____

4. Mark, do me a favor! But don't do it for them (*m.*)!

_____

5. Mary, go downtown with us! Don't go there with him!

_____

6. Mrs. Verdi, go downtown with us! Don't go there with her!

_____

C. *Rewrite each sentence by replacing the italicized object pronoun words or phrases with the appropriate unstressed pronouns and by making all other necessary changes.*

1. Marco *mi* darà *il portatile* domani.

_____

2. Io *ti* ho dato *le scarpe* ieri.

_____

3. Loro hanno dato *le matite alla loro amica.*

_____

4. Prima di mangiare *gli gnocchi*, voglio mangiare l'antipasto.

_____

5. Ecco *il fratello e sua sorella.*

_____

6. Lui ha comprato *le scarpe nuove* ieri.

_____

7. Non voglio mangiare *la carne.*

_____

8. Claudia, mangia *le patate*!

_____

9. Giovanni, dammi due *matite*!

_____

10. Mio fratello è andato *in Italia* ieri.

_____

11. Lei ha comprato molte *mele* ieri.

_____

12. Ci sono quattro *matite* nello zaino.

_____

D. *Rewrite each sentence by replacing each italicized phrase with the appropriate unstressed object pronoun. Then, rewrite the sentence again by making the italicized phrase plural and resubstituting the appropriate unstressed object pronoun. Make all other necessary changes.*

EXAMPLE   Io ho sempre detto *la stessa cosa.*

Io l'ho sempre detta.

Io ho sempre detto le stesse cose.

Io le ho sempre dette.

1. Bruno mi ha comprato *quell'orologio.*

2. Marco, mangia *quella mela*!

3. Paola vi darà *quel libro* domani.

4. Anche tu mi hai comprato *quella camicia* nello stesso negozio, vero?

5. Lui ha bevuto *quel caffè* volentieri.

Grammar in culture

Whether a pronoun comes before or after the verb depends on the structure of the sentence. In some cases, however, as in the negative imperative, the pronoun may come before or after; this is a matter of style or emphasis. The difference between **Marco, non lo mangiare** and **Marco, non mangiarlo** (*Marco, don't eat it!*) is that the latter command stresses the verb more, thus giving the action more emphasis.

ESERCIZIO
6·4

Provide the emphatic or nonemphatic version of each sentence.

EMPHATIC	NONEMPHATIC
1. Gina, non darmela!	_____
2. _____	Luca, non ci andare!
3. Posso darti questo libro?	_____
4. _____	Ti voglio chiamare subito.

Demonstratives

Demonstratives are special kinds of adjectives (see Unit 4). They mark nouns as referring to someone or something that is relatively near or far from someone or something else.

RELATIVELY NEAR		RELATIVELY FAR	
questo bambino	*this child*	**quel bambino**	*that child*
questa porta	*this door*	**quella porta**	*that door*

The demonstrative of nearness

As listed in the dictionary, the demonstrative indicating *nearness* is **questo** (*this*). Like any adjective, it modifies the noun—that is, it changes in form to indicate the gender and number of the noun. Its forms are given below.

The form **questo** is used before a masculine noun. Its plural form is **questi**.

SINGULAR		PLURAL	
questo amico	*this friend*	**questi amici**	*these friends*
questo cane	*this dog*	**questi cani**	*these dogs*
questo ragazzo	*this boy*	**questi ragazzi**	*these boys*
questo studente	*this student*	**questi studenti**	*these students*
questo zio	*this uncle*	**questi zii**	*these uncles*

And the form **questa** is used before a feminine noun. Its plural form is **queste**.

SINGULAR		PLURAL	
questa amica	*this friend*	**queste amiche**	*these friends*
questa camicia	*this shirt*	**queste camicie**	*these shirts*
questa ragazza	*this girl*	**queste ragazze**	*these girls*
questa studentessa	*this student*	**queste studentesse**	*these students*
questa zia	*this aunt*	**queste zie**	*these aunts*

The form **quest'** can be used (optionally) in front of a singular noun (masculine or feminine) beginning with a vowel.

questo orologio	(or)	**quest'orologio**	*this watch*
questa amica	(or)	**quest'amica**	*this friend*

Be careful!

Unlike in English, in Italian you must repeat the demonstrative before each noun.

questo zio e **questa zia**	*this uncle and aunt*
questi ragazzi e **queste ragazze**	*these boys and girls*

ESERCIZIO 7·1

A. *Rewrite each of the following phrases in the plural. If you have forgotten the meanings of the nouns used in this and the next Esercizio, look them up in the glossary at the back of this book.*

1. quest'affare _____
2. quest'attrice _____
3. questo biologo _____
4. questa bugia _____
5. questo cameriere _____
6. questa cameriera _____

B. *Now, rewrite each phrase in the singular. Some of the items are tricky, although you have come across the grammar behind them in previous units. So, be careful!*

1. questi diagrammi _____
2. queste dita _____
3. questi francesi _____
4. queste francesi _____
5. questi giornali _____

The demonstrative of farness

The demonstrative adjective indicating farness is **quello** (*that*). Its forms vary as follows.

◆ The form **quello** is used before a masculine noun beginning with **z**, **s + consonant**, **gn**, or **ps**. Its plural form is **quegli**.

SINGULAR		PLURAL	
quello zio	*that uncle*	**quegli zii**	*those uncles*
quello studente	*that student*	**quegli studenti**	*those students*
quello gnocco	*that dumpling*	**quegli gnocchi**	*those dumplings*
quello psicologo	*that psychologist*	**quegli psicologi**	*those psychologists*

◆ The form **quel** is used before a masculine noun beginning with any other consonant. Its plural form is **quei**.

SINGULAR		PLURAL	
quel cane	*that dog*	**quei cani**	*those dogs*
quel giornale	*that newspaper*	**quei giornali**	*those newspapers*
quel giorno	*that day*	**quei giorni**	*those days*
quel ragazzo	*that boy*	**quei ragazzi**	*those boys*

◆ The form **quell'** is used before a masculine noun beginning with any vowel. Its plural form is **quegli**.

SINGULAR		PLURAL	
quell'amico	*that friend*	**quegli amici**	*those friends*
quell'avvocato	*that lawyer*	**quegli avvocati**	*those lawyers*
quell'impermeabile	*that raincoat*	**quegli impermeabili**	*those raincoats*
quell'orologio	*that watch*	**quegli orologi**	*those watches*

◆ The form **quella** is used before a feminine noun beginning with any consonant. Its plural form is **quelle**.

SINGULAR		PLURAL	
quella camicia	*that shirt*	**quelle camicie**	*those shirts*
quella ragazza	*that girl*	**quelle ragazze**	*those girls*
quella studentessa	*that student*	**quelle studentesse**	*those students*
quella zia	*that aunt*	**quelle zie**	*those aunts*

◆ And the form **quell'** is used before a feminine noun beginning with any vowel. Its plural form is also **quelle**.

SINGULAR		PLURAL	
quell'amica	*that friend*	**quelle amiche**	*those friends*
quell'attrice	*that actress*	**quelle attrici**	*those actresses*
quell'infermiera	*that nurse*	**quelle infermiere**	*those nurses*
quell'ora	*that hour*	**quelle ore**	*those hours*

Tips and reminders!

As with the articles, when an adjective precedes a noun, you will have to change the demonstrative according to the adjective's initial sound.

quello zio	*that uncle*	but	**quel simpatico zio**	*that nice uncle*
quegli amici	*those friends*	but	**quei simpatici amici**	*those nice friends*

Remember to repeat the demonstratives before every noun:

quel ragazzo e **quella ragazza**   *that boy and girl*

As was the case with **bello** (see Unit 4), **quello** undergoes the same kinds of form changes as the definite article (see Unit 3).

lo	→	**quello**
l'	→	**quell'**
gli	→	**quegli**
il	→	**quel**
i	→	**quei**
la	→	**quella**
le	→	**quelle**

A. *Rewrite each of the following phrases in the plural. If you have forgotten the meanings of the nouns and adjectives used in this and the next Esercizio, look them up in the glossary at the back of this book.*

1. quell'architetto _____

2. quell'autrice _____

3. quel braccio _____

4. quella cameriera _____

5. quello zaino _____

6. quell'ipotesi _____

7. quella macchina _____

8. quel simpatico bambino _____

9. quel bel ragazzo _____

10. quella bella ragazza _____

B. *Now, rewrite each phrase in the singular.*

1. quei programmi _____

2. quei problemi _____

3. quegli inglesi _____

4. quelle inglesi _____

5. quei nomi _____

6. quelle notti _____

7. quegli occhi _____

8. quelle paia _____

9. quegli spagnoli simpatici _____

10. quei teoremi e quelle tesi _____

Demonstrative pronouns

Demonstrative pronouns replace noun phrases formed with demonstrative adjectives.

Questa ragazza è americana.	*This girl is American.*
Questa è americana.	*This one is American.*
Quel ragazzo è italiano.	*That boy is Italian.*
Quello è italiano.	*That one is Italian.*

The pronouns retain the gender and number of the demonstratives they replace. However, once you do this you will have to make adjustments. Here are all the possibilities.

MASCULINE DEMONSTRATIVES

SINGULAR ADJECTIVE FORM		CORRESPONDING PRONOUN FORM	
questo (or) **quest'**		**questo**	
questo zaino	*this backpack*	**questo**	*this one* (*referring to* zaino)
quest'uomo	*this man*	**questo**	*this one* (*referring to* uomo)
quel, quello, (or) **quell'**		**quello**	
quel ragazzo	*that boy*	**quello**	*that one* (*referring to* ragazzo)
quello psicologo	*that psychologist*	**quello**	*that one* (*referring to* psicologo)
quell'orologio	*that watch*	**quello**	*that one* (*referring to* orologio)

PLURAL ADJECTIVE FORM		CORRESPONDING PRONOUN FORM	
questi		**questi**	
questi zaini	*these backpacks*	**questi**	*these ones* (*referring to* zaini)
questi uomini	*these men*	**questi**	*these ones* (*referring to* uomini)
quei (or) **quegli**		**quelli**	
quei ragazzi	*those boys*	**quelli**	*those ones* (*referring to* ragazzi)
quegli psicologi	*those psychologists*	**quelli**	*those ones* (*referring to* psicologi)
quegli orologi	*those watches*	**quelli**	*those ones* (*referring to* orologi)

FEMININE DEMONSTRATIVES

SINGULAR ADJECTIVE FORM		CORRESPONDING PRONOUN FORM	
questa (or) **quest'**		**questa**	
questa ragazza	*this girl*	**questa**	*this one* (*referring to* ragazza)
quest'amica	*this friend*	**questa**	*this one* (*referring to* amica)
quella		**quella**	
quella ragazza	*that girl*	**quella**	*that one* (*referring to* ragazza)
quell'amica	*that friend*	**quella**	*that one* (*referring to* amica)

PLURAL ADJECTIVE FORM		CORRESPONDING PRONOUN FORM	
queste		**queste**	
queste ragazze	*these girls*	**queste**	*these ones* (*referring to* ragazze)
queste amiche	*these friends*	**queste**	*these ones* (*referring to* amiche)
quelle		**quelle**	
quelle ragazze	*these girls*	**quelle**	*those ones* (*referring to* ragazze)
quelle amiche	*these friends*	**quelle**	*those ones* (*referring to* amiche)

A. *Provide the appropriate demonstrative pronoun for each phrase.*

1. quel vestito rosa _____

2. quelle sciarpe rosse _____

3. quell'uomo alto _____

4. quegli zaini marrone _____

5. quel fratello simpatico _____

6. quegli zii _____

7. quegli psicologi simpatici _____

8. quegli orologi _____

9. quelle isole _____

10. questa macchina _____

11. quest'ora _____

12. queste amiche _____

13. questo bambino _____

14. quest'impermeabile _____

15. questi bambini _____

16. questi ingegneri _____

B. *You are asked if you want this item or these items nearby. Answer that, no, you want that one or those ones farther away.*

EXAMPLE   Desidera questa macchina?

      _____ *No, quella.* _____

Desidera...

1. quest'orologio? _____

2. questi impermeabili? _____

3. questa camicia? _____

4. queste sciarpe? _____

5. questo libro? _____

6. questi zaini? _____

7. questo vestito? _____

8. quest'arancia? _____

Indicating words and expressions

The adverbs **qui** (*here*), **qua** (*right here*), **lì** (*there*), **là** (*over there*) can be used alone, of course, or with demonstratives to emphasize the nearness or farness of someone or something, or else to indicate their relative farness or nearness.

questo ragazzo	*this boy*	**questo ragazzo qui**	*this boy here*
questa ragazza	*this girl*	**questa ragazza qua**	*this girl right here*
quei libri	*those books*	**quei libri lì**	*those books there*
quelle sciarpe	*those scarves*	**quelle sciarpe là**	*those scarves over there*

The verb **essere** (*to be*) combined with **ci** (*there*) produces the construction **esserci** (*to be there*). It is conjugated like **essere** with **ci** before the verb. Note, however, that it can only be used in the third person (singular and plural). The conjugations of **essere** are found in the irregular verb section at the back of this book.

C'è troppo zucchero nel caffè.	*There is too much sugar in the coffee.*
Ci sono molte persone alla festa.	*There are many people at the party.*

Ecco means *here is, here are, there is,* or *there are*. But it is used to indicate or point out something or someone directly. **Essere, esserci,** and **ecco** are often confusing to learners. Note the differences between them.

SINGULAR		PLURAL	
Che cosa **è**?	*What is it?*	Che cosa **sono**?	*What are they?*
È un libro.	*It's a book.*	**Sono** dei libri.	*They are books.*
C'è Dino?	*Is Dino there?*	**Ci sono** Dino e Maria?	*Are Dino and Mary there?*
Sì, **c'è**.	*Yes, he is (there/here).*	Sì, **ci sono**.	*Yes, they are (there/here).*
No, **non c'è**.	*No, he is not (there/here).*	No, **non ci sono**.	*No, they are not (there/here).*
Dov'**è** Dino?	*Where is Dino?*	Dove **sono** Dino e Maria?	*Where are Dino and Mary?*
Ecco Dino.	*Here/There is Dino.*	**Ecco** Dino e Maria.	*Here/There Dino and Mary are.*

ESERCIZIO
7·4

A. *You are asked if you want this item or these items nearby. Answer that, no, you want that item or those items farther away.*

EXAMPLE   Desidera questa penna qui?

No, quella penna lì.

Desidera...

1. quest'orologio qui? _____

2. questi impermeabili qui? _____

3. questa camicia qua? _____

4. queste sciarpe qua? _____

5. questo libro qui? _____

6. questi zaini qua? _____

B. *Answer each question with an appropriate form of* **essere, esserci,** *or* **ecco,** *as required. If you have forgotten how to conjugate* **essere** *look it up in the irregular verb section at the back of this book.*

1. Dov'è la penna? _____

2. C'è un'americano qui? _____

3. È uno studente d'italiano? _____

4. Dove sono quelle persone? _____

5. Ci sono persone italiane lì? _____

6. Sono amici? _____

C. *Provide the corresponding demonstrative of nearness or farness, as required. Note that you could be given an adjective or pronoun form of the demonstrative. If you have forgotten the meanings of the nouns and adjectives in this and the next sets of exercises, look them up in the glossary at the back of this book.*

NEARNESS	FARNESS
1. questo ragazzo	_____
2. _____	quella nuova macchina
3. questo qui	_____
4. _____	quegli studenti là
5. queste amiche simpatiche	_____
6. _____	quei simpatici psicologi
7. questi gnocchi lì	_____
8. _____	quelle paia di pantaloni

D. *A friend says that he or she wants, buys, needs, etc., this or these. Indicate instead that you want, will buy, need, etc., that or those of the same item or items.*

EXAMPLE   Voglio (*I want*) questa sciarpa.

       Io, invece, voglio quella sciarpa.

1. Voglio questo impermeabile.

_____

2. Voglio questi libri.

_____

3. Voglio questa camicia.

_____

4. Voglio queste giacche.

_____

5. Voglio questo zaino.

_____

6. Voglio questi orologi.

_____

7. Voglio queste foto.

_____

E. *How do you say the following in Italian? (Note: **dove** = where; **che cosa** = what.)*

1. John and Mary are not here.

_____

2. Where are those shirts? Here are the shirts.

_____

3. What is it? It is a new car.

_____

4. Where are the students? There are the students.

_____

5. Are they right here? No, they are over there.

_____

Grammar in culture

The form **ecco** has many social and conversational uses. Here are a few:

- As a conversational hedge or support:

  Ecco, quello che voglio dire è questo.   *Well, what I want to say is this.*
  Eccoci finalmente arrivati.   *Well, we have arrived at last.*

- With the meaning *this is*:

  Ecco perché ho fatto questo.   *This is why I did it.*

- To indicate that something is done or complete:

  Ecco fatto.   *All done. / It's done.*
  Ecco tutto.   *This is all of it. / That's all.*

How do you say the following in Italian?

1. This is why he didn't do it.

   _____

2. Well, this is the truth (**la verità**).

   _____

3. This is all of it. There is nothing else (**altro**) to (**da**) say.

   _____

4. Well, here we are at last.

   _____

Possessives

Possessives are adjectives that indicate ownership of, or relationship to, something or someone. Like all other adjectives, they modify nouns.

il mio libro	*my book (ownership of)*	**i miei libri**	*my books*
la nostra amica	*our friend (relationship to)*	**le nostre amiche**	*our friends*

Possessive adjective forms

Like descriptive adjectives (see Unit 4), demonstratives (see Unit 7), and ordinal number words (see Unit 19), possessives agree in number and gender with the noun or nouns they modify. One of the possessives, however, is invariable: **loro**. Unlike most descriptive adjectives, however, they come before the noun (as do demonstratives and ordinals).

Unlike English, the definite article is part of the possessive. It is not optional. Here are the forms of the possessive adjective:

◆ **mio**   *my*

	SINGULAR		PLURAL	
MASCULINE	**il mio amico**	*my (male) friend*	**i miei amici**	*my (male) friends*
FEMININE	**la mia amica**	*my (female) friend*	**le mie amiche**	*my (female) friends*

◆ **tuo**   *your* (*fam., sing.*)

	SINGULAR		PLURAL	
MASCULINE	**il tuo orologio**	*your watch*	**i tuoi orologi**	*your watches*
FEMININE	**la tua giacca**	*your jacket*	**le tue giacche**	*your jackets*

◆ **suo**   *his/her, its*

	SINGULAR		PLURAL	
MASCULINE	**il suo espresso**	*his/her espresso*	**i suoi espressi**	*his/her espressos*
FEMININE	**la sua bibita**	*his/her soft drink*	**le sue bibite**	*his/her soft drinks*

◆ **Suo**   *your (pol., sing.)*

	SINGULAR		PLURAL	
MASCULINE	**il Suo espresso**	*your espresso*	**i Suoi espressi**	*your espressos*
FEMININE	**la Sua bibita**	*your soft drink*	**le Sue bibite**	*your soft drinks*

◆ **nostro**   *our*

	SINGULAR		PLURAL	
MASCULINE	**il nostro amico**	*our friend*	**i nostri amici**	*our friends*
FEMININE	**la nostra amica**	*our friend*	**le nostre amiche**	*our friends*

◆ **vostro**   *your (fam., pl.)*

	SINGULAR		PLURAL	
MASCULINE	**il vostro orologio**	*your watch*	**i vostri orologi**	*your watches*
FEMININE	**la vostra giacca**	*your jacket*	**le vostre giacche**	*your jackets*

◆ **loro**   *their (invariable)*

	SINGULAR		PLURAL	
MASCULINE	**il loro espresso**	*their espresso*	**i loro espressi**	*their espressos*
FEMININE	**la loro bibita**	*their soft drink*	**le loro bibite**	*their soft drinks*

◆ **Loro**   *your (pol., pl., invariable)*

	SINGULAR		PLURAL	
MASCULINE	**il Loro cellulare**	*your cell phone*	**i Loro cellulari**	*your cell phones*
FEMININE	**la Loro macchina**	*your car*	**le Loro macchine**	*your cars*

Note: The possessive adjective can be put after the noun for emphasis.

È **il mio cane**.	*It's my dog.*	È **il cane mio**!	*It's my dog!*
Chiama **il tuo amico**.	*Call your friend.*	Chiama **l'amico tuo**!	*Call your friend!*

When preceded by the indefinite, rather than the definite, article, the possessive adjective renders the same concept as can be found in English phrases such as *of mine, of yours,* etc.

un mio zio	*an uncle of mine*
una sua amica	*a friend of his/hers*

To express *(very) own*, use the adjective **proprio**.

il mio proprio cane	*my (very) own dog*
la sua propria motocicletta	*his/her (very) own motorcycle*
il loro proprio indirizzo	*their (very) own address*
la nostra propria casa	*our (very) own house*

A. *Complete the chart as indicated, providing the appropriate forms of the indicated possessives. The first one is done for you.*

	MY	YOUR (FAM., SING.)	OUR	THEIR
1. bibita	*la mia bibita*	*la tua bibita*	*la nostra bibita*	*la loro bibita*
2. cappuccino				
3. bicchieri				
4. braccia (*Be careful!*)				
5. cappotto				
6. cravatta				
7. dita (*Be careful!*)				
8. diagrammi				

B. *You are asked a question. Answer in the negative, providing the correct information indicated in parentheses, which tells you which possessive to use.*

EXAMPLE   È la sua macchina? (*your, fam., pl.*)

_____*No, è la vostra macchina.*_____

1. È il suo espresso? (*their*)

_____

2. Sono i vostri figli? (*her*)

_____

3. Sono le vostre figlie? (*his*)

_____

4. È il tuo giornale? (*their*)

_____

5. È la sua professoressa? (*your, fam., sing.*)

_____

6. Sono i vostri amici? (*his*)

_____

7. Sono le sue chiavi? (*my*)

_____

The third-person forms

Both *his* and *her* are expressed by the same possessive form **suo** (which takes on its appropriate form before the noun). This is a constant source of blunders for many learners.

HIS		HER	
il suo orologio	*his watch*	**il suo orologio**	*her watch*
i suoi orologi	*his watches*	**i suoi orologi**	*her watches*
la sua bibita	*his soft drink*	**la sua bibita**	*her soft drink*
le sue bibite	*his soft drinks*	**le sue bibite**	*her soft drinks*

To avoid making potential blunders, keep this simple rule in mind—make the possessive adjective agree with the noun, without worrying about what it means in English. Otherwise, you will confuse its form with its meaning.

You can also figure out the meaning by using a corresponding genitive phrase, which is introduced by **di**. This is equivalent to English forms such as *John's, the boy's*, etc. If you have forgotten how to contract the preposition **di** with the definite article, jump forward to Unit 9. The genitive phrase provides information on the meaning, not the form of the possessive.

GENITIVE		CORRESPONDING POSSESSIVE	
il cappotto di Marco	*Mark's coat*	**il suo cappotto**	*his coat*
il cappotto di Maria	*Mary's coat*	**il suo cappotto**	*her coat*
la giacca del ragazzo	*the boy's jacket*	**la sua giacca**	*his jacket*
la giacca della ragazza	*the girl's jacket*	**la sua giacca**	*her jacket*
i libri di Marco	*Mark's books*	**i suoi libri**	*his books*
i libri di Maria	*Mary's books*	**i suoi libri**	*her books*
le giacche del ragazzo	*the boy's jackets*	**le sue giacche**	*his jackets*
le giacche della ragazza	*the girl's jackets*	**le sue giacche**	*her jackets*

Notice that there are familiar and polite possessives that correspond to the English possessive *your*. As these terms imply, you must use familiar forms with the people you know well and with whom you are on familiar terms; otherwise, you must use the polite forms.

Basically, you use the familiar forms (**tuo** in the singular and **vostro** in the plural) with people with whom you are on a first-name basis (family members, friends, children, colleagues, etc.). Otherwise, you use the polite forms (**Suo** in the singular and **Loro** in the plural) with anyone else (strangers, store clerks, etc.).

The polite forms are identical to the **suo** forms in the singular, and to the **loro** forms in the plural. To keep the two types distinct in writing, the polite forms are often capitalized, as has been done here.

HIS/HER		YOUR (POL., SING.)	
il suo cane	*his/her dog*	**il Suo cane**	*your dog*
i suoi cani	*his/her dogs*	**i Suoi cani**	*your dogs*
la sua bibita	*his/her soft drink*	**la Sua bibita**	*your soft drinks*
le sue bibite	*his/her soft drinks*	**le Sue bibite**	*your soft drinks*

THEIR		YOUR (POL., PL.)	
il loro amico	*their friend*	**il Loro amico**	*your friend*
i loro amici	*their friends*	**i Loro amici**	*your friends*
la loro fotografia	*their photograph*	**la Loro fotografia**	*your photograph*
le loro fotografie	*their photographs*	**le Loro fotografie**	*your photographs*

Thus, when you see or hear these forms, you will have to figure out what they mean from the context.

In current Italian, it is not unusual to find the **vostro** forms used as the plural of both the familiar and polite forms. The use of **Loro** as the polite plural possessive is restricted to very formal situations.

ESERCIZIO

8·2

A. *Answer each question affirmatively, using the appropriate form of the possessive.*

EXAMPLE   È la macchina di Maria?

_____ *Sì, è la sua macchina.* _____

1. È la macchina di Paolo?

_____

2. È il caffè di quell'uomo?

_____

3. È il caffè di quella donna?

_____

4. Sono gli amici del bambino?

_____

5. Sono gli amici della bambina?

_____

6. Sono le amiche del bambino?

_____

7. Sono le amiche della bambina?

_____

8. È la foto di quella donna?

_____

9. Sono le foto di quell'uomo?

B. *Complete each question with the missing possessive adjective. Insert the familiar or polite form of the appropriate possessive, as required.*

EXAMPLE 1   Marco, è _____ *il tuo* _____ libro?

EXAMPLE 2   Signor Dini, è _____ *il Suo* _____ libro?

1. Maria, è _____ caffè?

2. Signora Rossi, è _____ caffè?

3. Gino, è _____ cappuccino?

4. Signor Bruni, è _____ cappuccino?

5. Claudia, sono _____ amiche?

6. Signorina Verdi, sono _____ amiche?

7. Giovanni, sono _____ forbici?

8. Professor Marchi, sono _____ forbici?

9. Maria e Claudia, è _____ caffè?

10. Signora Rossi e signorina Verdi, è _____ caffè?

11. Gino e Marco, è _____ cappuccino?

12. Signor Bruni e dottor Rossini, è _____ cappuccino?

13. Claudia e Maria, sono _____ amiche?

14. Signorina Verdi e dottoressa Dini, sono _____ amiche?

15. Giovanni e Claudia, sono _____ forbici?

16. Professor Marchi e dottoressa Bruni, sono _____ forbici?

Possessives with kinship nouns

The definite article is dropped from all forms except **loro** when the noun to which the possessive refers is a singular, unmodified kinship noun (**padre**, **madre**, etc.).

The most common kinship terms

il padre	*father*
la madre	*mother*
il figlio	*son*
la figlia	*daughter*
il fratello	*brother*
la sorella	*sister*
il nonno	*grandfather*
la nonna	*grandmother*
lo zio	*uncle*
la zia	*aunt*
il cugino / la cugina	*cousin*
il genero	*son-in-law*
il suocero / la suocera	*father-in-law / mother-in-law*
la nuora	*daughter-in-law*
il cognato / la cognata	*brother-in-law / sister-in-law*

SINGULAR KINSHIP NOUN		PLURAL KINSHIP NOUN	
tuo cugino	*your cousin*	**i tuoi cugini**	*your cousins*
sua zia	*his/her aunt*	**le sue zie**	*his/her aunts*
mia sorella	*my sister*	**le mie sorelle**	*my sisters*
nostro fratello	*our brother*	**i nostri fratelli**	*our brothers*

SINGULAR KINSHIP NOUN		MODIFIED OR ALTERED KINSHIP NOUN	
tuo cugino	*your cousin*	**il tuo cugino americano**	*your American cousin*
sua zia	*his/her aunt*	**la sua zia vecchia**	*his/her old aunt*
mia sorella	*my sister*	**la mia sorella minore**	*my little sister*
nostra cugina	*our cousin*	**la nostra cugina italiana**	*our Italian cousin*

The article is always retained with **loro**, even in the singular possessive forms.

il loro figlio	*their son*
la loro figlia	*their daughter*
il loro fratello	*their brother*
la loro sorella	*their sister*

The above set of rules are optional in the case of the following kinship nouns (when singular and unmodified, of course).

nonno	*grandfather*			
nonna	*grandmother*			
mamma	*mom*			
papà (or) **babbo**	*dad*			
mia mamma	*my mom*	(or)	**la mia mamma**	*my mom*
tuo papà / tuo babbo	*your dad*	(or)	**il tuo papà / il tuo babbo**	*your dad*
mio nonno	*my grandfather*	(or)	**il mio nonno**	*my grandfather*
mia nonna	*my grandmother*	(or)	**la mia nonna**	*my grandmother*

Be careful!

As in the case of articles and demonstratives, you must repeat the possessive before each noun.

mio zio e **mia sorella**	*my uncle and sister*
tuo fratello e **la tua amica**	*your brother and friend*

ESERCIZIO
8·3

A. *How do you say the following in Italian?*

1. Marco è...

a. *my cousin* _____

b. *her younger brother* _____

c. *your (fam., sing.) father* _____

d. *our Italian uncle* _____

e. *their friend* _____

2. Maria è...

    a. *my cousin* _____

    b. *his older sister* _____

    c. *your (fam., sing.) mother* _____

    d. *your (fam., pl.) aunt* _____

    e. *their friend* _____

3. Il signor Verdi e la signora Verdi sono...

    a. *my grandfather and grandmother* _____

    b. *his Italian uncle and aunt* _____

    c. *your (fam., sing.) father-in-law and mother-in-law* _____

    d. *your (fam., pl.) son-in-law and daughter-in-law* _____

    e. *their Italian brother-in-law and sister-in-law* _____

B. *Rewrite each phrase in the plural.*

1. mio cugino   _____

2. mia nonna   _____

3. tuo fratello   _____

4. tua sorella   _____

5. suo zio   _____

6. sua zia   _____

7. nostro genero   _____

8. nostra suocera   _____

9. vostro cognato   _____

10. vostra cognata   _____

11. il loro fratello   _____

12. la loro sorella   _____

Possessive pronouns

A possessive pronoun replaces a noun phrase containing a possessive adjective. The pronouns correspond to English *mine, yours, his, hers, ours,* and *theirs.* There is a perfect match between the adjective and pronoun forms of the possessive.

mio

Il mio amico è italiano.
My friend is Italian.
La mia amica è simpatica.
My friend is nice.
I miei professori sono italiani.
My professors are Italian.
Le mie professoresse sono italiane.
My professors (f.) are Italian.

Il mio è italiano.
Mine is Italian.
La mia è simpatica.
Mine is nice.
I miei sono italiani.
Mine are Italian.
Le mie sono italiane.
Mine are Italian.

tuo

Il tuo amico è italiano.
Your friend is Italian.
La tua amica è simpatica.
Your friend is nice.
I tuoi professori sono italiani.
Your professors are Italian.
Le tue professoresse sono italiane.
Your professors (f.) are Italian.

Il tuo è italiano.
Yours is Italian.
La tua è simpatica.
Yours is nice.
I tuoi sono italiani.
Yours are Italian.
Le tue sono italiane.
Yours are Italian.

suo

Il suo amico è italiano.
His/Her friend is Italian.
La sua amica è simpatica.
His/Her friend is nice.
I suoi professori sono italiani.
His/Her professors are Italian.
Le sue professoresse sono italiane.
His/Her professors (f.) are Italian.

Il suo è italiano.
His/Hers is Italian.
La sua è simpatica.
His/Hers is nice.
I suoi sono italiani.
His/Hers are Italian.
Le sue sono italiane.
His/Hers are Italian.

nostro

Il nostro amico è italiano.
Our friend is Italian.
La nostra amica è simpatica.
Our friend is nice.
I nostri professori sono italiani.
Our professors are Italian.
Le nostre professoresse sono italiane.
Our professors (f.) are Italian.

Il nostro è italiano.
Ours is Italian.
La nostra è simpatica.
Ours is nice.
I nostri sono italiani.
Ours are Italian.
Le nostre sono italiane.
Ours are Italian.

vostro

Il vostro amico è italiano.
Your friend is Italian.
La vostra amica è simpatica.
Your friend is nice.
I vostri professori sono italiani.
Your professors are Italian.
Le vostre professoresse sono italiane.
Your professors (f.) are Italian.

Il vostro è italiano.
Yours is Italian.
La vostra è simpatica.
Yours is nice.
I vostri sono italiani.
Yours are Italian.
Le vostre sono italiane.
Yours are Italian.

loro

Il loro amico è italiano.	**Il loro** è italiano.
Their friend is Italian.	*Theirs is Italian.*
La loro amica è simpatica.	**La loro** è simpatica.
Their friend is nice.	*Theirs is nice.*
I loro professori sono italiani.	**I loro** sono italiani.
Their professors are Italian.	*Theirs are Italian.*
Le loro professoresse sono italiane.	**Le loro** sono italiane.
Their professors (f.) are Italian.	*Theirs are Italian.*

The article is always used with the pronoun forms, even when the noun phrase replaced contained singular, unmodified, kinship nouns.

Sua sorella è simpatica.	*His/Her sister is pleasant.*
La sua è simpatica.	*His/Hers is pleasant.*
Nostro zio è giovane.	*Our uncle is young.*
Il nostro è giovane.	*Ours is young.*

The article can be dropped if the pronoun occurs as a predicate; that is, if it occurs after the verb **essere** (*to be*), or some other linking verb.

Questo cappotto **è mio**.	*This coat is mine.*
È tua questa camicia?	*Is this shirt yours?*
Quei libri **sono suoi**.	*Those books are his/hers.*

ESERCIZIO

8·4

A. *Answer each question affirmatively using the appropriate possessive pronoun.*

EXAMPLE   Giovanni è tuo fratello? (*Is John your brother?*)

_____Sì, è il mio._____

1. Maria è la tua amica? _____

2. La signora Verdi è la loro nonna? _____

3. Io sono il vostro amico? _____

4. Tu sei sua zia? _____

5. Lui è suo zio? _____

6. Marco è il loro amico? _____

7. Quegli uomini sono i tuoi cugini? _____

8. Quelle donne sono le vostre cugine? _____

B. *Answer each question as suggested by the italicized word in parentheses.*

EXAMPLE   Di chi è questo cappotto? (*Whose coat is it?*) (*mine*)

_____*È il mio.*_____

1. Di chi è questa giacca? (*mine*)   _____

2. Di chi è questo impermeabile? *(his)*   _____

3. Di chi è quella macchina? (*hers*)   _____

4. Di chi è quello zaino? (*ours*)   _____

5. Di chi sono quei vestiti rossi? (*theirs*)   _____

6. Di chi sono quelle sciarpe verdi? (*mine*)   _____

7. Di chi sono questi bicchieri? (*his*)   _____

8. Di chi sono quelle bibite? (*hers*)   _____

C. *Provide the corresponding singular or plural form, as required.*

SINGULAR	PLURAL
1. il mio orologio	_____
2. _____	le nostre amiche
3. la mia camicia	_____
4. _____	i nostri libri
5. il tuo cane	_____
6. _____	le vostre amiche
7. la tua macchina	_____
8. _____	i vostri amici
9. il suo gatto	_____
10. _____	le sue amiche
11. il loro amico	_____
12. _____	le loro case

D. *Complete each sentence with the appropriate form of the indefinite or definite article, if needed. If the article is not needed, leave the space blank.*

1. Lui è _____ mio fratello. (*He is my brother.*)

2. Lei è _____ nostra sorella maggiore. (*She is our older sister.*)

3. Quel ragazzo è _____ loro figlio. (*That boy is their son.*)

4. Lei è _____ sua figlia più grande. (*She is his oldest daughter.*)

5. Signora Marchi, come si chiama _____ Sua figlia? (*Mrs. Marchi, what's your daughter's name?*)

6. Signora e signor Marchi, come si chiama _____ Loro figlio? (*Mrs. and Mr. Marchi, what's your son's name?*)

7. Lui è _____ mio amico, tra molti amici. (*He is one of my friends, among many friends.*)

8. Anche lei è _____ mia amica, tra molte amiche. (*She is also one of my friends, among many friends.*)

9. Questo libro è mio. Dov'è _____ tuo? (*This book is mine. Where is yours?*)

Grammar in culture

The omission of the article in kinship possessives is probably due to convention and frequency of usage. The article is used, in fact, with other people to whom you have a social or emotional attachment.

amico (*friend*)	il mio amico, il tuo amico...
amica (*friend*)	la mia amica, la tua amica...
fidanzato (*fiancé*)	il mio fidanzato, il tuo fidanzato...
fidanzata (*fiancée*)	la mia fidanzata, la tua fidanzata...
ragazzo (*boyfriend*)	il mio ragazzo, il tuo ragazzo...
ragazza (*girlfriend*)	la mia ragazza, la tua ragazza...
amante (*m./f.*) (*lover*)	il mio amante, la mia amante...

ESERCIZIO
8·5

How do you say the following in Italian?

1. She's my sister, not my lover!

_____

2. Here's my boyfriend and your brother.

_____

3. She's my girlfriend, not yet my fiancée.

_____

4. My sister is also my friend.

_____

Partitives

Partitives are forms used with nouns to indicate a part of something as distinct from its whole.

l'acqua	*water*	**dell'**acqua	*some water*
un esame	*an exam*	**degli** esami	*some exams*
un'amica	*a (female) friend*	**delle** amiche	*some friends*
lo zucchero	*sugar*	**dello** zucchero	*some sugar*

Partitives with count nouns

Before count nouns (nouns that have a plural form), the partitive functions grammatically as the plural of the indefinite article. The most commonly used type of partitive in this case consists of the preposition **di** + *the appropriate plural forms of the definite article.*

Contractions of **di** with the masculine plural forms of the definite article

di + i → dei	di + i libri → dei libri	*some books*
di + gli → degli	di + gli studenti → degli studenti	*some students*

Contractions of **di** with the feminine plural forms of the definite article

di + le → delle	di + le penne → delle penne	*some pens*

MASCULINE SINGULAR		MASCULINE PLURAL	
uno, un (*before a vowel*)		**degli**	
uno sbaglio	*a mistake*	**degli sbagli**	*some mistakes*
un albero	*a tree*	**degli alberi**	*some trees*
un		**dei**	
un bicchiere	*a glass*	**dei bicchieri**	*some glasses*
un coltello	*a knife*	**dei coltelli**	*some knives*

FEMININE SINGULAR		FEMININE PLURAL	
una		**delle**	
una forchetta	*a fork*	**delle forchette**	*some forks*
una sedia	*a chair*	**delle sedie**	*some chairs*
un'		**delle**	
un'automobile	*an automobile*	**delle automobili**	*some automobiles*
un'arancia	*an orange*	**delle arance**	*some oranges*

As always, be careful when an adjective precedes the noun. You must adjust the form of the partitive accordingly.

degli zii	*some uncles*	**dei simpatici zii**	*some nice uncles*
degli zaini	*some backpacks*	**dei nuovi zaini**	*some new backpacks*

Useful vocabulary

The following words, referring to items in the house, will come in handy. They are used in the Esercizio that follows.

il bagno	*bathroom*	**la cucina**	*kitchen*
il bicchiere	*drinking glass*	**la forchetta**	*fork*
la bottiglia	*bottle*	**il salotto**	*living room*
la camera	*bedroom*	**la sedia**	*chair*
il coltello	*knife*	**la stanza**	*room*
il cucchiaino	*teaspoon*	**la tavola**	*eating table*
il cucchiaio	*spoon*		

ESERCIZIO
9·1

A. *Provide the singular or plural form of each phrase, as required.*

SINGULAR	PLURAL PARTITIVE
1. un coltello	_____
2. _____	degli sbagli
3. una forchetta	_____
4. _____	dei salotti
5. uno zio	_____
6. _____	delle cucine
7. uno psicologo	_____
8. _____	dei bagni
9. una camera	_____
10. _____	delle bottiglie

11. una sedia   _____

12. _____   delle tavole

13. un bicchiere   _____

14. _____   dei cucchiai

15. un cucchiaino   _____

16. _____   delle forchette

17. un coltello   _____

18. _____   degli gnocchi

19. un'automobile   _____

20. _____   degli amici

B. *For each question provide an answer in the plural, using the indicated adjective.*

EXAMPLE   È un coltello? (nuovo)

Sono dei coltelli nuovi. / Sono dei nuovi coltelli.

1. È un'automobile? (italiano) _____

2. È una sedia? (nuovo) _____

3. È uno psicologo? (bravo) _____

4. È un amico? (vecchio) _____

5. È un'amica? (vecchio) _____

6. È un bagno? (grande) _____

7. È una camera? (piccolo) _____

8. È un salotto? (bello) _____

9. È una cucina? (bello) _____

Alternative forms

In place of **di** + *definite article*, the pronouns **alcuni** (*m., pl.*) and **alcune** (*f., pl.*) can be used to correspond more precisely to the idea of *several*.

degli zii	*some uncles*	**alcuni zii**	*several (a few) uncles*
dei bicchieri	*some glasses*	**alcuni bicchieri**	*several (a few) glasses*
delle forchette	*some forks*	**alcune forchette**	*several (a few) forks*
delle amiche	*some friends*	**alcune amiche**	*several (a few) friends*

The invariable pronoun **qualche** can also be used to express the partitive with count nouns. But be careful with this one! It must be followed by a singular noun, even though the meaning is plural.

degli zii	*some uncles*	**qualche zio**	*some uncles*
dei bicchieri	*some glasses*	**qualche bicchiere**	*some glasses*
delle forchette	*some forks*	**qualche forchetta**	*some forks*
delle amiche	*some friends*	**qualche amica**	*some friends*

The pronoun forms (**qualche** or **alcuni/alcune**) are often used at the start of sentences, rather than the partitive forms with **di**. Once again, be careful with **qualche**. It requires a singular verb!

Alcuni studenti studiano il francese.	*Some students study French.*
Qualche studente studia il francese.	*Some students study French.*

ESERCIZIO
9·2

A. *Provide the equivalent partitive phrase with* **alcuni/alcune**.

1. dei coltelli _____

2. delle sedie _____

3. degli gnocchi _____

4. delle automobili _____

5. dei cucchiai _____

6. degli amici _____

B. *Now, provide the equivalent partitive phrase with* **qualche**.

1. dei cucchiaini _____

2. delle tavole _____

3. degli zaini _____

4. delle automobili _____

5. dei bicchieri _____

6. degli sbagli _____

C. *Complete each sentence with the appropriate form of the verb* **essere**, **è** *(is) or* **sono** *(are), as required.*

1. Alcuni amici nostri _____ italiani.

2. Qualche amico nostro _____ italiano.

3. Alcune ragazze _____ americane.

4. Qualche ragazza _____ americana.

Partitives with mass nouns

With mass nouns (nouns that do not, normally, have a plural form), the partitive is rendered by either **di** + *the singular forms of the definite article*, or by the expression **un po' di** (*a bit of*).

Contractions of **di** with the masculine singular forms of the definite article

di + il → del	di + il pane → del pane	*some bread*
di + lo → dello	di + lo zucchero → dello zucchero	*some sugar*
di + l' → dell'	di + l'orzo → dell'orzo	*some barley*

Contractions of **di** with the feminine singular forms of the definite article

di + la → della	di + la carne → della carne	*some meat*
di + l' → dell'	di + l'acqua → dell'acqua	*some water*

PARTITIVE FORM		ALTERNATIVE FORM	
del pane	*some bread*	**un po' di pane**	*a little bread*
dell'orzo	*some barley*	**un po' d'orzo**	*a little barley*
dello zucchero	*some sugar*	**un po' di zucchero**	*a little sugar*
della pasta	*some pasta*	**un po' di pasta**	*a little pasta*
dell'acqua	*some water*	**un po' d'acqua**	*a little water*

Useful vocabulary

Mass nouns		Count nouns	
l'acqua	*water*	**la carota**	*carrot*
la carne	*meat*	**il fagiolino**	*string bean*
l'insalata	*salad*	**il fagiolo**	*bean*
la minestra	*soup*	**la patata**	*potato*
l'orzo	*barley*	**il pomodoro**	*tomato*
la pasta	*pasta*		
il pesce	*fish (as a food)*		
il riso	*rice*		
l'uva	*grapes*		
lo zucchero	*sugar*		

A. *Provide the corresponding partitive phrase.*

PARTITIVE	ALTERNATIVE FORM
1. dell'insalata	_____
2. _____	un po' d'uva
3. del pesce	_____
4. _____	un po' di carne
5. della minestra	_____
6. _____	un po' di riso
7. dello zucchero	_____
8. _____	un po' d'orzo
9. della pasta	_____
10. _____	un po' d'acqua

B. *Say that you want both the items indicated. Follow the example, using only partitive forms (not their alternatives).*

EXAMPLE meat and potatoes

_____*Voglio della carne e delle patate.*_____

1. fish and beans _____

2. salad and carrots _____

3. pasta and string beans _____

4. meat and apples _____

5. coffee and sugar _____

6. grapes and potatoes _____

Partitives in the negative

In negative sentences, the partitive is omitted.

AFFIRMATIVE SENTENCE		NEGATIVE SENTENCE	
Ho dei biglietti.	*I have some tickets.*	**Non ho biglietti.**	*I don't have (any) tickets.*
Ho alcune riviste.	*I have some magazines.*	**Non ho riviste.**	*I don't have (any) magazines.*

The negative partitive can also be rendered by **non... nessuno**. As we will see in the unit on numbers (see Unit 19), **nessuno** is made up of **ness** + *indefinite article*. It renders the idea of *not ... any*. This means that in Italian the noun is always in the singular, even though the meaning is plural.

Non ho nessun biglietto.	*I don't have any tickets.*
Non ho nessuna rivista.	*I don't have any magazines.*

This cannot be used with mass nouns.

AFFIRMATIVE SENTENCE		NEGATIVE SENTENCE	
Prendo dello zucchero.	*I'll take some sugar.*	**Non prendo zucchero.**	*I don't take sugar.*
Mangio un po' di pasta.	*I'll eat a little pasta.*	**Non mangio pasta.**	*I don't eat pasta.*

ESERCIZIO
9·4

A. *Rewrite each sentence in the negative, as required. Do not use* **nessuno** *in this exercise.*

1. Mario mangia delle patate.

   _____

2. Io voglio dei fagiolini.

   _____

3. Il ragazzo prende un po' di carne.

   _____

4. La ragazza vuole dello zucchero.

   _____

5. Anch'io voglio alcuni biglietti.

   _____

6. Maria prende qualche pomodoro. (*Be careful!*)

   _____

B. *Now, rewrite each phrase in the negative with* **nessuno**.

1. delle carote   _____

2. dei fagiolini   _____

3. dei cucchiai   _____

4. delle patate   _____

5. degli zaini   _____

6. delle arance   _____

Adjectives indicating quantity

In addition to descriptive, demonstrative, ordinal, and possessive adjectives (see Units 4, 7, 8, and 19), there are certain words that have various adjectival functions. Some grammar texts classify them as adjectives (as we do here), others as different types of structures. Here are the most common. Most of these indicate quantity of some sort. Notice also that these come before the noun they modify.

abbastanza	*enough*
assai	*quite a lot, enough*
certo	*certain*
molto	*much, a lot*
ogni	*each, every*
parecchio	*several, quite a few, a lot*
poco	*little, few*
qualsiasi	*whichever, any*
qualunque	*whichever, any*
stesso	*the same*
tanto	*much, a lot*
troppo	*too much*
tutto	*all*
ultimo	*last*

The adjectives **abbastanza**, **assai**, **ogni**, **qualsiasi**, and **qualunque** are invariable (that is, they do not change).

Non ho **abbastanza soldi**.	*I do not have enough money.*
Lui mangia **assai carne**.	*He eats quite a lot of meat.*
Ogni mattina legge il giornale.	*Every morning he reads the newspaper.*
Possiamo andare a **qualsiasi ristorante**.	*We can go to any restaurant.*

The others are treated like any regular adjective.

Conosco un **certo signore** che si chiama Roberto.	*I know a certain gentleman named Robert.*
Lui mangia **molti (tanti) dolci**.	*He eats a lot of sweets.*
Ci sono **poche studentesse** in questa classe.	*There are few female students in this class.*
Parecchi turisti visitano Venezia.	*A lot of tourists visit Venice.*
Abbiamo mangiato **troppa carne**.	*We ate too much meat.*
Questa è **l'ultima volta** che ti chiamo.	*This is the last time I'm going to call you.*

Notice that **tutto** is separated from the noun by the definite article.

Lei ha mangiato **tutto il formaggio**.	*She ate all the cheese.*
Giovanni ha mangiato **tutta la minestra**.	*John ate all the soup.*

A. *Provide the missing adjective ending for each phrase.*

1. l'ultim_____ donna

2. poc_____ studenti

3. tutt_____ la minestra

4. parecch_____ bambini

5. una cert_____ signora

6. qualsias_____ città

7. qualunqu_____ ristorante

8. abbastanz_____ soldi

9. assa_____ studenti

10. ogn_____ settimana

B. *Write a sentence to indicate that you need much, many, little, etc., of the item or items indicated.*

EXAMPLE   dei fagioli / molto

_____*Ho bisogno di*_____ (*I need*) _____*molti fagioli.*_____

1. delle patate / poco   _____

2. dei fagioli / tutto   _____

3. delle carote / tanto   _____

4. alcuni fagiolini / molto   _____

5. qualche mela / poco   _____

6. un po' di minestra / tutto   _____

7. della pasta / tanto   _____

8. dei cucchiai / molto   _____

C. *Provide the equivalent partitive noun phrases for each item. The first item is done completely for you.*

1. _____*dei bambini*_____   alcuni bambini   _____*qualche bambino*_____

2. delle patate   _____   _____

3. _____   _____   qualche fagiolo

4. _____   alcune mele   _____

5. degli zaini   _____   _____

6. _____   _____   qualche forchetta

D. *Choose the correct response to complete each sentence.*

1. Non ho _____.

   a. degli amici   b. amici

2. Non ho mangiato _____.

   a. delle patate   b. nessuna patata

3. Prendo _____ zucchero.

   a. qualche   b. un po' di

4. Non prendo _____.

   a. nessun pane   b. pane

5. Voglio _____.

   a. dell'acqua   b. qualche acqua

6. Ecco _____ buono zucchero.

   a. del   b. dello

Grammar in culture

Classifying a noun as count or mass is a matter of cultural convention, even though there is a great deal of correspondence between lists of English and Italian nouns in this respect. This correspondence deviates for the following important Italian nouns.

◆ **Informazione** (*information*) is a count noun when it refers to a piece of information or similar item; as a general concept, **informazione** is a mass noun.

◆ **Comunicazione** (*communication*) is a count noun when it refers to correspondence or a message of some sort; as a general concept, **comunicazione** is a mass noun.

AS A COUNT NOUN	AS A MASS NOUN
Ho ricevuto poche informazioni da lui. *I received little information from him.*	L'informazione oggi controlla tutto. *Information controls everything today.*
Tutte le sue comunicazioni sono brevi. *All his messages are brief.*	La comunicazione scritta è importante. *Written communication is important.*

◆ **Uva** (*grapes*) is a mass noun. **Chicco** is used to refer to a single grape.

Quest'uva è molto buona.   Questo chicco d'uva è marcio.
These grapes are very good.   *This grape is rotten.*

How do you say the following in Italian?

1. I love grapes.

   _____

2. She sent me a few messages yesterday.

   _____

3. This grape is blue!

   _____

4. He always sends me little information.

   _____

Present tenses

Verbs are words that convey the action performed by the subject of a sentence. For this reason, they agree with the subject's person (first, second, or third) and number (singular or plural). Verbs are also marked for tense (present, past, future, etc.) to indicate the time an action occurred—now (present tense), before (past tense), or after (future tense); and they are marked for mood (indicative, imperative, conditional, etc.).

io mangio	*I eat*	**tu mangi**	*you eat*
io ho mangiato	*I ate*	**tu hai mangiato**	*you ate*
io mangerò	*I will eat*	**tu mangerai**	*you will eat*

The infinitive is the verb form that you will find in a dictionary. It is the "default" form of the verb. Italian verbs are divided into three main conjugations according to their infinitive endings. Verbs of the first conjugation end in **-are**, those of the second in **-ere**, and those of the third in **-ire**.

FIRST CONJUGATION		SECOND CONJUGATION		THIRD CONJUGATION	
parlare	*to speak*	**vendere**	*to sell*	**dormire**	*to sleep*
arrivare	*to arrive*	**cadere**	*to fall*	**finire**	*to finish*

The present indicative of regular verbs

The indicative mood is used to express or indicate facts. It is the most commonly used mood in everyday conversation. The **present indicative**, as its name implies, is used to express or indicate facts in the present or related to the present in some way.

To conjugate regular verbs in the present indicative, drop the infinitive ending, and add the appropriate ending according to person and number shown below.

First conjugation

parlare *to speak, talk* → **parl-**

io	parl**o**	*I speak, am speaking, do speak*
tu	parl**i**	*you (fam., sing.) speak, are speaking, do speak*
Lei	parl**a**	*you (pol., sing.) speak, are speaking, do speak*
lui/lei	parl**a**	*he/she speaks, is speaking, does speak*
noi	parl**iamo**	*we speak, are speaking, do speak*
voi	parl**ate**	*you (fam., pl.) speak, are speaking, do speak*
Loro	parl**ano**	*you (pol., pl.) speak, are speaking, do speak*
loro	parl**ano**	*they speak, are speaking, do speak*

Second conjugation

vendere *to sell* → **vend-**

io	vend**o**	*I sell, am selling, do sell*
tu	vend**i**	*you (fam., sing.) sell, are selling, do sell*
Lei	vend**e**	*you (pol., sing.) sell, are selling, do sell*
lui/lei	vend**e**	*he/she sells, is selling, does sell*
noi	vend**iamo**	*we sell, are selling, do sell*
voi	vend**ete**	*you (fam., pl.) sell, are selling, do sell*
Loro	vend**ono**	*you (pol., pl.) sell, are selling, do sell*
loro	vend**ono**	*they sell, are selling, do sell*

Third conjugation (type 1)

dormire *to sleep* → **dorm-**

io	dorm**o**	*I sleep, am sleeping, do sleep*
tu	dorm**i**	*you (fam., sing.) sleep, are sleeping, do sleep*
Lei	dorm**e**	*you (pol., sing.) sleep, are sleeping, do sleep*
lui/lei	dorm**e**	*he/she sleeps, is sleeping, does sleep*
noi	dorm**iamo**	*we sleep, are sleeping, do sleep*
voi	dorm**ite**	*you (fam., pl.) sleep, are sleeping, do sleep*
Loro	dorm**ono**	*you (pol., pl.) sleep, are sleeping, do sleep*
loro	dorm**ono**	*they sleep, are sleeping, do sleep*

Third conjugation (type 2)

finire *to finish* → **fin-**

io	fin**isco**	*I finish, am finishing, do finish*
tu	fin**isci**	*you (fam., sing.) finish, are finishing, do finish*
Lei	fin**isce**	*you (pol., sing.) finish, are finishing, do finish*
lui/lei	fin**isce**	*he/she finishes, is finishing, does finish*
noi	fin**iamo**	*we finish, are finishing, do finish*
voi	fin**ite**	*you (fam., pl.) finish, are finishing, do finish*
Loro	fin**iscono**	*you (pol., pl.) finish, are finishing, do finish*
loro	fin**iscono**	*they finish, are finishing, do finish*

Note that there are two sets of endings for third-conjugation verbs, and this fact is a constant source of blunders for learners. Essentially, you will have to learn to which category (type 1 or 2) a third-conjugation verb belongs. This information is contained in a good dictionary.

Type 1 verbs		Type 2 verbs	
aprire	*to open*	**capire**	*to understand*
dormire	*to sleep*	**finire**	*to finish*
partire	*to leave*	**preferire**	*to prefer*

The subject pronouns are optional. The reason for this is obvious: the endings generally make it clear which person is the subject of the verb.

Second-person forms are used for familiar (informal) address; third-person forms are used instead for polite (formal) address. The pronouns for the latter are normally capitalized in writing (**Lei, Loro**) to keep them distinct from the pronouns standing for *she* (**lei**) and *they* (**loro**).

Familiar

Maria, (**tu**) cosa preferisci?	*Mary, what do you prefer?*
Marco e Maria, capite (**voi**)?	*Mark and Mary, do you understand?*

Polite

Professore, (**Lei**) cosa preferisce?	*Professor, what do you prefer?*
Signor Marchi e Signora Verdi, capiscono (**Loro**)?	*Mr. Marchi and Mrs. Verdi, do you understand?*

The English subject pronouns *it* and *they* are not normally expressed in Italian.

Apre a mezzogiorno.	*It opens at noon.*
Chiudono alle sei.	*They close at six.*

Verbs that undergo spelling changes

If a verb ends in -**care** or -**gare**, the hard sound is preserved by inserting an **h** before the endings -**i** and -**iamo**.

cercare *to look for* → **cerc-**

io	cerco	*I look for, am looking for, do look for*
tu	cer**chi**	*you (fam., sing.) look for, are looking for, do look for*
Lei	cerca	*you (pol., sing.) look for, are looking for, do look for*
lui/lei	cerca	*he/she looks for, is looking for, does look for*
noi	cer**chiamo**	*we look for, are looking for, do look for*
voi	cercate	*you (fam., pl.) look for, are looking for, do look for*
Loro	cercano	*you (pol., pl.) look for, are looking for, do look for*
loro	cercano	*they look for, are looking for, do look for*

pagare *to pay* → **pag-**

io	pago	*I pay, am paying, do pay*
tu	pa**ghi**	*you (fam., sing.) pay, are paying, do pay*
Lei	paga	*you (pol., sing.) pay, are paying, do pay*
lui/lei	paga	*he/she pays, is paying, does pay*
noi	pa**ghiamo**	*we pay, are paying, do pay*
voi	pagate	*you (fam., pl.) pay, are paying, do pay*
Loro	pagano	*you (pol., pl.) pay, are paying, do pay*
loro	pagano	*they pay, are paying, do pay*

If a verb ends in -**ciare** or -**giare**, the -**i** of these endings is dropped before adding the conjugated endings -**i** and -**iamo**.

cominciare *to start, begin* → **cominci-**

io	comincio	*I start, am starting, do start*
tu	cominc**i**	*you (fam., sing.) start, are starting, do start*
Lei	comincia	*you (pol., sing.) start, are starting, do start*
lui/lei	comincia	*he/she starts, is starting, does start*
noi	cominc**iamo**	*we start, are starting, do start*
voi	cominciate	*you (fam., pl.) start, are starting, do start*
Loro	cominciano	*you (pol., pl.) start, are starting, do start*
loro	cominciano	*they start, are starting, do start*

mangiare *to eat* → **mangi-**

io	mangio	*I eat, am eating, do eat*
tu	mang**i**	*you (fam., sing.) eat, are eating, do eat*
Lei	mangia	*you (pol., sing.) eat, are eating, do eat*
lui/lei	mangia	*he/she eats, is eating, does eat*
noi	mang**iamo**	*we eat, are eating, do eat*
voi	mangiate	*you (fam., pl.) eat, are eating, do eat*
Loro	mangiano	*you (pol., pl.) eat, are eating, do eat*
loro	mangiano	*they eat, are eating, do eat*

Uses

The present indicative is used mainly to state facts in the present, to indicate an ongoing action, to refer to a continuous or habitual action, or to indicate an immediate future action.

Facts in the present

Studio l'italiano.	*I study Italian.*
Finisco di lavorare alle sei.	*I finish working at six.*

Ongoing actions

In questo momento **mangio** una pizza.	*At this moment I am eating a pizza.*
Loro **guardano** la TV.	*They are watching TV.*

Continuous or habitual actions

Il lunedì **mangio** sempre la pizza.	*On Mondays I always eat pizza.*
Ogni giorno **studio** l'italiano.	*Every day I study Italian.*

Immediate future actions

Domani **mangio** gli spaghetti.	*Tomorrow I am going to eat spaghetti.*
Loro **arrivano** la settimana prossima.	*They are arriving next week.*

As you will see in Unit 17, the present indicative can also be used with the preposition **da**, meaning both *since* and *for*, to correspond to English progressive tenses such as those below.

Aspetto da lunedì.	*I have been waiting since Monday.*
Aspetto da due giorni.	*I have been waiting for two days.*
Lui **dorme** da ieri.	*He has been sleeping since yesterday.*
Lui **dorme** da 48 ore.	*He has been sleeping for 48 hours.*

ESERCIZIO 10·1

A. *Provide the complete present indicative conjugation for each verb.*

1. First-conjugation verbs

   a. arrivare _____

   _____

   b. cercare _____

   _____

   c. cominciare _____

   _____

   d. mangiare _____

   _____

   e. pagare _____

   _____

2. Second-conjugation verbs

   a. chiedere _____

   _____

   b. rispondere _____

   _____

   c. vendere _____

   _____

   d. leggere _____

   _____

   e. chiudere _____

   _____

3. Third-conjugation verbs type 1

   a. aprire _____

   _____

   b. dormire _____

   _____

   c. partire _____

   _____

4. Third-conjugation verbs type 2

   a. capire _____

   _____

   b. finire _____

   _____

   c. preferire _____

   _____

B. *Rewrite each sentence by changing the verb to indicate that the subject in parentheses also does the same thing. Be careful! If the sentence is affirmative the appropriate form to use is* **anche**; *if it is negative the form is* **neanche** *(or* **nemmeno** *or* **neppure***).*

EXAMPLE 1   Giovanni mangia la pizza. (io)

          Anch'io mangio la pizza.

EXAMPLE 2   I miei amici non giocano a tennis. (noi)

          Neanche (Nemmeno/Neppure) noi giochiamo a tennis.

1. Marco non capisce la lezione. (io)

   _____

2. Loro partono domani. (noi)

   _____

3. La ragazza gioca a calcio da molti anni. (tu)

   _____

4. I miei cugini non aspettano mai. (voi)

   _____

5. Io telefono spesso a mia sorella. (Luigi)

   _____

6. Tu giochi sempre a tennis. (le mie amiche)

   _____

C. *Rewrite each question by changing the verb to direct the question to the subject in parentheses. Remember to use the polite form when appropriate.*

EXAMPLE   Maria, mangi la pizza stasera? (Signora Marchi)

   _____*Signora Marchi, mangia la pizza stasera?*_____

1. Alessandro, capisci la lezione? (Signor Verdi)

   _____

2. Signora Rossini, cerca qualcosa? (Sara)

   _____

3. Marco e Maria, partite domani? (Signori [*Gentlemen*])

   _____

4. Signore (*Ladies*), cominciano a studiare la matematica? (Ragazze)

   _____

Irregular verbs in the present indicative

Irregular verbs—that is, verbs that are not conjugated according to the pattern indicated above— are always problematic, since they have to be learned by memory. It is not possible to cover all the irregular verbs here. Below are the most commonly used and their present indicative conjugations.

andare (*to go*)	vado	vai	va	andiamo	andate	vanno
avere (*to have*)	ho	hai	ha	abbiamo	avete	hanno
bere (*to drink*)	bevo	bevi	beve	beviamo	bevete	bevono
dare (*to give*)	do	dai	dà	diamo	date	danno
dire (*to say, tell*)	dico	dici	dice	diciamo	dite	dicono

dovere (*to have to*)	devo	devi	deve	dobbiamo	dovete	devono
essere (*to be*)	sono	sei	è	siamo	siete	sono
fare (*to do, make*)	faccio	fai	fa	facciamo	fate	fanno
potere (*to be able to*)	posso	puoi	può	possiamo	potete	possono
sapere (*to know*)	so	sai	sa	sappiamo	sapete	sanno
stare (*to stay*)	sto	stai	sta	stiamo	state	stanno
tenere (*to hold, keep*)	tengo	tieni	tiene	teniamo	tenete	tengono
uscire (*to go out*)	esco	esci	esce	usciamo	uscite	escono
venire (*to come*)	vengo	vieni	viene	veniamo	venite	vengono
volere (*to want*)	voglio	vuoi	vuole	vogliamo	volete	vogliono

Special uses of avere, fare, and stare

avere caldo	*to be (feel) hot*	**stare bene**	*to be (feel) well*
avere freddo	*to be (feel) cold*	**stare male**	*to be (feel) bad*
fare bel tempo	*to be good weather*	**stare così così**	*to be so-so*
fare brutto tempo	*to be bad weather*		
fare cattivo tempo	*to be awful weather*		

ESERCIZIO
10·2

A. *Provide the appropriate present indicative forms for each verb.*

	IO	TU	LUI/LEI	NOI	VOI	LORO
1. volere						
2. venire						
3. uscire						
4. tenere						
5. stare						
6. sapere						
7. potere						
8. fare						
9. essere						
10. dovere						
11. dire						
12. dare						
13. bere						
14. avere						
15. andare						

B. *Complete the following dialogue between Maria and Marco with the missing forms of the verbs* **avere**, **fare**, *and* **stare**. *Note that* **ciao** *means both* hi *and* bye *in informal speech.*

1. Marco: Ciao, Maria, come _____?

2. Maria: Ciao, Marco, io _____ molto bene. E tu?

3. Marco: Io _____ così così. Anzi, _____ male.

4. Maria: Perché?

5. Marco: _____ male quando _____ cattivo o brutto tempo.
   _____ freddo!

6. Maria: Domani, per fortuna, dovrebbe (*it should*) _____ bel tempo.

7. Marco: Meno male! (*Thank heavens!*) E allora spero di (*I hope to*) _____ caldo!

C. *Rewrite each question by changing the form of the verb to direct the question to the subject in parentheses. Remember to use the polite form when appropriate.*

1. Marco, dove vai? (Signor Rossi)

   _____

2. Signora, come sta? (Maria)

   _____

3. Alessandro, cosa vuoi? (Signorina Verdi)

   _____

4. Signor Rossini, quando viene alla festa? (Giovanni)

   _____

5. Marco e Maria, quando uscite stasera? (Signor Verdi e Signora Verdi)

   _____

The present subjunctive of regular verbs

Verbs also allow you to convey a specific manner of thinking. This characteristic of a verb is known as its mood.

While the indicative mood is used to express facts, the subjunctive mood allows you to express a point of view, fear, doubt, hope, possibility, etc.—that is, anything that is not a sure fact. The subjunctive is, thus, a counterpart to the indicative, the mood that allows you to convey facts and information.

The subjunctive is formed by dropping the infinitive ending of the verb, and then adding on the appropriate ending according to person and number.

First conjugation

aspettare *to wait (for)* → **aspett-**

io	aspett**i**	*I wait*
tu	aspett**i**	*you (fam., sing.) wait*
Lei	aspett**i**	*you (pol., sing.) wait*
lui/lei	aspett**i**	*he/she waits*
noi	aspett**iamo**	*we wait*
voi	aspett**iate**	*you (fam., pl.) wait*
Loro	aspett**ino**	*you (pol., pl.) wait*
loro	aspett**ino**	*they wait*

Second conjugation

chiudere *to close* → **chiud-**

io	chiud**a**	*I close*
tu	chiud**a**	*you (fam., sing.) close*
Lei	chiud**a**	*you (pol., sing.) close*
lui/lei	chiud**a**	*he/she closes*
noi	chiud**iamo**	*we close*
voi	chiud**iate**	*you (fam., pl.) close*
Loro	chiud**ano**	*you (pol., pl.) close*
loro	chiud**ano**	*they close*

Third conjugation (type 1)

aprire *to open* → **apr-**

io	apr**a**	*I open*
tu	apr**a**	*you (fam., sing.) open*
Lei	apr**a**	*you (pol., sing.) open*
lui/lei	apr**a**	*he/she opens*
noi	apr**iamo**	*we open*
voi	apr**iate**	*you (fam., pl.) open*
Loro	apr**ano**	*you (pol., pl.) open*
loro	apr**ano**	*they open*

Third conjugation (type 2)

preferire *to prefer* → **prefer-**

io	prefer**isca**	*I prefer*
tu	prefer**isca**	*you (fam., sing.) prefer*
Lei	prefer**isca**	*you (pol., sing.) prefer*
lui/lei	prefer**isca**	*he/she prefers*
noi	prefer**iamo**	*we prefer*
voi	prefer**iate**	*you (fam., pl.) prefer*
Loro	prefer**iscano**	*you (pol., pl.) prefer*
loro	prefer**iscano**	*they prefer*

To preserve the hard **c** and **g** sounds of verbs ending -**care** and -**gare**, an **h** must be inserted before adding the appropriate ending for all forms of the conjugation.

cercare (*to look for*) → **cerch-**

cerchi	**cerchi**	**cerchi**	**cerchiamo**	**cerchiate**	**cerchino**

pagare (*to pay*) → **pagh-**

paghi	**paghi**	**paghi**	**paghiamo**	**paghiate**	**paghino**

The -**i** of verbs ending in -**ciare** and -**giare** is not repeated.

cominciare (*to begin*) → **cominc-**
cominci   **cominci**   **cominci**   **cominciamo**   **cominciate**   **comincino**

mangiare (*to eat*) → **mang-**
mangi   **mangi**   **mangi**   **mangiamo**   **mangiate**   **mangino**

Because the endings are often the same, the subject pronouns are used much more frequently with the subjunctive than with the indicative.

È necessario che **tu finisca** quel lavoro.	*It is important that you finish that job.*
È necessario che **lui finisca** quel lavoro.	*It is important that he finish that job.*

The subjunctive is used mainly in subordinate clauses introduced by **che** (see Unit 18). So, when a verb in the main clause (the verb to the left of **che**) expresses something that is a doubt, an opinion, etc., then the verb in the subordinate clause (the verb to the right of **che**) is normally in the subjunctive.

Spero che loro **parlino** italiano.	*I hope that they speak Italian.*
Penso che lui **cominci** a lavorare alle nove.	*I think that he starts working at nine.*
Crede che loro **arrivino** domani.	*He thinks (that) they are arriving tomorrow.*
Immagino che lei **capisca** tutto.	*I imagine (that) she understands everything.*
Dubitiamo che voi **finiate** in tempo.	*We doubt that you will finish in time.*

Not all verbs in subordinate clauses necessarily require the subjunctive—only those connected to a main clause verb that expresses a "nonfact" (opinion, fear, supposition, anticipation, wish, hope, doubt, etc.) will require the subjunctive.

INDICATIVE	SUBJUNCTIVE
Sa che **arriva** dopo.	Pensa che **arrivi** dopo.
He knows she is arriving later.	*He thinks she is arriving later.*
Sono sicuro che **parlano** italiano.	Credo che **parlino** italiano.
I am sure that they speak Italian.	*I believe that they speak Italian.*

Be careful!

Note that **che** is always used in Italian, whereas it is often dropped in English. Needless to say, this is a frequent source of blunders for learners.

Common verbs that, when used in the main clause, require the use of the subjunctive in the subordinate clause are the following.

credere	*to believe*
desiderare	*to desire*
dubitare	*to doubt*
immaginare	*to imagine*
pensare	*to think*
sembrare	*to seem*
sperare	*to hope*
volere	*to want*

A. *Provide the complete present subjunctive conjugation for each verb.*

1. First-conjugation verbs

   a. telefonare _____

   _____

   b. cercare _____

   _____

   c. cominciare _____

   _____

   d. mangiare _____

   _____

   e. pagare _____

   _____

2. Second-conjugation verbs

   a. scrivere _____

   _____

   b. leggere _____

   _____

3. Third-conjugation verbs (type 1)

   a. aprire _____

   _____

   b. partire _____

   _____

4. Third-conjugation verbs (type 2)

   a. capire _____

   _____

   b. preferire _____

   _____

B. *Rewrite each sentence using the verb in parentheses in the main clause. Adjust the verb in the subordinate clause to the subjunctive or indicative, as required.*

1. So che Mario dorme fino a tardi. (pensare)

   _____

2. Lui dice che tu finisci alle sei? (credere)

   _____

3. Desideriamo che voi scriviate un'e-mail. (sapere)

   _____

4. Sara dubita che tu capisca tutto. (sapere)

   _____

5. La professoressa Marchi immagina che noi studiamo molto. (dire)

   _____

6. È vero che lui studia molto. (sembrare)

   _____

7. Marco dice che io pago il conto (*the bill*). (sperare)

   _____

8. Loro dicono che lui comincia a studiare. (volere)

   _____

Irregular verbs in the present subjunctive

The following common verbs are irregular in the present subjunctive. By the way, the verbs that are irregular in the present indicative (see the preceding section of this unit) are also irregular in the present subjunctive.

andare	vada	vada	vada	andiamo	andiate	vadano
avere	abbia	abbia	abbia	abbiamo	abbiate	abbiano
bere	beva	beva	beva	beviamo	beviate	bevano
dare	dia	dia	dia	diamo	diate	diano
dire	dica	dica	dica	diciamo	diciate	dicano
dovere	deva (debba)	deva (debba)	deva (debba)	dobbiamo	dobbiate	devano (debbano)
essere	sia	sia	sia	siamo	siate	siano
fare	faccia	faccia	faccia	facciamo	facciate	facciano
potere	possa	possa	possa	possiamo	possiate	possano
sapere	sappia	sappia	sappia	sappiamo	sappiate	sappiano
stare	stia	stia	stia	stiamo	stiate	stiano
tenere	tenga	tenga	tenga	teniamo	teniate	tengano
uscire	esca	esca	esca	usciamo	usciate	escano
venire	venga	venga	venga	veniamo	veniate	vengano
volere	voglia	voglia	voglia	vogliamo	vogliate	vogliano

A. *Provide the corresponding subjunctive form of each verb.*

1. io

   a. voglio _____

   b. vengo _____

   c. esco _____

2. tu

   a. tieni _____

   b. stai _____

   c. sai _____

3. lui/lei; Lei

   a. può _____

   b. fa _____

   c. è _____

4. noi

   a. dobbiamo _____

   b. diciamo _____

   c. diamo _____

5. voi

   a. bevete _____

   b. avete _____

   c. andate _____

6. loro; Loro

   a. sono _____

   b. fanno _____

   c. danno _____

B. *Rewrite each sentence by using the verb in parentheses as the new main clause. Follow the example. Remember to adjust accordingly the verb in the subordinate clause to the subjunctive.*

EXAMPLE   Mario beve solo il latte. (penso)

Penso che Mario beva solo il latte.

1. È vero. (penso)

_____

2. Domani fa caldo. (crediamo)

_____

3. Sara sta bene. (sembra)

_____

4. Alessandro dà i soldi a sua sorella. (dubito)

_____

5. Lui può venire alla festa. (speriamo)

_____

6. Loro devono studiare di più. (sembra)

_____

7. Marco vuole uscire. (penso)

_____

8. Lui dice sempre la verità (*truth*). (crediamo)

_____

Special uses of the subjunctive

Impersonal verbs and expressions also require that the subordinate clause verb be in the subjunctive. These are verbs and expressions that have only third-person forms.

È probabile che lui **non venga** alla festa.	*It's probable that he will not come to the party.*
Bisogna che loro **studino** di più.	*It is necessary that they study more.*

Superlative expressions also require that the verb in the subordinate clause be in the subjunctive. (Note that **conoscere** = *to know someone*.)

Lei è **la persona più intelligente che io conosca**.	*She is the most intelligent person I know.*
Tu sei **la persona più elegante che io conosca**.	*You are the most elegant person I know.*

Certain conjunctions and indefinite structures also require that the verb that immediately follows be in the subjunctive.

Dovunque tu vada, io ti seguirò.	*Wherever you go, I will follow you.*
Benché piova, esco lo stesso.	*Although it is raining, I'm going out just the same.*

The most common ones are the following.

a meno che	*unless*
affinché	*so that*
benché	*although*
dovunque	*wherever*
nel caso che	*in the event that*
nonostante che	*despite*
prima che	*before*
purché	*provided that*
sebbene	*although*
senza che	*without*

Finally, the subjunctive is used in wish expressions.

Che piova, se vuole!	*Let it rain, if it wants to!*
Che Dio ce la mandi buona!	*May God help us!*

Note: When the subjects of two clauses are the same, then **di** + *infinitive* is used, even if the sentence expresses opinion, doubt, and so on.

Different subjects

Lui crede che **io scriva** bene.	*He believes that I write well.*
Maria pensa che **loro parlino** italiano bene.	*Mary thinks that they speak Italian well.*

Same subjects

Lui crede di scrivere bene.	*He believes that he writes well.*
Maria pensa di parlare italiano bene.	*Mary thinks that she speaks Italian well.*

ESERCIZIO 10·5

A. *Complete each sentence with the appropriate subjunctive form of the verb in parentheses.*

1. È probabile che domani non (fare) _____ caldo.

2. Bisogna che tu (dire) _____ la verità.

3. Lui è la persona più elegante che (esserci) _____.

4. Vengo anch'io alla festa, a meno che non (esserci) _____ la tua amica.

5. Devi studiare di più, affinché tu (potere) _____ parlare italiano meglio.

6. Benché (fare) _____ brutto tempo, esco lo stesso (*just the same*).

7. Dovunque tu (andare) _____, vengo anch'io.

8. Nel caso che (venire) _____ tuo cugino alla festa, io sto a casa.

9. Nonostante che tu (dire) _____ questo, io non ci credo.

10. Prima che loro (uscire) _____, devono studiare.

11. Faccio quello che dici, purché (essere) _____ facile.

12. Sebbene lui (volere) _____ uscire stasera, io devo stare a casa a studiare.

13. Faccio tutto, senza che tu (dire) _____ niente.

14. Che (fare) _____ brutto tempo!

B. *How do you say the following in Italian?*

1. She believes that I can go out tonight.

_____

2. We believe that he speaks Italian well.

_____

3. He thinks that he (himself) writes well.

_____

4. They believe that they (themselves) speak Italian well.

_____

C. *Choose the appropriate form of the verb to complete each sentence. (Note:* **lavorare** = *to work;* **vivere** = *to live;* **piovere** = *to rain.)*

1. Immaginiamo che loro _____ domani.

   a. arrivano   b. arrivino

2. Penso che loro _____ di lavorare alle sei.

   a. finiscono   b. finiscano

3. Pensiamo che loro _____ domani per l'Italia.

   a. partono   b. partano

4. È probabile che lei non _____ l'italiano.

   a. capisce   b. capisca

5. Dubitiamo che voi _____ prima delle sei.

   a. uscite   b. usciate

6. Io so che lui _____ una brava persona.

   a. è   b. sia

7. È certo che _____ anche lui alla festa.

   a. viene   b. venga

8. È probabile che lui non _____ dov'è la festa.

   a. sa   b. sappia

9. Bisogna che loro _____ di più.

   a. lavorano   b. lavorino

10. Lui è il professore più intelligente che io _____.

    a. conosco   b. conosca

11. Tu sei la persona più simpatica che _____ in quella città.

    a. vive   b. viva

12. Dovunque tu _____, ci vengo anch'io.

    a. vai   b. vada

13. Benché _____, lui vuole uscire lo stesso.

    a. piove   b. piova

14. Che _____, se vuole!

    a. piove   b. piova

D. *How do you say the following in Italian?*

1. Mary, are you studying Italian?

   _____

2. Mrs. Verdi, are you studying mathematics?

   _____

3. I think that Mary is going out tonight.

   _____

4. Although it is cold, I am going out just the same.

   _____

Grammar in culture

A common grammar-culture myth is that English has no subjunctive. In fact, it does. Consider the English equivalents of the subjunctive Italian verbs in the following sentences.

È necessario che lui parta subito.	*It is necessary that he leave* (not *leaves*) *right away.*
È importante che lei lo faccia.	*It is important that she do* (not *does*) *this.*

ESERCIZIO
10·6

Translate the following Italian sentences into English, so that you can compare how the two languages express the subjunctive.

1. Bisogna che lui dica sempre la verità.

   _____

2. Spero che lui dica sempre la verità.

   _____

3. È cruciale (*crucial*) che lei faccia questo.

   _____

4. Dubito che lei faccia questo spesso.

   _____

Past tenses

Past tenses allow you to talk about events that occurred before the present time. There are three main past tenses in Italian: the **present perfect**, the **past subjunctive**, and the **past absolute**.

PRESENT PERFECT	Ieri ho mangiato la pizza.	*Yesterday I ate pizza.*
PAST SUBJUNCTIVE	Penso che lui abbia mangiato la pizza ieri.	*I think that he ate pizza yesterday.*
PAST ABSOLUTE	Mangiammo la pizza alla napoletana molto tempo fa.	*We ate a Neapolitan pizza a long time ago.*

The present perfect

The present perfect tense is used to express actions that have been completed at the present time (at the time of speaking). It is a compound tense formed with the present indicative form of the auxiliary verb (**avere** or **essere**) plus the past participle of the verb of meaning, in that order.

Ieri **ho mangiato** tutto.	*Yesterday I ate everything.*
Marco **è andato** al cinema ieri.	*Mark went to the movies yesterday.*

The present indicative conjugations of the auxiliary verbs **avere** and **essere** are found in the previous unit. The regular past participle is formed by replacing the infinitive ending with the appropriate ending shown below.

FIRST CONJUGATION		SECOND CONJUGATION		THIRD CONJUGATION	
aspett**are**	*to wait*	vend**ere**	*to sell*	fin**ire**	*to finish*
aspett**ato**	*waited*	vend**uto**	*sold*	fin**ito**	*finished*

Verbs conjugated with **avere**

Here are the complete conjugations of three verbs conjugated with **avere** in the present perfect.

parlare   *to speak*

io	**ho parlato**	*I have spoken, spoke, did speak*
tu	**hai parlato**	*you (fam., sing.) have spoken, spoke, did speak*
Lei	**ha parlato**	*you (pol., sing.) have spoken, spoke, did speak*
lui/lei	**ha parlato**	*he/she has spoken, spoke, did speak*
noi	**abbiamo parlato**	*we have spoken, spoke, did speak*
voi	**avete parlato**	*you (fam., pl.) have spoken, spoke, did speak*
Loro	**hanno parlato**	*you (pol., pl.) have spoken, spoke, did speak*
loro	**hanno parlato**	*they have spoken, spoke, did speak*

vendere   *to sell*

io	**ho venduto**	*I have sold, sold, did sell*
tu	**hai venduto**	*you (fam., sing.) have sold, sold, did sell*
Lei	**ha venduto**	*you (pol., sing.) have sold, sold, did sell*
lui/lei	**ha venduto**	*he/she has sold, sold, did sell*
noi	**abbiamo venduto**	*we have sold, sold, did sell*
voi	**avete venduto**	*you (fam., pl.) have sold, sold, did sell*
Loro	**hanno venduto**	*you (pol., pl.) have sold, sold, did sell*
loro	**hanno venduto**	*they have sold, sold, did sell*

finire   *to finish*

io	**ho finito**	*I have finished, finished, did finish*
tu	**hai finito**	*you (fam., sing.) have finished, finished, did finish*
Lei	**ha finito**	*you (pol., sing.) have finished, finished, did finish*
lui/lei	**ha finito**	*he/she has finished, finished, did finish*
noi	**abbiamo finito**	*we have finished, finished, did finish*
voi	**avete finito**	*you (fam., pl.) have finished, finished, did finish*
Loro	**hanno finito**	*you (pol., pl.) have finished, finished, did finish*
loro	**hanno finito**	*they have finished, finished, did finish*

Verbs conjugated with **essere**

The past participle of verbs conjugated with **essere** agrees in number and gender with the subject of the verb. Here are the complete conjugations of three verbs conjugated with **essere** in the present perfect.

arrivare   *to arrive*

io	**sono arrivato (-a)**	*I have arrived, arrived, did arrive*
tu	**sei arrivato (-a)**	*you (fam., sing.) have arrived, arrived, did arrive*
Lei	**è arrivato (-a)**	*you (pol., sing.) have arrived, arrived, did arrive*
lui	**è arrivato**	*he has arrived, arrived, did arrive*
lei	**è arrivata**	*she has arrived, arrived, did arrive*
noi	**siamo arrivati (-e)**	*we have arrived, arrived, did arrive*
voi	**siete arrivati (-e)**	*you (fam., pl.) have arrived, arrived, did arrive*
Loro	**sono arrivati (-e)**	*you (pol., pl.) have arrived, arrived, did arrive*
loro	**sono arrivati (-e)**	*they have arrived, arrived, did arrive*

cadere   *to fall*

io	**sono caduto (-a)**	*I have fallen, fell, did fall*
tu	**sei caduto (-a)**	*you (fam., sing.) have fallen, fell, did fall*
Lei	**è caduto (-a)**	*you (pol., sing.) have fallen, fell, did fall*
lui	**è caduto**	*he has fallen, fell, did fall*
lei	**è caduta**	*she has fallen, fell, did fall*
noi	**siamo caduti (-e)**	*we have fallen, fell, did fall*
voi	**siete caduti (-e)**	*you (fam., pl.) have fallen, fell, did fall*
Loro	**sono caduti (-e)**	*you (pol., pl.) have fallen, fell, did fall*
loro	**sono caduti (-e)**	*they have fallen, fell, did fall*

partire *to leave*

io	**sono partito (-a)**	*I have left, left, did leave*
tu	**sei partito (-a)**	*you (fam., sing.) have left, left, did leave*
Lei	**è partito (-a)**	*you (pol., sing.) have left, left, did leave*
lui	**è partito**	*he has left, left, did leave*
lei	**è partita**	*she has left, left, did leave*
noi	**siamo partiti (-e)**	*we have left, left, did leave*
voi	**siete partiti (-e)**	*you (fam., pl.) have left, left, did leave*
Loro	**sono partiti (-e)**	*you (pol., pl.) have left, left, did leave*
loro	**sono partiti (-e)**	*they have left, left, did leave*

Selecting the auxiliary verb

When do you use **avere** or **essere**? The best learning strategy is to assume that most verbs are conjugated with **avere** (which is true), and then memorize those verbs which are conjugated with **essere**. All the latter are intransitive (that is, they do not take a direct object). Moreover, many of them generally refer to some kind of motion (going, arriving, staying, entering, etc.).

Common verbs conjugated with **essere** in compound tenses

andare	*to go*	partire	*to leave*
arrivare	*to arrive*	sembrare	*to seem*
cadere	*to fall*	stare	*to stay*
diventare	*to become*	tornare	*to return*
entrare	*to enter*	uscire	*to go out*
essere	*to be*	venire	*to come*
nascere	*to be born*		

Impersonal verbs are all conjugated with **essere**. These are verbs that have only third-person forms.

durare — *to last*

Lo spettacolo **è durato** tre ore. — *The show lasted three hours.*

costare — *to cost*

Quanto **sono costate** le arance? — *How much did the oranges cost?*

Uses

Basically, the present perfect covers three English past tenses: for example, *I spoke, I have spoken,* and *I did speak.*

Ieri **ho parlato** al signor Verdi.	*Yesterday, I spoke to Mr. Verdi.*
Maria **ha venduto** la sua macchina.	*Mary sold her car.*
Loro **hanno dormito** troppo ieri.	*They slept too much yesterday.*
Ho già **mangiato**.	*I have already eaten.*
Il nostro amico **è arrivato** ieri.	*Our friend arrived yesterday.*
Tua cugina **è arrivata** la settimana scorsa.	*Your cousin arrived last week.*
Quando **siete venuti**?	*When did you come?*
Quando **è partita**, signora Verdi?	*When did you leave, Mrs. Verdi?*

Remember that third-person forms are used in polite address. When using **Lei** or **Loro**, be sure that the past participle of verbs conjugated with **essere** indicates the gender of the person or people you are addressing.

Signor Verdi, **è uscito** ieri?	*Mr. Verdi, did you go out yesterday?*
Signora Verdi, **è uscita** ieri?	*Mrs. Verdi, did you go out yesterday?*
Signor e signora Verdi, **sono usciti** ieri?	*Mr. and Mrs. Verdi, did you go out yesterday?*

Adverbs that generally indicate use of the past tense

appena	*just*
fa	*ago*
già	*already*
ieri	*yesterday*
prima	*before*

Of these, **già** and **appena** are put generally between the auxiliary verb and the past participle.

Ho **già** mangiato.	*I have eaten already.*
Sono **appena** arrivati.	*They have just arrived.*

ESERCIZIO
11·1

A. *Provide the complete present perfect conjugation for each verb.*

1. First-conjugation verbs

   a. cercare

   _____

   _____

   b. andare

   _____

   _____

2. Second-conjugation verbs

   a. conoscere

   _____

   _____

   b. volere

   _____

   _____

3. Third-conjugation verbs

   a. capire

   _____

   _____

   b. uscire

   _____

   _____

B. *Rewrite each sentence by changing the verb to indicate that the subject in parentheses also does the same thing.*

EXAMPLE   Giovanni ha mangiato la pizza ieri. (io)

   Anch'io ho mangiato la pizza ieri.

1. Marco non ha capito la lezione. (io)

   _____

2. Loro sono già partiti. (noi)

   _____

3. La ragazza ha già studiato la lezione. (tu)

   _____

4. I miei cugini sono appena usciti. (voi)

   _____

5. Io ho telefonato prima a mia sorella. (Luigi)

   _____

6. Tu sei andato in Italia un anno fa. (le mie amiche)

   _____

C. *Rewrite each question by changing the verb to direct the question to the subject in parentheses. Remember to use the polite form when appropriate.*

EXAMPLE   Maria, hai mangiato la pizza ieri? (Signora Marchi)

   Signora Marchi, ha mangiato la pizza ieri?

1. Alessandro, hai capito la lezione? (Signor Verdi)

   _____

2. Signora Rossini, ha pagato il conto? (Sara)

   _____

3. Marco e Maria, siete usciti ieri sera? (Signori)

_____

4. Signore (_Ladies_), hanno cominciato a studiare la matematica? (Ragazze)

_____

Irregular past participles

The following common verbs have irregular past participles. The verbs conjugated with **essere** are identified by a notation in parentheses.

VERB		PAST PARTICIPLE	
aprire	_to open_	**aperto**	_opened_
bere	_to drink_	**bevuto**	_drunk_
chiedere	_to ask (for)_	**chiesto**	_asked_
chiudere	_to close_	**chiuso**	_closed_
dare	_to give_	**dato**	_given_
decidere	_to decide_	**deciso**	_decided_
dire	_to say, tell_	**detto**	_said_
essere (essere)	_to be_	**stato**	_been_
fare	_to do, make_	**fatto**	_done, made_
leggere	_to read_	**letto**	_read_
mettere	_to put_	**messo**	_put_
nascere (essere)	_to be born_	**nato**	_born_
perdere	_to lose_	**perso**	_lost_
prendere	_to take_	**preso**	_taken_
scegliere	_to choose, select_	**scelto**	_chosen, selected_
scendere (essere)	_to descend, go down_	**sceso**	_descended, gone down_
scrivere	_to write_	**scritto**	_written_
stare (essere)	_to stay_	**stato**	_stayed_
vedere	_to see_	**visto**	_seen_
venire (essere)	_to come_	**venuto**	_come_
vincere	_to win_	**vinto**	_won_

Note: The verb **scegliere** is also irregular in the present indicative and present subjunctive.

PRESENT INDICATIVE	(io) **scelgo**, (tu) **scegli**, (lui/lei; Lei) **sceglie**,
	(noi) **scegliamo**, (voi) **scegliete**, (loro; Loro) **scelgono**
PRESENT SUBJUNCTIVE	(io) **scelga**, (tu) **scelga**, (lui/lei; Lei) **scelga**,
	(noi) **scegliamo**, (voi) **scegliate**, (loro; Loro) **scelgano**

A. *Rewrite each sentence by changing the verb to the present perfect form.*

EXAMPLE   Lui vince spesso.

_____Lui ha vinto spesso._____

1. Io apro la finestra.   _____

2. Tu bevi l'espresso.   _____

3. Marco chiede qualcosa.   _____

4. Quando chiudono?   _____

5. A chi dà la rivista tuo fratello?   _____

6. Voi non decidete, vero?   _____

7. Anche loro dicono la verità.   _____

8. Loro sono in Italia.   _____

9. Che tempo fa?   _____

10. Che cosa leggi?   _____

11. Dove metti quel libro?   _____

12. Chi perde spesso?   _____

13. Cosa prendete voi?   _____

14. Quale scegli, Maria?   _____

15. A che ora scendono?   _____

16. A chi scrivete?   _____

17. Io sto in casa.   _____

18. Vedo i miei amici.   _____

19. A che ora vengono le ragazze?   _____

B. *Provide the present indicative, present subjunctive, and present perfect forms of each phrase according to the subject of the verb in parentheses. (Note:* **adesso** = *now.)*

EXAMPLE   vincere la partita (voi)

PRESENT INDICATIVE   _Voi vincete la partita adesso._

PRESENT SUBJUNCTIVE   _Penso che voi vinciate la partita adesso._

PRESENT PERFECT   _Voi avete già vinto la partita._

1. scegliere la borsa (tu)

   PRESENT INDICATIVE _____

   PRESENT SUBJUNCTIVE _____

   PRESENT PERFECT _____

2. scrivere l'e-mail (tu)

   PRESENT INDICATIVE _____

   PRESENT SUBJUNCTIVE _____

   PRESENT PERFECT _____

3. scegliere lo zaino (loro)

   PRESENT INDICATIVE _____

   PRESENT SUBJUNCTIVE _____

   PRESENT PERFECT _____

4. venire (lei)

   PRESENT INDICATIVE _____

   PRESENT SUBJUNCTIVE _____

   PRESENT PERFECT _____

5. venire (lui)

   PRESENT INDICATIVE _____

   PRESENT SUBJUNCTIVE _____

   PRESENT PERFECT _____

6. dire la verità (loro)

   PRESENT INDICATIVE _____

   PRESENT SUBJUNCTIVE _____

   PRESENT PERFECT _____

7. fare niente (voi)

   PRESENT INDICATIVE _____

   PRESENT SUBJUNCTIVE _____

   PRESENT PERFECT _____

The past subjunctive

Like the present perfect, the past subjunctive is a compound tense. It is formed with the present subjunctive of the auxiliary verb plus the past participle of the verb, in that order. Here are two verbs conjugated completely for you, one conjugated with **avere** and the other with **essere**.

parlare *to speak*

io	**abbia parlato**	*I have spoken, spoke*
tu	**abbia parlato**	*you (fam., sing.) have spoken, spoke*
Lei	**abbia parlato**	*you (pol., sing.) have spoken, spoke*
lui/lei	**abbia parlato**	*he/she has spoken, spoke*
noi	**abbiamo parlato**	*we have spoken, spoke*
voi	**abbiate parlato**	*you (fam., pl.) have spoken, spoke*
Loro	**abbiano parlato**	*you (pol., pl.) have spoken, spoke*
loro	**abbiano parlato**	*they have spoken, spoke*

arrivare *to arrive*

io	**sia arrivato (-a)**	*I have arrived, arrived*
tu	**sia arrivato (-a)**	*you (fam., sing.) have arrived, arrived*
Lei	**sia arrivato (-a)**	*you (pol., sing.) have arrived, arrived*
lui	**sia arrivato**	*he has arrived, arrived*
lei	**sia arrivata**	*she has arrived, arrived*
noi	**siamo arrivati (-e)**	*we have arrived, arrived*
voi	**siate arrivati (-e)**	*you (fam., pl.) have arrived, arrived*
Loro	**siano arrivati (-e)**	*you (pol., pl.) have arrived, arrived*
loro	**siano arrivati (-e)**	*they have arrived, arrived*

Essentially, the past subjunctive expresses in the subordinate clause an action that occurred in the past with respect to the main clause verb.

Non credo che lui **abbia capito**.	*I don't believe he understood.*
Non è possibile che loro **siano** già **partiti**.	*It's not possible that they have already left.*
Benché **abbia piovuto** ieri, è uscito lo stesso.	*Although it rained yesterday, he went out just the same.*

ESERCIZIO

11·3

A. *Rewrite each sentence by using the main clause in parentheses and by making all other necessary changes. (Note: **probabile** = probable; **possibile** = possible.)*

EXAMPLE   Marco ha mangiato la pizza ieri. (Penso che…)

Penso che Marco abbia mangiato la pizza ieri.

1. Io ho appena scritto quell'e-mail. (Mio fratello crede che…)

   _____

2. Io sono già stato in Italia. (Tutti pensano che…)

   _____

3. Anche tu non hai capito, no? (Credo che…)

   _____

4. Quella donna ha finito di lavorare presto. (È probabile che...)

_____

5. Quella donna è uscita al cinema con gli amici. (Dubito che...)

_____

6. Marco ha visto la sua professoressa in centro ieri. (Non è possibile che...)

_____

7. Quell'uomo è uscito al cinema con gli amici. (Immagino che...)

_____

8. Noi abbiamo già letto quel libro. (Lui dubita che...)

_____

9. Tu sei stato a Roma due anni fa, vero? (Non credo che...)

_____

10. Noi siamo andati al cinema ieri sera. (Lei non crede che...)

_____

11. Voi siete tornati tardi ieri sera. (Dubito che...)

_____

12. Voi non avete mai studiato l'italiano, vero? (È probabile che...)

_____

13. I miei amici hanno preso un caffellatte. (Penso che...)

_____

14. I tuoi amici sono venuti tardi alla festa. (Credo che...)

_____

15. Le nostre amiche hanno detto la verità. (Dubito che...)

_____

16. Quelle camicie sono costate così tanto. (Non è possibile che...)

_____

B. *Complete each sentence with the appropriate form of the verb in parentheses (the verb of the subordinate clause).*

EXAMPLE   Sono uscito lo stesso ieri, benché _____*abbia piovuto*_____ (piovere).

1. Siamo andati al cinema lo stesso, sebbene _____ (fare brutto tempo).

2. Mio fratello è venuto alla festa, nonostante _____ (piovere).

3. Marco e Maria sono usciti lo stesso ieri sera, benché _____ (lavorare fino a tardi).

4. Io ho scritto quell'e-mail, sebbene _____ (non avere tanto tempo).

The past absolute

The past absolute covers many of the same uses of the present perfect, except the one referring to present past actions. Thus, it is never translated with the English compound verb forms *I have gone, you have eaten,* and so on. It corresponds only to the forms *I went, you ate,* and so on. The past absolute is used more than the present perfect to refer to actions that occurred in the distant past.

Ieri loro **sono andati** in Italia.	*Yesterday they went to Italy.*
Andarono in Italia molti anni fa.	*They went to Italy many years ago.*

The past absolute is formed by dropping the infinitive ending and adding the appropriate ending according to person and number.

First conjugation

cantare *to sing* → **cant-**

io	cant**ai**	*I sang*
tu	cant**asti**	*you (fam., sing.) sang*
Lei	cant**ò**	*you (pol., sing.) sang*
lui/lei	cant**ò**	*he/she sang*
noi	cant**ammo**	*we sang*
voi	cant**aste**	*you (fam., pl.) sang*
Loro	cant**arono**	*you (pol., pl.) sang*
loro	cant**arono**	*they sang*

Second conjugation

vendere *to sell* → **vend-**

io	vend**ei** (vend**etti**)	*I sold*
tu	vend**esti**	*you (fam., sing.) sold*
Lei	vend**é** (vend**ette**)	*you (pol., sing.) sold*
lui/lei	vend**é** (vend**ette**)	*he/she sold*
noi	vend**emmo**	*we sold*
voi	vend**este**	*you (fam., pl.) sold*
Loro	vend**erono** (vend**ettero**)	*you (pol., pl.) sold*
loro	vend**erono** (vend**ettero**)	*they sold*

Third conjugation

finire *to finish* → **fin-**

io	fin**ii**	*I finished*
tu	fin**isti**	*you (fam., sing.) finished*
Lei	fin**ì**	*you (pol., sing.) finished*
lui/lei	fin**ì**	*he/she finished*
noi	fin**immo**	*we finished*
voi	fin**iste**	*you (fam., pl.) finished*
Loro	fin**irono**	*you (pol., pl.) finished*
loro	fin**irono**	*they finished*

As mentioned, the past absolute can be used in place of the present perfect in most cases. It is, however, the only tense to be used in reference to historical events and events that occurred in the distant past.

I miei genitori **tornarono** in Italia anni fa.	*My parents returned to Italy years ago.*
Marco Polo **portò** tanti tesori indietro.	*Marco Polo brought back many treasures.*
Finirono quel lavoro tanto tempo fa.	*They finished that job a long time ago.*

The past absolute cannot be used with temporal adverbs such as **fa** (*ago*), **già** (*already*), and **poco fa** (a *little while ago*), which limit the action to the immediate past. Only the present perfect can be used in such cases.

Alessandro **è arrivato** poco tempo fa. *Alexander arrived a little while ago.*
Ho già **telefonato** a lei. *I already phoned her.*

Outside of this restriction, the past absolute can be used (judiciously) as an alternative to the present perfect.

Maria **è venuta** in America (or) Maria **venne** in America *Mary came to America*
 nel 2004. nel 2004. *in 2004.*
Ieri ti **ho telefonato** alle (or) Ieri ti **telefonai** *Yesterday I phoned you*
 due. alle due. *at two.*

The past absolute is primarily a literary past tense. It is used in particular in the narration of historical events.

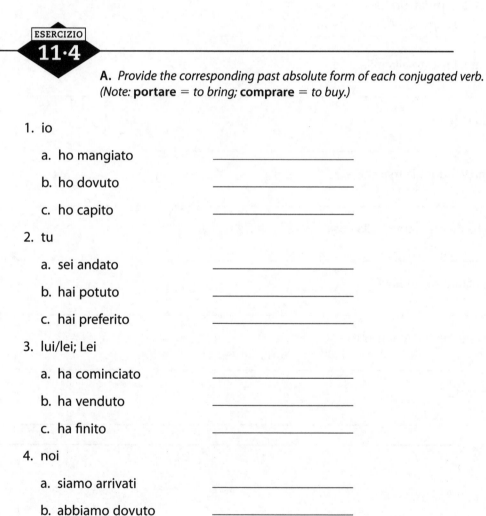

ESERCIZIO

11·4

A. *Provide the corresponding past absolute form of each conjugated verb.*
*(Note: **portare** = to bring; **comprare** = to buy.)*

1. io

 a. ho mangiato _____

 b. ho dovuto _____

 c. ho capito _____

2. tu

 a. sei andato _____

 b. hai potuto _____

 c. hai preferito _____

3. lui/lei; Lei

 a. ha cominciato _____

 b. ha venduto _____

 c. ha finito _____

4. noi

 a. siamo arrivati _____

 b. abbiamo dovuto _____

 c. siamo partiti _____

5. voi

    a. avete portato   _____

    b. avete potuto   _____

    c. siete usciti   _____

6. loro; Loro

    a. hanno comprato   _____

    b. hanno venduto   _____

    c. hanno dormito   _____

B. *Rewrite each sentence by changing the verb to the past absolute and indicating that the action was done many years ago.*

EXAMPLE   Maria è andata in Italia.

        Maria andò in Italia molti anni fa.

1. Io ho mangiato il risotto alla milanese.

    _____

2. Tu sei andata in Italia.

    _____

3. Mia sorella ha venduto la macchina.

    _____

4. Mio fratello ha dovuto fare quella cosa.

    _____

5. Noi abbiamo finito di studiare.

    _____

6. Anche voi avete mangiato il risotto.

    _____

7. Loro sono tornati.

    _____

Irregular verbs in the past absolute

As with other tenses, there are irregular verbs in the past absolute. Here are the most common ones.

> ## Tip!
>
> Note that most of the verbs have regular **tu** (second-person singular), **noi** (first-person plural), and **voi** (second-person plural) forms. For example, the verb **avere** is conjugated as a regular second-conjugation verb in these three persons: **(tu) avesti, (noi) avemmo, (voi) aveste**. The other forms are irregular: **(io) ebbi, (lui/lei; Lei) ebbe, (loro; Loro) ebbero**

avere (*to have*)	ebbi	avesti	ebbe	avemmo	aveste	ebbero
bere (*to drink*)	bevvi (bevetti)	bevesti	bevve (bevette)	bevemmo	beveste	bevvero (bevettero)
cadere (*to fall*)	caddi	cadesti	cadde	cademmo	cadeste	caddero
chiedere (*to ask for*)	chiesi	chiedesti	chiese	chiedemmo	chiedeste	chiesero
chiudere (*to close*)	chiusi	chiudesti	chiuse	chiudemmo	chiudeste	chiusero
conoscere (*to know, be familiar with*)	conobbi	conoscesti	conobbe	conoscemmo	conosceste	conobbero
dare (*to give*)	diedi	desti	diede	demmo	deste	diedero
decidere (*to decide*)	decisi	decidesti	decise	decidemmo	decideste	decisero
dire (*to say, tell*)	dissi	dicesti	disse	dicemmo	diceste	dissero
essere (*to be*)	fui	fosti	fu	fummo	foste	furono
fare (*to do, make*)	feci	facesti	fece	facemmo	faceste	fecero
leggere (*to read*)	lessi	leggesti	lesse	leggemmo	leggeste	lessero
mettere (*to put*)	misi	mettesti	mise	mettemmo	metteste	misero
nascere (*to be born*)	nacqui	nascesti	nacque	nascemmo	nasceste	nacquero
perdere (*to lose*)	persi	perdesti	perse	perdemmo	perdeste	persero
prendere (*to take*)	presi	prendesti	prese	prendemmo	prendeste	presero
sapere (*to know*)	seppi	sapesti	seppe	sapemmo	sapeste	seppero
scegliere (*to choose, select*)	scelsi	scegliesti	scelse	scegliemmo	sceglieste	scelsero
scendere (*to descend, go down*)	scesi	scendesti	scese	scendemmo	scendeste	scesero
scrivere (*to write*)	scrissi	scrivesti	scrisse	scrivemmo	scriveste	scrissero
stare (*to stay*)	stetti	stesti	stette	stemmo	steste	stettero
vedere (*to see*)	vidi	vedesti	vide	vedemmo	vedeste	videro
venire (*to come*)	venni	venisti	venne	venimmo	veniste	vennero
volere (*to want*)	volli	volesti	volle	volemmo	voleste	vollero

Other past tenses

There are also **past infinitive** and **past gerund** forms. The latter will be discussed in Unit 13. The past infinitive is a compound form consisting of the infinitive of the auxiliary verb and the past participle of the verb of meaning, in that order.

aver(e) parlato	*having spoken*	**esser(e) arrivato (-a)**	*having arrived*
aver(e) venduto	*having sold*	**esser(e) caduto (-a)**	*having fallen*
aver(e) dormito	*having slept*	**esser(e) partito (-a)**	*having left*

Note that the final **-e** of the auxiliary may be dropped.

Dopo **essere arrivato**, Marco ha chiamato.	*After having arrived, Mark called.*
Dopo **essere arrivata**, Maria ha chiamato.	*After having arrived, Mary called.*
Dopo **essere arrivati**, i miei amici hanno chiamato.	*After having arrived, my friends called.*
Dopo **essere arrivate**, le mie amiche hanno chiamato.	*After having arrived, my (female) friends called.*

A. *Provide the past absolute forms for each verb.*

	IO	TU	LUI/LEI	NOI	VOI	LORO
1. volere						
2. venire						
3. vedere						
4. stare						
5. scrivere						
6. scendere						
7. scegliere						
8. sapere						
9. prendere						
10. perdere						
11. nascere						
12. mettere						
13. leggere						
14. fare						
15. essere						
16. dire						
17. decidere						
18. dare						
19. conoscere						
20. chiudere						
21. chiedere						

22. cadere   _____ _____ _____ _____ _____ _____

23. bere   _____ _____ _____ _____ _____ _____

24. avere   _____ _____ _____ _____ _____ _____

B. *Use each sequence of words to create a sentence; use the past absolute form of the verb. Each sentence tells you something about Italian history or culture. (Note:* **inventare** = *to invent.)*

EXAMPLE   Dante / scrivere / la *Divina Commedia*

           Dante scrisse la Divina Commedia. _____

1. Galileo / inventare / il telescopio

_____

2. Colombo / venire / nel Nuovo Mondo nel 1492

_____

3. Leonardo Fibonacci / essere / un grande matematico

_____

4. Leonardo Da Vinci / fare / molte scoperte (*discoveries*)

_____

5. Il compositore Giuseppe Verdi / nascere / nel 1813.

_____

6. Alessandro Manzoni / scrivere / *I promessi sposi.*

_____

C. *How do you say the following in Italian?*

1. After having eaten, we went to the movies.

_____

2. After having bought that car, we sold our other car.

_____

3. After having gone to Italy, my (female) friends started to speak Italian very well.

_____

D. *Provide the present perfect, past subjunctive, and past absolute forms of each verb. The first one is done for you.*

	PRESENT PERFECT	PAST SUBJUNCTIVE	PAST ABSOLUTE
1. (tu) cantare	*hai cantato*	*abbia cantato*	*cantasti*
2. (io) mangiare	_____	_____	_____
3. (lui) pagare	_____	_____	_____
4. (noi) vendere	_____	_____	_____

5. (voi) leggere _____ _____ _____

6. (loro) scrivere _____ _____ _____

7. (lei) nascere _____ _____ _____

8. (io) capire _____ _____ _____

9. (tu) finire _____ _____ _____

10. (lui) venire _____ _____ _____

11. (loro) dire _____ _____ _____

12. (voi) dare _____ _____ _____

13. (noi) fare _____ _____ _____

14. (io) chiedere _____ _____ _____

15. (lui) essere _____ _____ _____

E. *Complete each sentence with the appropriate form of the auxiliary verb and with the missing final vowel of the past participle.*

1. Marco _____ vendut_____ la sua macchina ieri.

2. Maria _____ andat_____ al cinema ieri.

3. Maria _____ comprat_____ le scarpe nuove ieri.

4. I miei amici _____ andat_____ in Italia la settimana scorsa.

5. Anche le sue amiche _____ andat_____ in Italia qualche giorno fa.

6. Loro _____ vist_____ quel film già.

7. Voi _____ già mangiat_____, non è vero?

8. Noi tutti _____ andat_____ al cinema ieri.

9. Signor Verdi, quando _____ uscit_____ ieri Lei?

10. Signora Verdi, quando _____ uscit_____ ieri Lei?

F. *How do you say the following in Italian?*

1. I think that the movie lasted three hours.

_____

2. How much did the meat cost?

_____

3. Although my sister sold her car, she has a motorcycle.

_____

4. Yesterday we spoke to Mr. Verdi.

_____

5. I think he slept too much yesterday.

   _____

6. Although I have already eaten, I want to eat again.

   _____

7. Our grandfather came to the United States in 1994.

   _____

Grammar in culture

The use of the past absolute tense to narrate historical events probably reflects how we wish to imprint them in our cultural memory. The past absolute seems to give these events significance and uniqueness.

ESERCIZIO
11·6

How do you say the following in Italian?

1. Michelangelo sculpted (**scolpire**) David.

   _____

2. Giuseppe Verdi wrote many beautiful operas.

   _____

3. Petrarch wrote some beautiful poems (**poesie**).

   _____

4. Pavarotti was a great tenor (**tenore**).

   _____

The imperfect and pluperfect tenses

The present perfect (see Unit 11) allows you, in essence, to refer to a finished past action—an action that can be visualized as having started and ended.

Ieri **ho dormito** quattro ore.	*Yesterday I slept for four hours.*

However, if it is necessary to refer to an action that continued for an indefinite period of time, then the **imperfect tense** is called for.

Ieri, mentre io dormivo, **tu guardavi** la TV.	*Yesterday, while I was sleeping, you were watching TV.*

The imperfect is also used to refer to habitual or repeated actions in the past, and to describe the characteristics of people and things as they used to be.

Quando ero giovane, **suonavo** il pianoforte.	*When I was young, I used to play the piano.*
Da giovane, lei **aveva** i capelli biondi.	*As a youth, she had (used to have) blond hair.*

The imperfect indicative

The imperfect is formed by dropping the infinitive ending and adding the appropriate ending according to person and number.

First conjugation

suonare *to play (an instrument)* → **suon-**

io	suon**avo**	*I was playing, used to play*
tu	suon**avi**	*you (fam., sing.) were playing, used to play*
Lei	suon**ava**	*you (pol., sing.) were playing, used to play*
lui/lei	suon**ava**	*he/she was playing, used to play*
noi	suon**avamo**	*we were playing, used to play*
voi	suon**avate**	*you (fam., pl.) were playing, used to play*
Loro	suon**avano**	*you (pol., pl.) were playing, used to play*
loro	suon**avano**	*they were playing, used to play*

Second conjugation

mettere *to put* → **mett-**

io	mett**evo**	*I was putting, used to put*
tu	mett**evi**	*you (fam., sing.) were putting, used to put*
Lei	mett**eva**	*you (pol., sing.) were putting, used to put*
lui/lei	mett**eva**	*he/she was putting, used to put*
noi	mett**evamo**	*we were putting, used to put*
voi	mett**evate**	*you (fam., pl.) were putting, used to put*
Loro	mett**evano**	*you (pol., pl.) were putting, used to put*
loro	mett**evano**	*they were putting, used to put*

Third conjugation

venire *to come* → **ven-**

io	ven**ivo**	*I was coming, used to come*
tu	ven**ivi**	*you (fam., sing.) were coming, used to come*
Lei	ven**iva**	*you (pol., sing.) were coming, used to come*
lui/lei	ven**iva**	*he/she was coming, used to come*
noi	ven**ivamo**	*we were coming, used to come*
voi	ven**ivate**	*you (fam., pl.) were coming, used to come*
Loro	ven**ivano**	*you (pol., pl.) were coming, used to come*
loro	ven**ivano**	*they were coming, used to come*

Tip!

Another way to conjugate verbs in the imperfect indicative is to drop the **-re** of the infinitive (**suona-**, **mette-**, **veni-**) and then add one set of endings to all three conjugations: **-vo**, **-vi**, **-va**, **-vamo**, **-vate**, **-vano**. Try it!

As mentioned, the imperfect allows you to refer to continuous past actions (actions that went on for a while), to states and conditions that were habitual or recurring, and to the characteristics of people and things as they used to be or once were. (Note: **guardare** = *to watch, look at.*)

Mentre tu **studiavi**, io **suonavo** il pianoforte.	*While you were studying, I played (was playing) the piano.*
Da giovane, lui **guardava** sempre la TV.	*As a youth, he always watched TV.*
Da bambina, io **avevo** i capelli biondi.	*As a child, I had blond hair.*

Note that sometimes English uses a perfect tense in place of the Italian imperfect.

Mentre **dormivo**, **tu guardavi** la TV.	*While I slept (was sleeping), you watched TV.*

You must, therefore, always look for clues among the other words in a sentence to determine whether the imperfect should or should not be used. Words such as the following generally indicate that the imperfect is required.

di solito	*usually*
mentre	*while*
sempre	*always*

Di solito i miei genitori **andavano** in Italia per le vacanze.	*Usually my parents went to Italy for their vacation.*
Da bambino, mio fratello **giocava** **sempre** al computer.	*As a child, my brother always played on the computer.*
Alcuni anni fa, **guardavo sempre** le partite di calcio in televisione.	*A few years ago, I used to always watch soccer games on television.*

Irregular forms

Predictably, there are irregular verb forms in the imperfect. Here are the most common.

bere (*to drink*)	bevevo	bevevi	beveva	bevevamo	bevevate	bevevano
dare (*to give*)	davo	davi	dava	davamo	davate	davano
dire (*to say, tell*)	dicevo	dicevi	diceva	dicevamo	dicevate	dicevano
essere (*to be*)	ero	eri	era	eravamo	eravate	erano
fare (*to do, make*)	facevo	facevi	faceva	facevamo	facevate	facevano
stare (*to stay*)	stavo	stavi	stava	stavamo	stavate	stavano

ESERCIZIO 12·1

A. *Provide the appropriate imperfect form of each verb. The first one is done for you.*

1. (io) cantare   *(io) cantavo*

2. (io) stare   _____

3. (io) fare   _____

4. (lui) cominciare   _____

5. (lui) essere   _____

6. (lui) dire   _____

7. (io) leggere   _____

8. (noi) dare   _____

9. (noi) bere   _____

10. (io) capire   _____

11. (tu) guardare   _____

12. (io) bere   _____

13. (tu) dormire   _____

14. (tu) vedere   _____

15. (tu) essere   _____

16. (lei) avere   _____

17. (noi) dare   _____

18. (lui) fare   _____

19. (voi) essere   _____

20. (voi) uscire   _____

21. (lei) dire   _____

22. (noi) sapere   _____

23. (voi) potere   _____

24. (noi) pagare   _____

25. (voi) mangiare   _____

26. (loro) arrivare   _____

27. (loro) avere   _____

28. (loro) venire   _____

29. (lei) preferire   _____

30. (noi) capire   _____

B. *Choose the appropriate form of the verb to complete each sentence.*

1. Da bambina, mia sorella _____ il pianoforte.

   a. ha suonato   b. suonava

2. Da giovane, mio fratello _____ i capelli lunghi.

   a. ha avuto   b. aveva

3. Ieri, mentre mio padre dormiva, io _____ la TV.

   a. ho guardato   b. guardavo

4. Ieri _____ tutta la giornata (*all day long*).

   a. ho dormito   b. dormivo

5. Mentre io studiavo, lui _____ al computer.

   a. ha giocato   b. giocava

6. Da bambino, nostro cugino _____ una sola volta (*only once*) in Italia.

   a. è andato   b. andava

7. Da bambina, lei non _____ mangiare la pasta.

   a. ha voluto   b. voleva

8. Alcuni anni fa, io _____ spesso al cinema, ma non più.

   a. sono andata   b. andavo

The imperfect subjunctive

The imperfect subjunctive is formed by dropping the infinitive ending and adding the appropriate ending according to person and number.

First conjugation

guardare *to watch* → **guard-**

io	guard**assi**	*I was watching, used to watch*
tu	guard**assi**	*you (fam., sing.) were watching, used to watch*
Lei	guard**asse**	*you (pol., sing.) were watching, used to watch*
lui/lei	guard**asse**	*he/she was watching, used to watch*
noi	guard**assimo**	*we were watching, used to watch*
voi	guard**aste**	*you (fam., pl.) were watching, used to watch*
Loro	guard**assero**	*you (pol., pl.) were watching, used to watch*
loro	guard**assero**	*they were watching, used to watch*

Second conjugation

potere *to be able to* → **pot-**

io	pot**essi**	*I was able to, used to be able to (could)*
tu	pot**essi**	*you (fam., sing.) were able to, used to be able to (could)*
Lei	pot**esse**	*you (pol., sing.) were able to, used to be able to (could)*
lui/lei	pot**esse**	*he/she was able to, used to be able to (could)*
noi	pot**essimo**	*we were able to, used to be able to (could)*
voi	pot**este**	*you (fam., pl.) were able to, used to be able to (could)*
Loro	pot**essero**	*you (pol., pl.) were able to, used to be able to (could)*
loro	pot**essero**	*they were able to, used to be able to (could)*

Third conjugation

uscire *to go out* → **usc-**

io	usc**issi**	*I was going out, used to go out*
tu	usc**issi**	*you (fam., sing.) were going out, used to go out*
Lei	usc**isse**	*you (pol., sing.) were going out, used to go out*
lui/lei	usc**isse**	*he/she was going out, used to go out*
noi	usc**issimo**	*we were going out, used to go out*
voi	usc**iste**	*you (fam., pl.) were going out, used to go out*
Loro	usc**issero**	*you (pol., pl.) were going out, used to go out*
loro	usc**issero**	*they were going out, used to go out*

Tip!

Another way to conjugate verbs in the imperfect subjunctive is to drop the **-re** of the infinitive (**guarda-**, **pote-**, **usci-**) and then add one set of endings to all three conjugations: **-ssi, -ssi, -sse, -ssimo, -ste, -ssero**. Try it!

As in the case of the imperfect indicative, the imperfect subjunctive is used in a subordinate clause to indicate a repeated or habitual action in the past.

Speravo che tu **avessi capito**.	*I was hoping that you had understood.*
Sembrava che lui **dicesse** la verità.	*It seemed that he was telling the truth.*
Credo che lei **avesse** i capelli biondi da bambina.	*I believe she had blond hair as a child.*
Hanno creduto che **venisse** anche lui.	*They believed that he was coming as well.*

Irregular forms

The verbs that are irregular in the imperfect indicative are also irregular in the imperfect subjunctive.

bere *(to drink)*	bevessi	bevessi	bevesse	bevessimo	beveste	bevessero
dare *(to give)*	dessi	dessi	desse	dessimo	deste	dessero
dire *(to say, tell)*	dicessi	dicessi	dicesse	dicessimo	diceste	dicessero
essere *(to be)*	fossi	fossi	fosse	fossimo	foste	fossero
fare *(to do, make)*	facessi	facessi	facesse	facessimo	faceste	facessero
stare *(to stay)*	stessi	stessi	stesse	stessimo	steste	stessero

A. *Provide the corresponding imperfect subjunctive forms of each verb. The first one is done for you.*

1. (io) cantavo   _(io) cantassi_

2. (io) facevo   _____

3. (io) stavo   _____

4. (lui) era   _____

5. (lui) cominciava   _____

6. (lui) leggeva   _____

7. (io) dicevo   _____

8. (noi) bevevamo   _____

9. (noi) davamo   _____

10. (io) guardavo   _____

11. (tu) capivi   _____

12. (io) bevevo   _____

13. (tu) dormivi   _____

14. (tu) vedevi   _____

15. (tu) eri   _____

16. (lei) aveva   _____

17. (noi) davamo   _____

18. (lui) faceva   _____

19. (voi) eravate   _____

20. (voi) uscivate   _____

21. (lei) diceva   _____

22. (noi) sapevamo   _____

23. (voi) potevate   _____

24. (noi) pagavamo   _____

25. (voi) mangiavate   _____

26. (loro) arrivavano   _____

27. (loro) venivano   _____

28. (loro) avevano   _____

29. (lei) preferiva   _____

30. (noi) capivamo   _____

B. *Rewrite each sentence by using the main clause in parentheses and by making all necessary changes.*

EXAMPLE   Tuo fratello suonava il pianoforte da bambino. (Penso che...)

             Penso che tuo fratello suonasse il pianoforte da bambino.

1. Da bambina, mia madre suonava il pianoforte. (È possibile che...)

2. Da giovane, mio padre aveva i capelli lunghi. (Credo che...)

3. Mentre lui dormiva, tu guardavi la TV. (Pensavamo che...)

4. Di solito lui studiava il sabato. (Sembra che...)

5. Mentre tu studiavi, lui giocava a calcio. (Credevamo che...)

6. Da bambini, i nostri amici andavano spesso in Italia. (È possibile che...)

7. Da bambina, lei non voleva mangiare la pasta. (Credo che...)

8. Alcuni anni fa, io andavo spesso al cinema. (Lui pensa che...)

The pluperfect tenses

The **pluperfect** is a compound tense. As such, it is conjugated with an auxiliary verb, either **avere** or **essere** in the imperfect (indicative or subjunctive as the case may be), and the past participle of the verb, in that order. So, there is nothing really new to learn in this case—the same verbs require either **avere** or **essere**, the same verbs have irregular past participles, and so on.

The pluperfect indicative

Here are the complete conjugations of one verb conjugated with **avere** and another conjugated with **essere** (in the pluperfect indicative).

comprare	*to buy*	
io	**avevo comprato**	*I had bought*
tu	**avevi comprato**	*you (fam., sing.) had bought*
Lei	**aveva comprato**	*you (pol., sing.) had bought*
lui/lei	**aveva comprato**	*he/she had bought*
noi	**avevamo comprato**	*we had bought*
voi	**avevate comprato**	*you (fam., pl.) had bought*
Loro	**avevano comprato**	*you (pol., pl.) had bought*
loro	**avevano comprato**	*they had bought*

partire	to leave	
io	**ero partito (-a)**	*I had left*
tu	**eri partito (-a)**	*you (fam., sing.) had left*
Lei	**era partito (-a)**	*you (pol., sing.) had left*
lui	**era partito**	*he had left*
lei	**era partita**	*she had left*
noi	**eravamo partiti (-e)**	*we had left*
voi	**eravate partiti (-e)**	*you (fam., pl.) had left*
Loro	**erano partiti (-e)**	*you (pol., pl.) had left*
loro	**erano partiti (-e)**	*they had left*

The pluperfect tense (literally, "more than perfect" or "more than past") is used primarily to indicate an action that occurred before a simple past action (as expressed by the present perfect, the imperfect, or the past absolute).

Dopo che **era arrivata**, ha telefonato.	*After she had arrived, she phoned.*
Lui ha detto che **aveva** già **parlato** al professore.	*He said that he had already talked to the professor.*

Essentially, this tense corresponds to the English pluperfect. But be careful! In colloquial usage of English, the pluperfect is sometimes only implied, whereas in Italian it must be used explicitly.

Sono andati in Italia dopo che **avevano finito** gli esami.	*They went to Italy after they finished (had finished) their exams.*

The pluperfect subjunctive

The pluperfect subjunctive is formed with the imperfect subjunctive of the auxiliary verb plus the past participle of the verb, in that order. Here are two verbs conjugated completely, one with **avere** and one with **essere**.

ascoltare	to listen to	
io	**avessi ascoltato**	*I had listened*
tu	**avessi ascoltato**	*you (fam., sing.) had listened*
Lei	**avesse ascoltato**	*you (pol., sing.) had listened*
lui/lei	**avesse ascoltato**	*he/she had listened*
noi	**avessimo ascoltato**	*we had listened*
voi	**aveste ascoltato**	*you (fam., pl.) had listened*
Loro	**avessero ascoltato**	*you (pol., pl.) had listened*
loro	**avessero ascoltato**	*they had listened*

venire	to come	
io	**fossi venuto (-a)**	*I had come*
tu	**fossi venuto (-a)**	*you (fam., sing.) had come*
Lei	**fosse venuto (-a)**	*you (pol., sing.) had come*
lui	**fosse venuto**	*he had come*
lei	**fosse venuta**	*she had come*
noi	**fossimo venuti (-e)**	*we had come*
voi	**foste venuti (-e)**	*you (fam., pl.) had come*
Loro	**fossero venuti (-e)**	*you (pol., pl.) had come*
loro	**fossero venuti (-e)**	*they had come*

This tense corresponds to the pluperfect indicative in usage. It expresses a past action in the subordinate clause that occurred before a past action in the main clause.

Sembrava che lui **fosse** già **arrivato**.   *It seemed that he had already arrived.*
Eravamo contenti che voi **foste venuti**.   *We were happy that you had come.*

A. *Provide the appropriate pluperfect indicative and pluperfect subjunctive forms for each verb. The first one is done for you.*

	PLUPERFECT INDICATIVE	PLUPERFECT SUBJUNCTIVE
1. ho mangiato	*avevo mangiato*	*avessi mangiato*
2. ho venduto		
3. sono partita		
4. ho avuto		
5. sei andato		
6. hai venduto		
7. sei uscito		
8. hai fatto		
9. è arrivato		
10. ha potuto		
11. ha preferito		
12. è stata		
13. abbiamo pagato		
14. abbiamo dovuto		
15. abbiamo dormito		
16. abbiamo detto		
17. avete cantato		
18. avete potuto		
19. siete partiti		
20. avete dato		
21. hanno cominciato		
22. hanno dovuto		
23. hanno capito		
24. sono nati		

B. *Choose the appropriate form of the verb to complete each sentence. (Note: **avere fame** = to be hungry; **chiamare** = to call; **rientrare** = to get back, return home.)*

1. I miei amici _____ già quando hai chiamato.

   a. fossero rientrati   b. erano rientrati

2. È possibile che i miei genitori _____ per l'Italia già.

   a. fossero partiti   b. erano partiti

3. Le tue amiche _____ già quando siamo arrivati.

   a. fossero uscite   b. erano uscite

4. Lui ha detto che tu _____ già quel libro.

   a. avessi letto   b. avevi letto

5. Pensavamo che lui _____ prima di noi.

   a. fosse uscito   b. era uscito

6. Ieri non avevo fame perché _____ già.

   a. avessi mangiato   b. avevo mangiato

7. Dopo che lui _____ a Roma, fece molte cose.

   a. fosse andato   b. era andato

C. *Provide the corresponding imperfect or pluperfect subjunctive form of each given verb.*

1. io ero arrivato _____

2. io vendevo _____

3. io avevo preferito _____

4. io andavo _____

5. io avevo avuto _____

6. tu mangiavi _____

7. tu avevi messo _____

8. tu mettevi _____

9. tu bevevi _____

10. tu eri caduto _____

11. lui cominciava _____

12. lei aveva chiesto _____

13. lui aveva capito _____

14. Lei dava _____

15. lei era _____

16. noi pagavamo _____

17. noi avevamo chiuso _____

18. noi avevamo finito _____

19. noi facevamo _____

20. noi potevamo _____

21. voi cercavate _____

22. voi mettevate _____

23. voi avevate preferito _____

24. voi sapevate _____

25. voi avevate tenuto _____

26. loro mangiavano _____

27. loro avevano chiesto _____

28. loro erano andati _____

29. loro vedevano _____

30. loro venivano _____

D. *Choose the appropriate form of the verb to complete each sentence. Note that more than one answer is possible in some cases.*

1. Penso che lui _____ già.

   a. abbia mangiato   b. mangiasse   c. avesse mangiato

2. Credevo che _____ quando ho chiamato ieri.

   a. abbia mangiato   b. mangiasse   c. avesse mangiato

3. Pensavamo che lui _____ già, quando abbiamo chiamato.

   a. abbia studiato   b. studiasse   c. avesse studiato

4. È improbabile che loro _____ già.

   a. siano partiti   b. partissero   c. fossero partiti

5. Benché _____ ieri, è uscito lo stesso.

   a. abbia piovuto   b. piovesse   c. avesse piovuto

6. Spero che voi _____.

   a. abbiate capito   b. capiste   c. aveste capito

7. Penso che lui _____ la verità.

   a. abbia detto   b. dicesse   c. avesse detto

8. Speravo che voi _____.

   a. abbiate capito   b. capiste   c. aveste capito

9. Sembrava che lui _____ la verità.

   a. abbia detto   b. dicesse   c. avesse detto

10. Benché _____ i soldi, non ha comprato la macchina.

    a. abbia avuto   b. avesse   c. avesse avuto

Grammar in culture

In comparison with the present perfect tense, the imperfect signals not only differences in the duration of past actions, but also nuances of meaning. Consider the verbs **sapere** and **conoscere**, which have slightly different meanings in the present perfect and imperfect tenses.

PRESENT PERFECT	IMPERFECT
Ho saputo che veniva anche lui.	Sapevo che veniva anche lui.
I found out that he was also coming.	*I knew that he was also coming.*
Ho conosciuto Maria due anni fa.	Conoscevo Maria da bambina.
I met Maria two years ago.	*I knew Maria when she was a child.*

ESERCIZIO
12·4

Choose the appropriate verb form according to context and meaning.

1. Quando _____ il tuo professore?

   a. hai conosciuto   b. conoscevi

2. Quando ero bambino, _____ la sua famiglia molto bene.

   a. ho conosciuto   b. conoscevo

3. Viene anche Maria? No, _____ che è ammalata (*sick*).

   a. ho saputo   b. sapevo

4. Lo sai che viene anche Maria alla festa? Sì, lo _____.

   a. ho saputo   b. sapevo

The progressive tenses

Progressive tenses are tenses that allow language users to zero in on an ongoing action.

In questo momento lui **sta guardando** la TV.	*At this moment he is watching TV.*
Mentre **stava studiando**, io ho chiamato.	*While he was studying, I called.*
Penso che lui **stia guardando** la TV.	*I think he is watching TV.*
Pensavo che **stesse guardando** la TV quando ho chiamato.	*I thought he was watching TV when I called.*

There are four main progressive tenses in Italian, two in the present and two in the imperfect. Other progressive tenses are rarely used and will not be discussed in this book.

The gerund

The **gerund** is used to conjugate verbs in progressive tenses. Gerunds are formed by dropping the infinitive ending of a verb and adding **-ando** to the stems of first-conjugation verbs and **-endo** to the stems of the verbs of the other two conjugations.

FIRST CONJUGATION		SECOND CONJUGATION		THIRD CONJUGATION	
parl**are**	*to speak*	cad**ere**	*to fall*	dorm**ire**	*to sleep*
parl**ando**	*speaking*	cad**endo**	*falling*	dorm**endo**	*sleeping*
arriv**are**	*to arrive*	vend**ere**	*to sell*	part**ire**	*to leave*
arriv**ando**	*arriving*	vend**endo**	*selling*	part**endo**	*leaving*

As you will soon see, the most important use of the gerund is in progressive tenses, which are made up of the verb **stare** plus the gerund.

The gerund is also used, as in English, to express indefinite actions, replacing **mentre** (*while*) + *imperfect* when the subjects of the two clauses are the same.

Mentre **camminavo**, ho visto Marco.	*While I was walking, I saw Mark.*

(or)

Camminando, ho visto Marco.	*While walking, I saw Mark.*

There is also a past gerund, consisting of the auxiliary verb in the gerund (**avendo** or **essendo**) and a past participle.

avendo parlato	*having spoken*		**essendo arrivato (-a)**	*having arrived*
avendo venduto	*having sold*		**essendo caduto (-a)**	*having fallen*
avendo dormito	*having slept*		**essendo partito (-a)**	*having left*

Once again, the past participle of verbs conjugated with **essere** is treated like an adjective.

Avendo mangiato tutto, **siamo usciti**.	*Having eaten everything, we went out.*
Essendo andati in Italia, visitarono tante città.	*Having gone to Italy, they visited many cities.*

There are very few irregular gerunds. The most important ones are:

bere	*to drink*	→	**bevendo**	*drinking*
dare	*to give*	→	**dando**	*giving*
dire	*to say*	→	**dicendo**	*saying*
fare	*to do, make*	→	**facendo**	*doing, making*
stare	*to stay*	→	**stando**	*staying*

ESERCIZIO
13·1

A. *Provide the missing infinitive, gerund, or past gerund, as required.*

INFINITIVE	GERUND	PAST GERUND
1. andare	_____	_____
2. _____	facendo	_____
3. _____	_____	essendo stato (-a)
4. leggere	_____	_____
5. _____	dando	_____
6. _____	_____	avendo detto
7. venire	_____	_____
8. _____	bevendo	_____

B. *How do you say the following in Italian?*

1. Watching TV, he became tired.

_____

2. Having done everything, he went out.

_____

3. Studying Italian last night, she became quite tired.

_____

4. Having gone to Italy, they learned to speak well.

_____

The progressive tenses 163

The present progressive tenses

Progressive tenses are made up of the verb **stare** plus the gerund. The **present progressive tense** is conjugated with the present indicative of **stare** plus the gerund; the **present subjunctive** form is conjugated with the present subjunctive of **stare** plus the gerund. Here are two verbs conjugated fully, one in the indicative and the other in the subjunctive.

Indicative

mangiare   *to eat*

io	**sto mangiando**	*I am eating*
tu	**stai mangiando**	*you (fam., sing.) are eating*
Lei	**sta mangiando**	*you (pol., sing.) are eating*
lui/lei	**sta mangiando**	*he/she is eating*
noi	**stiamo mangiando**	*we are eating*
voi	**state mangiando**	*you (fam., pl.) are eating*
Loro	**stanno mangiando**	*you (pol., pl.) are eating*
loro	**stanno mangiando**	*they are eating*

Subjunctive

uscire   *to go out*

io	**stia uscendo**	*I am going out*
tu	**stia uscendo**	*you (fam., sing.) are going out*
Lei	**stia uscendo**	*you (pol., sing.) are going out*
lui/lei	**stia uscendo**	*he/she is going out*
noi	**stiamo uscendo**	*we are going out*
voi	**stiate uscendo**	*you (fam., pl.) are going out*
Loro	**stiano uscendo**	*you (pol., pl.) are going out*
loro	**stiano uscendo**	*they are going out*

The present progressive tenses are alternatives to the present indicative and present subjunctive, allowing you to zero in on an ongoing action.

| In questo momento, mia sorella **sta mangiando**. | *At this moment, my sister is eating.* |
| Penso che in questo momento, lei **stia mangiando**. | *I think that at this moment, she is eating.* |

Note that the present progressive is always translated with English progressive forms such as *I am reading, you are going*, etc.

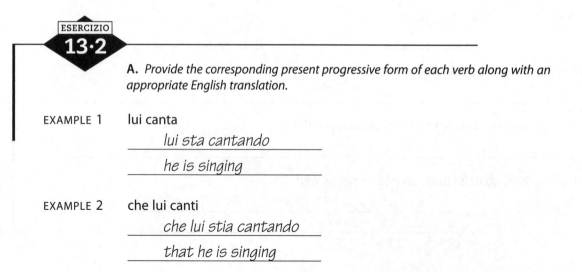

ESERCIZIO
13·2

A. *Provide the corresponding present progressive form of each verb along with an appropriate English translation.*

EXAMPLE 1   lui canta

   lui sta cantando

   he is singing

EXAMPLE 2   che lui canti

   che lui stia cantando

   that he is singing

	PROGRESSIVE FORM	TRANSLATION
1. io mangio	_____	_____
2. tu leggi	_____	_____
3. Lei finisce	_____	_____
4. noi guardiamo	_____	_____
5. voi vedete	_____	_____
6. lui dice	_____	_____
7. lei fa	_____	_____
8. loro imparano	_____	_____
9. che io aspetti	_____	_____
10. che tu scriva	_____	_____
11. che Lei beva	_____	_____
12. che noi andiamo	_____	_____
13. che voi usciate	_____	_____
14. che loro vadano	_____	_____
15. che lui faccia	_____	_____
16. che lei veda	_____	_____

B. *Rewrite each sentence by using the main clause in parentheses and by making all other necessary changes.*

EXAMPLE   In questo momento mia sorella sta leggendo. (Penso che...)

_____*Penso che in questo momento mia sorella stia leggendo.*_____

1. Giovanni sta mangiando in questo momento. (Penso che...)

   _____

2. Voi state guardando un programma alla televisione adesso. (Maria crede che...)

   _____

3. Mio fratello sta dormendo. (Sembra che...)

   _____

4. Io sto scrivendo un'e-mail. (Lui crede che...)

   _____

5. I miei amici stanno uscendo. (Lei pensa che...)

   _____

6. Noi stiamo bevendo un caffè. (Loro credono che...)

   _____

7. Voi state leggendo quel romanzo (*novel*) in questo momento. (Dubito che...)

   _____

8. Lui sta suonando il pianoforte. (Sembra che...)

   _____

C. *How do you say the following in Italian?*

1. Frank, what are you drinking? Are you drinking an espresso?

   _____

2. What program are they watching at this moment?

   _____

3. Mrs. Marchi, what are you saying?

   _____

4. Mark and Mary are going out at this moment.

   _____

5. Where is Alexander? He's sleeping.

   _____

6. What are they drinking? I think that they are drinking a cappuccino.

   _____

The imperfect progressive tenses

The imperfect progressive is conjugated with the imperfect of **stare** (indicative or subjunctive as the case may be). Here are two verbs conjugated fully, one in the indicative and the other in the subjunctive.

Indicative

imparare	*to learn*	
io	**stavo imparando**	*I was learning*
tu	**stavi imparando**	*you (fam., sing.) were learning*
Lei	**stava imparando**	*you (pol., sing.) were learning*
lui/lei	**stava imparando**	*he/she was learning*
noi	**stavamo imparando**	*we were learning*
voi	**stavate imparando**	*you (fam., pl.) were learning*
Loro	**stavano imparando**	*you (pol., pl.) were learning*
loro	**stavano imparando**	*they were learning*

Subjunctive

sentire *to feel, hear*

io	**stessi sentendo**	*I was feeling*
tu	**stessi sentendo**	*you (fam., sing.) were feeling*
Lei	**stesse sentendo**	*you (pol., sing.) were feeling*
lui/lei	**stesse sentendo**	*he/she was feeling*
noi	**stessimo sentendo**	*we were feeling*
voi	**steste sentendo**	*you (fam., pl.) were feeling*
Loro	**stessero sentendo**	*you (pol., pl.) were feeling*
loro	**stessero sentendo**	*they were feeling*

The imperfect progressive tenses are alternatives to the imperfect indicative and subjunctive (see Unit 12), allowing you to zero in on an ongoing action in the past. Note that the imperfect progressive is always translated with English progressive forms such as *I was reading, you were going*, etc.

Mentre lei **stava studiando**, io guardavo la TV.	*While she was studying, I was watching TV.*
Penso che ieri **stesse studiando**, quando è arrivato.	*I think she was studying yesterday, when he arrived.*

ESERCIZIO
13·3

A. *Rewrite each phrase in the corresponding imperfect progressive form.*

EXAMPLE 1 lui mangiava

_____*lui stava mangiando*_____

EXAMPLE 2 che lui mangiasse

_____*che lui stesse mangiando*_____

1. io andavo _____

2. tu cominciavi _____

3. noi scrivevamo _____

4. loro leggevano _____

5. voi preferivate _____

6. lei dormiva _____

7. che io cominciassi _____

8. tu bevevi _____

9. noi davamo _____

10. loro facevano _____

11. voi dicevate _____

12. lui studiava _____

13. che tu leggessi _____

14. che lei uscisse _____

15. che lui mangiasse _____

16. che noi venissimo _____

17. che voi usciste _____

B. *Choose the appropriate imperfect form of the verb to complete each sentence. Note: both choices, a and b, may be correct in some cases.*

1. Mentre lei _____ una rivista, io parlavo al telefono ieri.

   a. stava leggendo   b. leggeva

2. Che cosa _____ tu ieri, quando sono arrivato?

   a. stavi facendo   b. facevi

3. Penso che la signora Marchi _____ un caffè, quando ho chiamato.

   a. stesse bevendo   b. bevesse

4. Mentre noi _____, ha squillato il telefono (*the phone rang*).

   a. stavamo uscendo   b. uscivamo

5. Penso che loro _____ quando sei rientrato.

   a. stessero studiando   b. studiassero

6. Di solito, lui _____ in Italia durante l'estate (*summer*).

   a. stava andando   b. andava

C. *Provide the missing infinitive, past infinitive, gerund, or past gerund as required. The first one is done for you.*

INFINITIVE	PAST INFINITIVE	GERUND	PAST GERUND
1. parlare	*aver(e) parlato*	*parlando*	*avendo parlato*
2. _____	esser(e) arrivato (-a)	_____	_____
3. _____	_____	cadendo	_____
4. _____	_____	_____	avendo venduto
5. dormire	_____	_____	_____
6. _____	esser(e) partito (-a)	_____	_____
7. fare	_____	_____	_____
8. _____	aver(e) detto	_____	_____

9. _____ _____ bevendo _____

10. dare _____ _____ _____

D. *Choose the correct form to complete each sentence.*

1. Dopo essere _____, loro hanno chiamato.

   a. arrivati   b. arrivato

2. Dopo _____ studiato, noi usciremo.

   a. avere   b. essere

3. Alessandro crede _____ molto intelligente.

   a. che sia   b. di essere

4. Devo imparare _____ italiano bene.

   a. a parlare   b. che parli

5. _____ di studiare, hanno guardato la TV.

   a. Finendo   b. Avendo finito

E. *Choose the appropriate progressive form of the verb to complete each sentence.*

1. Dubito che lei _____ ieri quando ho chiamato.

   a. stava mangiando   b. stesse mangiando

2. Mentre Sara _____, io ho chiamato.

   a. stava mangiando   b. stesse mangiando

3. Pensavo che Alessandro _____ quando voi avete chiamato.

   a. stava studiando   b. stesse studiando

4. Daniela, che cosa _____ ieri quando ho chiamato?

   a. stavi facendo   b. stessi facendo

5. Non so cosa _____ ieri Cristofero quando ho chiamato.

   a. stava facendo   b. stesse facendo

Grammar in culture

Another verb form, the present participle, is often confused with the gerund. It is formed by adding **-ante** to first-conjugation verb stems (**parlare** → **parl-** → **parlante**) and **-ente** to second- and third-conjugation verb stems (**ridere** (*to laugh*) → **rid-** → **ridente** and **bollire** (*to boil*) → **boll-** → **bollente**).

A present participle may be used as an adjective or noun; its meaning depends on social context and historical convention. **Parlante** commonly means *speaker*; **ridente**, *smiling, laughing, joyful*; and **bollente**, *boiling*.

ESERCIZIO
13·4

Write the present participle for each verb, then provide its likely meaning in English.

VERB	PRESENT PARTICIPLE	LIKELY MEANING
1. pesare (*to weigh*)	_____	_____
2. pendere (*to hang*)	_____	_____
3. eccitare (*to excite*)	_____	_____
4. insegnare (*to teach*)	_____	_____

The future and conditional tenses

The **simple future**, as its name implies, allows you to talk about an action that will occur in the future. The **future perfect** refers, instead, to actions that occurred before simple future actions.

Domani **andremo** in centro.	*Tomorrow we will be going downtown.*
Dopo che **saremo andati** in centro, **chiameremo**.	*After we have gone downtown, we'll call.*

The **conditional** (present and past) allows you basically to express a condition of the present or past, as the case may be: *I would go . . . ; We would have done it . . . ;* etc.

Uscirei oggi, ma devo studiare.	*I would go out today, but I have to study.*
Avrei comprato questa, ma non avevo soldi.	*I would have bought this one, but I didn't have money.*

The future

The simple future is formed by dropping the final **-e** of the infinitives of all three conjugations, changing the **-ar** of first-conjugation verbs to **-er**, and then adding on the same set of endings for all three conjugations.

First conjugation

incontrare *to run into, meet* → **incontrer-**

io	incontrer**ò**	*I will meet*
tu	incontrer**ai**	*you (fam., sing.) will meet*
Lei	incontrer**à**	*you (pol., sing.) will meet*
lui/lei	incontrer**à**	*he/she will meet*
noi	incontrer**emo**	*we will meet*
voi	incontrer**ete**	*you (fam., pl.) will meet*
Loro	incontrer**anno**	*you (pol., pl.) will meet*
loro	incontrer**anno**	*they will meet*

Second conjugation

mettere *to put* → **metter-**

io	metter**ò**	*I will put*
tu	metter**ai**	*you (fam., sing.) will put*
Lei	metter**à**	*you (pol., sing.) will put*
lui/lei	metter**à**	*he/she will put*

171

noi	metter**emo**	*we will put*
voi	metter**ete**	*you (fam., pl.) will put*
Loro	metter**anno**	*you (pol., pl.) will put*
loro	metter**anno**	*they will put*

Third conjugation

sentire *to feel* → **sentir-**

io	sentir**ò**	*I will feel*
tu	sentir**ai**	*you (fam., sing.) will feel*
Lei	sentir**à**	*you (pol., sing.) will feel*
lui/lei	sentir**à**	*he/she will feel*
noi	sentir**emo**	*we will feel*
voi	sentir**ete**	*you (fam., pl.) will feel*
Loro	sentir**anno**	*you (pol., pl.) will feel*
loro	sentir**anno**	*they will feel*

To preserve the hard **c** and **g** sounds of verbs ending in -**care** and -**gare**, an **h** is added to the stem.

cercare *to look for* → **cercher-**

io	cercherò	*I will look for*
tu	cercherai	*you (fam., sing.) will look for*
Lei	cercherà	*you (pol., sing.) will look for*
lui/lei	cercherà	*he/she will look for*
noi	cercheremo	*we will look for*
voi	cercherete	*you (fam., pl.) will look for*
Loro	cercheranno	*you (pol., pl.) will look for*
loro	cercheranno	*they will look for*

pagare *to pay* → **pagher-**

io	pagherò	*I will pay*
tu	pagherai	*you (fam., sing.) will pay*
Lei	pagherà	*you (pol., sing.) will pay*
lui/lei	pagherà	*he/she will pay*
noi	pagheremo	*we will pay*
voi	pagherete	*you (fam., pl.) will pay*
Loro	pagheranno	*you (pol., pl.) will pay*
loro	pagheranno	*they will pay*

The **i** of verbs ending in -**ciare** or -**giare** is not maintained.

cominciare *to start* → **comincer-**

io	comincerò	*I will start*
tu	comincerai	*you (fam., sing.) will start*
Lei	comincerà	*you (pol., sing.) will start*
lui/lei	comincerà	*he/she will start*
noi	cominceremo	*we will start*
voi	comincerete	*you (fam., pl.) will start*
Loro	cominceranno	*you (pol., pl.) will start*
loro	cominceranno	*they will start*

mangiare *to eat* → **manger-**

io	mangerò	*I will eat*
tu	mangerai	*you (fam., sing.) will eat*
Lei	mangerà	*you (pol., sing.) will eat*
lui/lei	mangerà	*he/she will eat*

noi	mangeremo	*we will eat*
voi	mangerete	*you (fam., pl.) will eat*
Loro	mangeranno	*you (pol., pl.) will eat*
loro	mangeranno	*they will eat*

The future tense corresponds, generally, to the same tense in English: *I will go, you will write,* and so on. It also conveys the idea expressed in English with forms such as *I am going to write* and *I will be writing.*

Note

Use the preposition **tra/fra** to indicate future time in expressions such as:

tra una settimana	*in a week (in a week's time)*
fra un anno	*in a year (in a year's time)*

Manderò un'e-mail al mio amico domani.	*I will send an e-mail to my friend tomorrow.*
	I will be sending an e-mail to my friend tomorrow.
	I am going to send an e-mail to my friend tomorrow.
Partiranno tra un mese.	*They will leave in a month.*
	They will be leaving in a month.
	They are going to leave in a month.

It is also used to convey probability.

Sai quanto costa quell'orologio?	*Do you know how much that watch costs?*
Costerà mille euro.	*It probably costs one thousand euros.*
Chi **sarà**?	*Who can that be?*
A quest'ora **sarà** tua sorella.	*At this hour it is probably your sister.*

Irregular forms

As with other tenses, there are irregular forms in the future. Here are the most common irregular verbs in the future.

andare (*to go*)	andrò	andrai	andrà	andremo	andrete	andranno
avere (*to have*)	avrò	avrai	avrà	avremo	avrete	avranno
bere (*to drink*)	berrò	berrai	berrà	berremo	berrete	berranno
cadere (*to fall*)	cadrò	cadrai	cadrà	cadremo	cadrete	cadranno
dare (*to give*)	darò	darai	darà	daremo	darete	daranno
dovere (*to have to*)	dovrò	dovrai	dovrà	dovremo	dovrete	dovranno
essere (*to be*)	sarò	sarai	sarà	saremo	sarete	saranno
fare (*to do, make*)	farò	farai	farà	faremo	farete	faranno
potere (*to be able to*)	potrò	potrai	potrà	potremo	potrete	potranno
sapere (*to know*)	saprò	saprai	saprà	sapremo	saprete	sapranno
stare (*to stay*)	starò	starai	starà	staremo	starete	staranno
tenere (*to hold, keep*)	terrò	terrai	terrà	terremo	terrete	terranno
vedere (*to see*)	vedrò	vedrai	vedrà	vedremo	vedrete	vedranno
venire (*to come*)	verrò	verrai	verrà	verremo	verrete	verranno
volere (*to want*)	vorrò	vorrai	vorrà	vorremo	vorrete	vorranno

Tip!

Note that many irregular forms involve simply dropping both vowels of the infinitive.

andare → andr-

avere → avr-

etc.

ESERCIZIO

14·1

A. *Provide the future forms for each verb. (Note: **mandare** = to send; **indicare** = to indicate; **navigare** = to navigate [especially on the Internet]; **baciare** = to kiss.)*

	IO	TU	LUI/LEI	NOI	VOI	LORO
1. mandare						
2. indicare						
3. navigare						
4. baciare						
5. leggere						
6. preferire						
7. volere						
8. venire						
9. vedere						
10. stare						
11. sapere						
12. potere						
13. fare						
14. essere						
15. dovere						
16. dare						
17. cadere						
18. bere						
19. avere						
20. andare						

B. *How do you say the following in Italian? (Note:* **la scarpa** = *shoe.)*

1. I will be sending an e-mail to my sister tomorrow.

   _____

2. She is going to navigate on the Internet shortly.

   _____

3. They are going to leave in a week.

   _____

4. Do you know how much those shoes cost? They probably cost 500 euros.

   _____

5. Who can that be? At this hour it is probably your brother.

   _____

C. *Rewrite each question by using the subject in parentheses and the polite form.*

EXAMPLE   Maria, andrai in centro domani? (Signora Verdi)

       Signora Verdi, andrà in centro domani?

1. Marcello, quando vedrai tua figlia? (Signor Dini)

   _____

2. Claudia, dove andrai in vacanza? (Signorina Marchi)

   _____

3. Marco e Alessandro, a che ora verrete alla festa? (Signor Verdi e signora Verdi)

   _____

4. Maria e Sara, quando uscirete? (Signora Rossini e signor Rossini)

   _____

The future perfect

Like the present perfect and the pluperfect (see Units 11 and 12), the future perfect is a compound tense. It is formed with the future of the auxiliary verb plus the past participle of the verb, in that order. Here are two verbs conjugated fully, one conjugated with **avere** and the other with **essere**.

portare	*to bring*	
io	**avrò portato**	*I will have brought*
tu	**avrai portato**	*you (fam., sing.) will have brought*
Lei	**avrà portato**	*you (pol., sing.) will have brought*
lui/lei	**avrà portato**	*he/she will have brought*
noi	**avremo portato**	*we will have brought*
voi	**avrete portato**	*you (fam., pl.) will have brought*
Loro	**avranno portato**	*you (pol., pl.) will have brought*
loro	**avranno portato**	*they will have brought*

guarire	*to get better, heal, cure*	
io	**sarò guarito (-a)**	*I will have healed*
tu	**sarai guarito (-a)**	*you (fam., sing.) will have healed*
Lei	**sarà guarito (-a)**	*you (pol., sing.) will have healed*
lui	**sarà guarito**	*he will have healed*
lei	**sarà guarita**	*she will have healed*
noi	**saremo guariti (-e)**	*we will have healed*
voi	**sarete guariti (-e)**	*you (fam., pl.) will have healed*
Loro	**saranno guariti (-e)**	*you (pol., pl.) will have healed*
loro	**saranno guariti (-e)**	*they will have healed*

Generally, this Italian future perfect corresponds to its English counterpart. It is used to refer to actions that occurred before simple future actions.

Andremo al cinema, dopo che **avrai finito** di lavorare.	*We will go to the movies, after you (will) have finished working.*

However, in conversational Italian, the simple future can often be used instead.

Andremo al cinema, appena **finirai** di lavorare.	*We will go to the movies, as soon as you finish working.*

Like the simple future, the future perfect can also be used to convey probability.

Quanto **sarà costata** quella macchina?	*How much did that car probably cost?*
Sarà costata molto.	*It must have cost a lot.*
A che ora ha telefonato?	*At what time did he phone?*
Avrà telefonato alle sei.	*He must have phoned at six.*

ESERCIZIO 14·2

A. *Provide the corresponding future perfect forms of each verb.*

1. (io) ho imparato _____

2. (io) sono uscita _____

3. (tu) hai fatto _____

4. (tu) sei venuto _____

5. (lui) ha scritto _____

6. (lui) è andato _____

7. (lei) ha letto _____

8. (lei) è tornata _____

9. (noi) abbiamo visto _____

10. (noi) siamo entrati _____

11. (voi) avete chiamato _____

12. (voi) siete stati _____

13. (loro) hanno bevuto _____

14. (loro) erano rientrati _____

15. (io) ho navigato _____

B. *Complete each sentence with the appropriate future or future perfect form of the verb.* (Note: **piatto** = dish, plate; **dolce** = sweet.)

1. Mangerò anche la carne, appena io _____ (finire) la pasta.

2. Sono sicura che lui _____ (uscire) già.

3. Claudia _____ (arrivare) domani verso il tardo pomeriggio.

4. Quando _____ (andare) in Italia, tu e tua sorella?

5. È vero che _____ (venire) anche loro alla festa?

6. A quest'ora Sara _____ (andare) già a dormire.

7. Appena _____ (arrivare), loro andranno al cinema insieme.

8. Quando loro _____ (vedere) quel film, diranno che è un grande film.

9. Dopo che tu _____ (mangiare) questo dolce, sono sicuro che vorrai un

   altro dolce.

10. Quanto _____ (costare) quella macchina che poi non avete comprato?

11. A che ora ha chiamato la tua amica? Lei _____ (chiamare) alle cinque.

The conditional (present and past)

The **present conditional** is formed like the simple future: the final **-e** of the infinitives of all three conjugations is dropped (changing the **-ar** of first-conjugation verbs to **-er**), and the same set of endings is added on.

comprare	*to buy* → **comprer-**	
io	comprer**ei**	*I would buy*
tu	comprer**esti**	*you (fam., sing.) would buy*
Lei	comprer**ebbe**	*you (pol., sing.) would buy*
lui/lei	comprer**ebbe**	*he/she would buy*
noi	comprer**emmo**	*we would buy*
voi	comprer**este**	*you (fam., pl.) would buy*
Loro	comprer**ebbero**	*you (pol., pl.) would buy*
loro	comprer**ebbero**	*they would buy*

leggere	*to read* → **legger-**	
io	legger**ei**	*I would read*
tu	legger**esti**	*you (fam., sing.) would read*
Lei	legger**ebbe**	*you (pol., sing.) would read*
lui/lei	legger**ebbe**	*he/she would read*
noi	legger**emmo**	*we would read*
voi	legger**este**	*you (fam., pl.) would read*
Loro	legger**ebbero**	*you (pol., pl.) would read*
loro	legger**ebbero**	*they would read*

pulire	*to clean* → **pulir-**	
io	puli**rei**	*I would clean*
tu	puli**resti**	*you (fam., sing.) would clean*
Lei	puli**rebbe**	*you (pol., sing.) would clean*
lui/lei	puli**rebbe**	*he/she would clean*
noi	puli**remmo**	*we would clean*
voi	puli**reste**	*you (fam., pl.) would clean*
Loro	puli**rebbero**	*you (pol., pl.) would clean*
loro	puli**rebbero**	*they would clean*

As with the simple future, to preserve the hard **c** and **g** sounds of verbs ending in -**care** and -**gare**, an **h** is added to the stem.

giocare	*to play* → **giocher-**	
io	gio**cherei**	*I would play*
tu	gio**cheresti**	*you (fam., sing.) would play*
Lei	gio**cherebbe**	*you (pol., sing.) would play*
lui/lei	gio**cherebbe**	*he/she would play*
noi	gio**cheremmo**	*we would play*
voi	gio**chereste**	*you (fam., pl.) would play*
Loro	gio**cherebbero**	*you (pol., pl.) would play*
loro	gio**cherebbero**	*they would play*

allegare	*to attach* → **allegher-**	
io	alleg**herei**	*I would attach*
tu	alleg**heresti**	*you (fam., sing.) would attach*
Lei	alleg**herebbe**	*you (pol., sing.) would attach*
lui/lei	alleg**herebbe**	*he/she would attach*
noi	alleg**heremmo**	*we would attach*
voi	alleg**hereste**	*you (fam., pl.) would attach*
Loro	alleg**herebbero**	*you (pol., pl.) would attach*
loro	alleg**herebbero**	*they would attach*

And, as in the case of the future, the **i** of verbs ending in -**ciare** or -**giare** is not maintained in the conditional.

cominciare	*to start* → **comincer-**	
io	cominc**erei**	*I would start*
tu	cominc**eresti**	*you (fam., sing.) would start*
Lei	cominc**erebbe**	*you (pol., sing.) would start*
lui/lei	cominc**erebbe**	*he/she would start*
noi	cominc**eremmo**	*we would start*
voi	cominc**ereste**	*you (fam., pl.) would start*
Loro	cominc**erebbero**	*you (pol., pl.) would start*
loro	cominc**erebbero**	*they would start*

mangiare	*to eat* → **manger-**	
io	mang**erei**	*I would eat*
tu	mang**eresti**	*you (fam., sing.) would eat*
Lei	mang**erebbe**	*you (pol., sing.) would eat*
lui/lei	mang**erebbe**	*he/she would eat*
noi	mang**eremmo**	*we would eat*
voi	mang**ereste**	*you (fam., pl.) would eat*
Loro	mang**erebbero**	*you (pol., pl.) would eat*
loro	mang**erebbero**	*they would eat*

The very same verbs that are irregular in the future are also irregular in the conditional in the same way. For example, conjugating the irregular future and conditional forms of **andare** involves dropping both vowels from the infinitive ending and then adding on the appropriate future or conditional endings. Here are a few forms compared for you.

FUTURE		CONDITIONAL	
io **andrò**	*I will go*	io **andrei**	*I would go*
noi **saremo**	*we will be*	noi **saremmo**	*we would be*
lui **potrà**	*he will be able to*	lui **potrebbe**	*he would be able to*
loro **verranno**	*they will come*	loro **verrebbero**	*they would come*

The conditional tense corresponds, generally, to the English conditional—*I would go; you would write;* etc.

Pagherei il conto, ma non ho soldi.	*I would pay the bill, but I have no money.*
Comprerebbe la macchina, ma non ha soldi.	*He would buy the car, but he doesn't have money.*

In addition, it is used to make a polite request.

Potrei parlare?	*May I speak?*
Mi **darebbe** la sua penna?	*Would you give me your pen?*

And it is used to convey that something is an opinion, rather than fact. (Note: **secondo** = *according to*; **opinione** (*f.*) = *opinion*.)

Secondo lui, lei **sarebbe** intelligente.	*According to him, she must be (is) intelligent.*
Nella loro opinione, lui **sarebbe** bravissimo.	*In their opinion, he is very good.*

The past conditional

The past conditional is a compound tense. It is formed with the conditional of the auxiliary verb plus the past participle of the verb, in that order. Here are two verbs conjugated fully, one conjugated with **avere** and the other with **essere**.

mangiare	*to eat*	
io	**avrei mangiato**	*I would have eaten*
tu	**avresti mangiato**	*you (fam., sing.) would have eaten*
Lei	**avrebbe mangiato**	*you (pol., sing.) would have eaten*
lui/lei	**avrebbe mangiato**	*he/she would have eaten*
noi	**avremmo mangiato**	*we would have eaten*
voi	**avreste mangiato**	*you (fam., pl.) would have eaten*
Loro	**avrebbero mangiato**	*you (pol., pl.) would have eaten*
loro	**avrebbero mangiato**	*they would have eaten*

partire	*to leave*	
io	**sarei partito (-a)**	*I would have left*
tu	**saresti partito (-a)**	*you (fam., sing.) would have left*
Lei	**sarebbe partito (-a)**	*you (pol., sing.) would have left*
lui	**sarebbe partito**	*he would have left*
lei	**sarebbe partita**	*she would have left*
noi	**saremmo partiti (-e)**	*we would have left*
voi	**sareste partiti (-e)**	*you (fam., pl.) would have left*
Loro	**sarebbero partiti (-e)**	*you (pol., pl.) would have left*
loro	**sarebbero partiti (-e)**	*they would have left*

Generally, the Italian past conditional corresponds to the English past conditional: *I would have eaten, you would have bought,* and so on. It is used to refer to conditional (hypothetical) actions that can only logically be expressed in a perfect tense, as shown below.

Mi ha detto che **sarebbe venuto**.	*He told me that he would (would have) come.*
Sapeva che io **avrei capito**.	*He knew I would have understood.*

As with the present conditional, it is also used to convey that something was (or has been) an opinion, rather than a fact.

Secondo lui, lei **avrebbe dovuto** studiare di più.	*According to him, she should have studied more.*
Nella loro opinione, io **avrei dovuto** vincere.	*In their opinion, I should have won.*

ESERCIZIO
14·3

A. *Provide the corresponding conditional and past conditional forms for each verb.*

	PRESENT CONDITIONAL	PAST CONDITIONAL
1. io arriverò	_____	_____
2. io venderò	_____	_____
3. io preferirò	_____	_____
4. io andrò	_____	_____
5. io avrò	_____	_____
6. tu mangerai	_____	_____
7. tu metterai	_____	_____
8. tu aprirai	_____	_____
9. tu berrai	_____	_____
10. tu cadrai	_____	_____
11. lui comincerà	_____	_____
12. lei chiederà	_____	_____
13. lui capirà	_____	_____
14. Lei darà	_____	_____
15. lei sarà	_____	_____
16. noi pagheremo	_____	_____
17. noi chiuderemo	_____	_____
18. noi finiremo	_____	_____
19. noi faremo	_____	_____
20. noi potremo	_____	_____

21. voi cercherete _____ _____

22. voi metterete _____ _____

23. voi preferirete _____ _____

24. voi saprete _____ _____

25. voi terrete _____ _____

26. loro mangeranno _____ _____

27. loro chiederanno _____ _____

28. loro preferiranno _____ _____

29. loro vedranno _____ _____

30. loro verranno _____ _____

31. voi verrete _____ _____

32. noi andremo _____ _____

B. *How do you say the following in Italian? (Note:* **tazza** = *cup;* **per favore** = *please;* **grazie** = *thank you.)*

1. I would like (want) to send an e-mail to my brother tomorrow.

   _____

2. They would have gone to Italy, but they didn't have enough money.

   _____

3. They would have bought that car, but they didn't know how to drive.

   _____

4. May I have a cup of coffee, please?

   _____

5. We would have gone to the movies yesterday, but we had to study.

   _____

6. He told me that he would (would have) come.

   _____

7. He knew I would have understood.

   _____

8. According to Sarah, I should have studied more.

   _____

9. In their opinion, we should have won.

   _____

10. May I say something?

   _____

11. Could you give me your pen, please? Thanks!

_____

12. In their opinion, he is a good person.

_____

Hypothetical sentences

The imperfect subjunctive is used after **se** (*if*) in hypothetical sentences (also called counterfactual) when the verb in the main clause is in the present conditional.

Se tu **andassi** a Roma, vedresti il Colosseo.	*If you were to go to Rome, you would see the Coliseum.*
Se **potessimo**, andremmo in Italia subito.	*If we could, we would go to Italy right away.*

It is also used after **magari** (*if only, I wish*) to express a wish or desire.

Magari non **piovesse**!	*If only it wouldn't rain!*
Magari **vincessi** la lotteria!	*If only I would win the lottery!*

The pluperfect subjunctive is also used after **se** in counterfactual sentences. In this case, it is used mainly when the main clause verb is in the past conditional.

Se **avessi avuto** i soldi, avrei comprato la macchina.	*If I had had the money, I would have bought the car.*
Se tu **avessi studiato** ieri, saresti potuto venire.	*If you had studied yesterday, you could have come.*

ESERCIZIO
14·4

A. *Complete each sentence with the present or past conditional form of the verb. (Note:* **sicuro** = *sure;* **compito** = *task, homework assignment;* **pace** [f.] = *peace.)*

1. Se noi potessimo, _____ (comprare) quella casa.

2. Se lui avesse soldi, _____ (andare) in Italia.

3. Se voi aveste più tempo, sono sicuro che _____ (andare) al cinema

    più spesso.

4. Se io vivessi in Italia, _____ (bere) solo il caffè espresso.

5. Se loro fossero stati in Italia, _____ (vedere) tante belle cose.

6. Se tu avessi fatto i compiti ieri, oggi _____ (potere) guardare la TV

    in pace.

B. *Now, complete each sentence with the imperfect or pluperfect subjunctive form of the verb.*

1. Se noi _____ (potere), compreremmo quella macchina.

2. Se io _____ (avere) soldi, andrei subito in Italia.

3. Se voi _____ (sapere) parlare italiano, sono sicuro che andreste in Italia.

4. Se io _____ (essere) in Italia, avrei visto molte belle cose.

5. Se loro _____ (conoscere) un buon ristorante, saremmo andati lì ieri sera.

6. Magari non _____ (piovere)!

C. *Provide the corresponding future, future perfect, conditional, and past conditional forms for each verb.*

	FUTURE	FUTURE PERFECT	CONDITIONAL	PAST CONDITIONAL
1. io arrivo				
2. io vendo				
3. io preferisco				
4. io vado				
5. io ho				
6. tu mangi				
7. tu metti				
8. tu apri				
9. tu bevi				
10. tu cadi				
11. lui comincia				
12. lei chiede				
13. lui capisce				
14. Lei dà				
15. lei è				
16. noi paghiamo				
17. noi chiudiamo				
18. noi finiamo				
19. noi facciamo				
20. noi possiamo				
21. voi cercate				
22. voi mettete				
23. voi preferite				
24. voi sapete				

25. voi tenete _____ _____ _____ _____

26. loro mangiano _____ _____ _____ _____

27. loro chiedono _____ _____ _____ _____

28. loro finiscono _____ _____ _____ _____

29. loro vedono _____ _____ _____ _____

30. loro vengono _____ _____ _____ _____

D. *Choose the appropriate form of each verb for each sentence. In some cases, more than one choice is possible. (Note:* **patente** *[f.] = driver's license;* **conto** *= bill, check.)*

1. Alessandro _____ il conto, ma non ha soldi.

   a. pagherà   b. avrà pagato   c. pagherebbe   d. avrebbe pagato

2. Sara _____ la macchina, ma non ha ancora la patente.

   a. comprerà   b. avrà comprato   c. comprerebbe   d. avrebbe comprato

3. Domani il mio amico _____ il conto di sicuro.

   a. pagherà   b. avrà pagato   c. pagherebbe   d. avrebbe pagato

4. _____ dire qualcosa, per favore?

   a. Potrò   b. Avrò potuto   c. Potrei   d. Avrei potuto

5. Mi _____ la Sua penna, professore?

   a. darà   b. avrà dato   c. darebbe   d. avrebbe dato

6. Dopo che _____ di mangiare, usciremo.

   a. finiremo   b. avremo finito   c. finiremmo   d. avremmo finito

7. Secondo mio fratello, quella ragazza _____ italiana.

   a. sarà   b. sarà stata   c. sarebbe   d. sarebbe stata

8. Quella ragazza _____ l'italiano l'anno prossimo.

   a. studierà   b. avrà studiato   c. studierebbe   d. avrebbe studiato

9. Se sua sorella fosse venuta alla festa, _____ le sue migliori amiche.

   a. vedrà   b. avrà visto   c. vedrebbe   d. avrebbe visto

10. Nella loro opinione, l'Italia _____ vincere l'anno scorso.

    a. dovrà   b. avrà dovuto   c. dovrebbe   d. avrebbe dovuto

Grammar in culture

As mentioned earlier in this chapter, the conditional may be used to make a polite request—a critical social function of language.

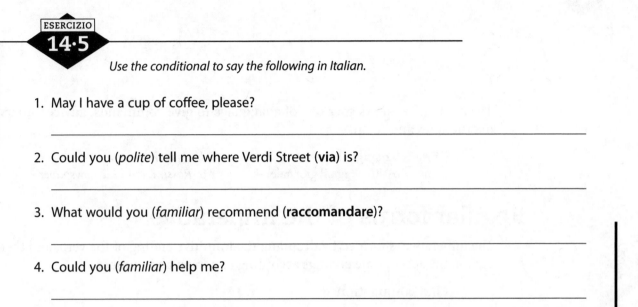

ESERCIZIO
14·5

Use the conditional to say the following in Italian.

1. May I have a cup of coffee, please?

   _____

2. Could you (*polite*) tell me where Verdi Street (**via**) is?

   _____

3. What would you (*familiar*) recommend (**raccomandare**)?

   _____

4. Could you (*familiar*) help me?

   _____

 **·15·**

The imperative

The imperative allows speakers of a language to give commands, advice, orders, instructions, and so on.

Giovanni, **mangia** la pesca!	*John, eat the peach!*
Signor Rossini, **legga** il giornale!	*Mr. Rossini, read the newspaper!*

Regular forms of the imperative

The imperative is formed by dropping the infinitive ending of the verb, and then adding the appropriate endings according to person and number.

First conjugation

aspettare *to wait (for)* → **aspett-**

tu	aspett**a**	*wait (fam., sing.)*
Lei	aspett**i**	*wait (pol., sing.)*
noi	aspett**iamo**	*let's wait*
voi	aspett**ate**	*wait (fam., pl.)*
Loro	aspett**ino**	*wait (pol., pl.)*

Second conjugation

chiudere *to close* → **chiud-**

tu	chiud**i**	*close (fam., sing.)*
Lei	chiud**a**	*close (pol., sing.)*
noi	chiud**iamo**	*let's close*
voi	chiud**ete**	*close (fam., pl.)*
Loro	chiud**ano**	*close (pol., pl.)*

Third conjugation (type 1)

aprire *to open* → **apr-**

tu	apr**i**	*open (fam., sing.)*
Lei	apr**a**	*open (pol., sing.)*
noi	apr**iamo**	*let's open*
voi	apr**ite**	*open (fam., pl.)*
Loro	apr**ano**	*open (pol., pl.)*

Third conjugation (type 2)

finire *to finish* → **fin-**

tu	fin**isci**	*finish (fam., sing.)*
Lei	fin**isca**	*finish (pol., sing.)*
noi	fin**iamo**	*let's finish*
voi	fin**ite**	*finish (fam., pl.)*
Loro	fin**iscano**	*finish (pol., pl.)*

To preserve the hard **c** and **g** sounds of verbs ending in **-care** and **-gare**, an **h** must be added before the **-i**, **-iamo**, and **-ino** endings.

cercare *to look for*

tu	cerca	*look for (fam., sing.)*
Lei	cer**chi**	*look for (pol., sing.)*
noi	cer**chiamo**	*let's look for*
voi	cercate	*look for (fam., pl.)*
Loro	cer**chino**	*look for (pol., pl.)*

pagare *to pay*

tu	paga	*pay (fam., sing.)*
Lei	pag**hi**	*pay (pol., sing.)*
noi	pag**hiamo**	*let's pay*
voi	pagate	*pay (fam., pl.)*
Loro	pag**hino**	*pay (pol., pl.)*

The **i** of verbs ending in **-ciare** and **-giare** is not repeated before the **-i**, **-iamo**, and **-ino** endings.

cominciare *to begin*

tu	comincia	*begin (fam., sing.)*
Lei	cominc**i**	*begin (pol., sing.)*
noi	cominc**iamo**	*let's begin*
voi	cominciate	*begin (fam., pl.)*
Loro	cominc**ino**	*begin (pol., pl.)*

mangiare *to eat*

tu	mangia	*eat (fam., sing.)*
Lei	mang**i**	*eat (pol., sing.)*
noi	mang**iamo**	*let's eat*
voi	mangiate	*eat (fam., pl.)*
Loro	mang**ino**	*eat (pol., pl.)*

Tip!

If you look carefully at the polite forms of the imperative (**Lei** and **Loro** forms), you will see that they are exactly the same as their corresponding present subjunctive forms.

Uses

As in English, the imperative allows you to issue commands, give orders, make requests, etc.

Giovanni, **aspetta** qui!	*John, wait here!*
Signora Rossi, **scriva** il Suo nome qui!	*Mrs. Rossi, write your name here!*
Maria e Carla, **aprite** i vostri libri!	*Mary and Carla, open your books!*
Signora Verdi e signor Rossi, **aspettino** qui!	*Mrs. Verdi and Mr. Rossi, wait here!*
Signor Dini, **cerchi** i Suoi occhiali!	*Mr. Dini, look for your glasses!*
Paghiamo il conto!	*Let's pay the bill!*
E ora, **mangiamo**!	*And now, let's eat!*

Pay close attention to the differences between the familiar and polite forms.

Tu (familiar singular)

Maria, **mangia** la pizza!   *Mary, eat the pizza!*
Alessandro, **finisci** gli spaghetti!   *Alexander, finish the spaghetti!*

Voi (familiar plural)

Marco e Maria, **mangiate** la pizza!   *Mark and Mary, eat the pizza!*
Alessandro e Sara, **finite** gli spaghetti!   *Alexander and Sarah, finish the spaghetti!*

Lei (polite singular)

Signora Verdi, **mangi** la pizza!   *Mrs. Verdi, eat the pizza!*
Signor Rossi, **finisca** gli spaghetti!   *Mr. Rossi, finish the spaghetti!*

Loro (polite plural)

Signora Verdi e signor Rossi, **mangino**
  la pizza!   *Mrs. Verdi and Mr. Rossi, eat the pizza!*
Signora Verdi e signor Rossi, **finiscano**   *Mrs. Verdi and Mr. Rossi, finish the spaghetti!*
  gli spaghetti!

ESERCIZIO
15·1

A. *Provide the imperative forms of each verb.*

	TU	LEI	NOI	VOI	LORO
1. parlare					
2. indicare					
3. allegare					
4. baciare					
5. mangiare					
6. leggere					
7. aprire (type 1)					
8. pulire (type 2)					

B. *Provide an appropriate command to tell each subject given to do the indicated things. (Note:* **finestra** *= window.)*

EXAMPLE   Tell Mark to speak Italian.

<u>*Marco, parla italiano!*</u>

1. Tell John to . . .

   a. eat the apple   _____

   b. call Mary   _____

   c. write an e-mail to his uncle   _____

   d. open the window   _____

   e. finish studying   _____

2. Tell Mrs. Verdi to . . .

   a. wait for the bus _____

   b. look for the book _____

   c. put the key in her purse _____

   d. open the door _____

   e. finish the coffee _____

3. Tell Mark and Mary to . . .

   a. start studying _____

   b. speak Italian _____

   c. shut the window _____

   d. open the door _____

   e. clean the house _____

4. Tell Mr. Rossini and Mrs. Rossini to . . .

   a. eat the meat _____

   b. wait here _____

   c. shut the window _____

   d. open the door _____

   e. clean the house _____

C. *Rewrite each command to tell the subject indicated in parentheses to do the same things, making all necessary changes.*

EXAMPLE   Marco, aspetta qui! (Professore)

_____*Professore, aspetti qui!*_____

1. Claudia, ascolta la radio! (Signorina Bruni)

   _____

2. Signor Marchi, prenda questa tazza! (Marco)

   _____

3. Ragazzi e ragazze, giocate a calcio! (Professori)

   _____

4. Signore e signori, leggano il giornale! (Ragazzi e ragazze)

   _____

The negative imperative

To form the negative imperative, add **non** in the usual way before the verb. However, you must make one adjustment in this case—you must change second-person singular forms to infinitives. As you might know, this is a frequent source of blunders.

Tu forms

AFFIRMATIVE		NEGATIVE	
Aspetta!	*Wait!*	**Non aspettare!**	*Don't wait!*
Scrivi!	*Write!*	**Non scrivere!**	*Don't write!*
Finisci!	*Finish!*	**Non finire!**	*Don't finish!*

Other forms

AFFIRMATIVE		NEGATIVE	
Aspetti!	*Wait! (pol., sing.)*	**Non aspetti!**	*Don't wait!*
Scriviamo!	*Let's write!*	**Non scriviamo!**	*Let's not write!*
Finite!	*Finish! (fam., pl.)*	**Non finite!**	*Don't finish!*
Aspettino!	*Wait! (pol., pl.)*	**Non aspettino!**	*Don't wait!*

ESERCIZIO
15·2

A. *Rewrite each command in the negative. (Note:* **torta** = *cake;* **romanzo** = *novel.)*

EXAMPLE   Maria, aspetta l'autobus!

   Maria, non aspettare l'autobus!

1. Maria...

   a. mangia la torta!   _____

   b. paga il conto!   _____

2. Signora Marchi...

   a. pulisca la casa!   _____

   b. chiuda la porta!   _____

3. Ragazzi e ragazze...

   a. aprite i vostri libri!   _____

   b. leggete quel romanzo!   _____

4. Signore e signori...

   a. paghino il conto!   _____

   b. ascoltino la radio!   _____

B. *Now, rewrite each negative command in the affirmative.*

1. Signore e signori...

   a. non mangino la torta! _____

   b. non paghino il conto! _____

2. Ragazzi e ragazze...

   a. non pulite la casa! _____

   b. non chiudete la porta! _____

3. Signora Verdi...

   a. non apra il Suo libro! _____

   b. non legga quel romanzo! _____

4. Maria...

   a. non finire tutta la torta! _____

   b. non ascoltare la radio! _____

Irregular forms

Here are the most common irregular verbs in the imperative.

andare (*to go*)	va'	vada	andiamo	andate	vadano
avere (*to have*)	abbi	abbia	abbiamo	abbiate	abbiano
bere (*to drink*)	bevi	beva	beviamo	bevete	bevano
dare (*to give*)	da'	dia	diamo	date	diano
dire (*to say, tell*)	di'	dica	diciamo	dite	dicano
essere (*to be*)	sii	sia	siamo	siate	siano
fare (*to do, make*)	fa'	faccia	facciamo	fate	facciano
salire (*to go up, climb*)	sali	salga	saliamo	salite	salgano
sapere (*to know*)	sappi	sappia	sappiamo	sappiate	sappiano
scegliere (*to choose, select*)	scegli	scelga	scegliamo	scegliete	scelgano
stare (*to stay*)	sta'	stia	stiamo	state	stiano
tenere (*to hold, keep*)	tieni	tenga	teniamo	tenete	tengano
uscire (*to go out*)	esci	esca	usciamo	uscite	escano
venire (*to come*)	vieni	venga	veniamo	venite	vengano

Be careful!

Remember, in the negative imperative you must use the infinitive for the **tu** forms.

AFFIRMATIVE		NEGATIVE	
Maria, **fa'** questo!	*Mary, do this!*	Maria, **non fare** questo!	*Mary, don't do this!*
Carla, **di'** questo!	*Carla, say this!*	Carla, **non dire** questo!	*Carla, don't say this!*

A. *Provide the imperative forms of each verb.*

	TU	LEI	NOI	VOI	LORO
1. venire	_____	_____	_____	_____	_____
2. uscire	_____	_____	_____	_____	_____
3. tenere	_____	_____	_____	_____	_____
4. stare	_____	_____	_____	_____	_____
5. scegliere	_____	_____	_____	_____	_____
6. sapere	_____	_____	_____	_____	_____
7. salire	_____	_____	_____	_____	_____
8. fare	_____	_____	_____	_____	_____
9. essere	_____	_____	_____	_____	_____
10. dire	_____	_____	_____	_____	_____
11. dare	_____	_____	_____	_____	_____
12. bere	_____	_____	_____	_____	_____
13. avere	_____	_____	_____	_____	_____
14. andare	_____	_____	_____	_____	_____

B. *Provide the affirmative or negative imperative form, as required. (Note: **andare via** = to go away;* **stare zitto** *= to be quiet.)*

AFFIRMATIVE	NEGATIVE
1. Claudia, vieni qui!	_____
2. _____	Signora Dini, non faccia quella cosa!
3. Marco, di' la verità!	_____
4. _____	Professore, non vada via!
5. Franca, sta' zitta!	_____
6. _____	Paolo, non andare via!
7. Professoressa, stia qui!	_____
8. _____	Bruno, non bere quella bibita!

C. *Provide the corresponding familiar or polite form of the singular or plural imperative, as required. (Note:* **pazienza** = *patience.)*

FAMILIAR	POLITE
1. Mangia la pizza!	_____
2. _____	Cominci a mangiare!
3. Aspetta qui!	_____
4. _____	Apra la porta!
5. Finisci la mela!	_____
6. _____	Cerchi la chiave!
7. Paga il conto!	_____
8. _____	Scriva l'e-mail!
9. Chiudi la porta!	_____
10. _____	Dorma!
11. Aprite le porte!	_____
12. _____	Chiudano le porte!
13. Finite di studiare!	_____
14. _____	Abbia pazienza!
15. Va' a dormire!	_____

D. *Provide the corresponding affirmative or negative form of the imperative singular or plural, as required.*

AFFIRMATIVE	NEGATIVE
1. Mangia la pesca!	_____
2. _____	Non guardi la televisione!
3. Finiamo di mangiare!	_____
4. _____	Non chiudere la porta!
5. Bevi tutta l'acqua!	_____
6. _____	Non dica questo!
7. Usciamo stasera!	_____

E. *Provide an appropriate command to tell each subject given to do the indicated things.*

1. Tell Claudia to . . .

   a. eat the apple _____

   b. not drink the water _____

   c. close the door _____

   d. open the window _____

2. Now, tell both Claudia and Paul to . . .

   a. eat the apple _____

   b. not drink the water _____

   c. close the door _____

   d. open the window _____

3. This time tell Mrs. Verdi to . . .

   a. eat the apple _____

   b. not drink the water _____

   c. close the door _____

   d. open the window _____

4. Finally, tell both Mrs. Verdi and Mr. Rossi to . . .

   a. eat the apple _____

   b. not drink the water _____

   c. close the door _____

   d. open the window _____

Grammar in culture

As discussed in the previous chapter, the conditional may be used to make a polite request. In a formal or delicate situation, a polite form of the present tense of **potere** may be used instead of the imperative.

Change each imperative sentence into a polite request using **può**, *as shown in the example.*

EXAMPLE   Signor Verdi, venga qui!

Signor Verdi, può venire qui?

1. Dottoressa Marchi, mi dia la ricetta (*prescription*)!

   _____

2. Cameriere, mi porti subito il caffè!

   _____

3. Signora, mi dica tutto!

   _____

4. Professore, mi aiuti!

   _____

Reflexive verbs

A **reflexive verb** is a verb, in any tense or mood, that requires reflexive pronouns. More technically, it is a verb having an identical subject and direct object, as in *I dressed myself.*

A reflexive infinitive in Italian is identifiable by the ending **-si** (*oneself*) attached to the infinitive (minus the final **-e**).

> **lavare** + **si** → **lavarsi** (*to wash oneself*)
> **divertire** + **si** → **divertirsi** (*to enjoy oneself*)

Below is a list of common reflexive verbs.

alzarsi	*to get up*
annoiarsi	*to become bored*
arrabbiarsi	*to become angry*
chiamarsi	*to be called (named)*
dimenticarsi	*to forget*
divertirsi	*to enjoy oneself, have fun*
lamentarsi	*to complain*
lavarsi	*to wash oneself*
mettersi	*to put on, wear; to set about, begin to*
preoccuparsi	*to worry*
prepararsi	*to prepare oneself*
sentirsi	*to feel*
sposarsi	*to marry, get married*
svegliarsi	*to wake up*
vergognarsi	*to be (feel) ashamed, embarrassed*
vestirsi	*to get dressed*

Forms

Reflexive verbs are conjugated in exactly the same manner as non-reflexive verbs with, of course, the addition of reflexive pronouns. These pronouns are: **mi, ti, si, ci, vi, si.**

Io **mi alzo** presto ogni giorno.	*I get up early every day.*
Sembra che tu **ti diverta** sempre in Italia.	*It seems that you always enjoy yourself in Italy.*
Lui **si sposerà** l'anno prossimo.	*He is getting married next year.*
Lei **si sposerebbe**, se avesse più soldi.	*She would get married if she had more money.*
Come **si chiama** suo fratello?	*What's her brother's name?*

(Noi) **ci divertivamo** sempre da bambini. — *We always used to have fun as children.*
Penso che voi **vi siate annoiati** ieri. — *I think that you became bored yesterday.*
Anche loro **si divertirono** in Italia. — *They also had fun in Italy.*

Note that some verbs are reflexive in Italian, but not in English. Needless to say, this is a common source of error for learners.

Reflexive pronouns are changed to **me**, **te**, **se**, **ce**, **ve**, and **se** before direct object pronouns.

Marco **si** mette sempre **la giacca**. — *Mark always puts on a jacket.*
Marco **se la** mette sempre. — *Mark always puts it on.*

Some verbs can be used with reflexive pronouns. These are the reciprocal forms of the verb.

VERB		RECIPROCAL	
parlare	*to speak, talk*	**parlarsi**	*to talk to each other*
telefonare	*to phone*	**telefonarsi**	*to phone each other*
vedere	*to see*	**vedersi**	*to see each other*
capire	*to understand*	**capirsi**	*to understand each other*

Loro **si parlano** spesso. — *They speak to each other often.*
Noi **ci telefoniamo** ogni giorno. — *We phone each other every day.*
Voi non **vi vedete** da molto, vero? — *You haven't seen each other for quite a while, no?*
Loro non **si capiscono** mai. — *They never understand each other.*

ESERCIZIO
16·1

A. *Provide the appropriate present indicative, present subjunctive, and past absolute forms of each reflexive verb. This is your chance to review the tenses, the irregular forms, and so on, covered so far in this book. The first one is done for you.*

	PRESENT INDICATIVE	PRESENT SUBJUNCTIVE	PAST ABSOLUTE
1. (tu) alzarsi	*(tu) ti alzi*	*(tu) ti alzi*	*(tu) ti alzasti*
2. (lei) annoiarsi			
3. (lui) arrabbiarsi			
4. (io) alzarsi			
5. (noi) dimenticarsi			
6. (voi) divertirsi			
7. (io) lamentarsi			
8. (loro) lavarsi			
9. (tu) mettersi			
10. (lei) preoccuparsi			
11. (lui) prepararsi			
12. (noi) sentirsi			

13. (voi) sposarsi   _____   _____   _____

14. (loro) svegliarsi   _____   _____   _____

15. (lui) vestirsi   _____   _____   _____

B. *Now, provide the appropriate future, conditional, and present progressive (both indicative and subjunctive) forms for each verb.*

	FUTURE	CONDITIONAL	PRESENT PROGRESSIVE (INDICATIVE AND SUBJUNCTIVE)
1. (tu) alzarsi	_____	_____	_____
2. (lei) annoiarsi	_____	_____	_____
3. (lui) arrabbiarsi	_____	_____	_____
4. (io) alzarsi	_____	_____	_____
5. (noi) dimenticarsi	_____	_____	_____
6. (voi) divertirsi	_____	_____	_____
7. (io) lamentarsi	_____	_____	_____
8. (loro) lavarsi	_____	_____	_____
9. (tu) mettersi	_____	_____	_____
10. (lei) preoccuparsi	_____	_____	_____
11. (lui) prepararsi	_____	_____	_____
12. (noi) sentirsi	_____	_____	_____
13. (voi) sposarsi	_____	_____	_____
14. (loro) svegliarsi	_____	_____	_____
15. (lui) vestirsi	_____	_____	_____

C. *And now, provide the appropriate imperfect indicative, imperfect subjunctive, and imperfect progressive (indicative and subjunctive) forms for each verb. By now, you should really know your tenses!*

	IMPERFECT INDICATIVE	IMPERFECT SUBJUNCTIVE	IMPERFECT PROGRESSIVE (INDICATIVE AND SUBJUNCTIVE)
1. (tu) alzarsi	_____	_____	_____
2. (lei) annoiarsi	_____	_____	_____
3. (lui) arrabbiarsi	_____	_____	_____
4. (io) alzarsi	_____	_____	_____
5. (noi) dimenticarsi	_____	_____	_____
6. (voi) divertirsi	_____	_____	_____
7. (io) lamentarsi	_____	_____	_____

8. (loro) lavarsi   _____   _____   _____

9. (tu) mettersi   _____   _____   _____

10. (lei) preoccuparsi   _____   _____   _____

11. (lui) prepararsi   _____   _____   _____

12. (noi) sentirsi   _____   _____   _____

13. (voi) sposarsi   _____   _____   _____

14. (loro) svegliarsi   _____   _____   _____

15. (lui) vestirsi   _____   _____   _____

D. *How do you say the following in Italian?*

1. We speak to each other often.

   _____

2. They phone each other every day.

   _____

3. They haven't seen each other in a while.

   _____

4. We never understand each other.

   _____

Compound tenses

In compound tenses, all reflexive verbs are conjugated with **essere**.

Io **mi sono alzato (-a)** tardi ieri.	*I got up late yesterday.*
Perché non **ti sei messa** la giacca?	*Why didn't you put a jacket on?*
Loro **si sono divertiti** molto a Roma.	*They had a lot of fun in Rome.*
Dopo che **ci saremo alzati**, usciremo.	*After we have gotten up, we'll be going out.*
Quando **si saranno sposati**, andranno via.	*When they will have gotten married, they will leave.*

With double pronouns—reflexive and direct object pronouns—agreement in compound tenses is between the past participle and the object pronoun, not the subject. So, be careful!

Agreement with the subject

Marco si è mess**o** la giacca ieri.	*Mark put on his jacket yesterday.*
Maria si è lav**ata** i capelli.	*Mary washed her hair.*

Agreement with the object pronoun

Marco se **la** è mess**a** ieri.	*Mark put it on yesterday.*
Maria se **li** è lav**ati**.	*Mary washed it (them).*

A. *Provide the appropriate present perfect, past subjunctive, and future perfect forms of each verb. This is your chance, once again, to review the tenses, the irregular forms, and so on, covered in this book. The first one is done for you.*

	PRESENT PERFECT	PAST SUBJUNCTIVE	FUTURE PERFECT
1. (tu) alzarsi	*(tu) ti sei alzato (-a)*	*(tu) ti sia alzato (-a)*	*(tu) ti sarai alzato (-a)*
2. (lei) annoiarsi			
3. (lui) arrabbiarsi			
4. (io) alzarsi			
5. (noi) dimenticarsi			
6. (voi) divertirsi			
7. (io) lamentarsi			
8. (loro) lavarsi			
9. (tu) mettersi			
10. (lei) preoccuparsi			
11. (lui) prepararsi			
12. (noi) sentirsi			
13. (voi) sposarsi			
14. (loro) svegliarsi			
15. (lui) vestirsi			

B. *Now, provide the past conditional, pluperfect indicative, and pluperfect subjunctive forms of each verb.*

	PAST CONDITIONAL	PLUPERFECT (INDICATIVE)	PLUPERFECT (SUBJUNCTIVE)
1. (tu) alzarsi			
2. (lei) annoiarsi			
3. (lui) arrabbiarsi			
4. (io) alzarsi			
5. (noi) dimenticarsi			
6. (voi) divertirsi			
7. (io) lamentarsi			
8. (loro) lavarsi			
9. (tu) mettersi			
10. (lei) preoccuparsi			

11. (lui) prepararsi _____ _____ _____

12. (noi) sentirsi _____ _____ _____

13. (voi) sposarsi _____ _____ _____

14. (loro) svegliarsi _____ _____ _____

15. (lui) vestirsi _____ _____ _____

C. *Rewrite each sentence by replacing the italicized words with the appropriate object pronoun and by making all necessary changes. (Note:* **testa** *= head;* **piede** *[m.] = foot.)*

1. Io mi sono messo *quella giacca* per la festa.

   _____

2. Tu ti sei già lavato *la testa*, vero?

   _____

3. Lui si è lavato *le mani* già.

   _____

4. Lei si è lavata *i piedi* già.

   _____

5. Noi ci siamo messi *il cappotto*, perché faceva freddo.

   _____

6. Voi vi siete dimenticati *il biglietto*.

   _____

7. Loro si sono messi *la camicia*.

   _____

Imperative forms

The reflexive pronouns are attached to the (**tu**), (**voi**), and (**noi**) forms of the affirmative imperative.

FAMILIAR		POLITE	
TU FORMS		LEI FORMS	
Dino, **vestiti!**	*Dino, get dressed!*	Signor Rossi, **si vesta!**	*Mr. Rossi, get dressed!*
Maria, **alzati!**	*Mary, get up!*	Signora Rossi, **si alzi!**	*Mrs. Rossi, get up!*
NOI FORMS			
Divertiamoci!	*Let's have fun!*	**Prepariamoci!**	*Let's get ready!*
Sposiamoci!	*Let's get married!*	**Vestiamoci!**	*Let's get dressed!*

VOI FORMS		LORO FORMS	
Divertitevi!	*Enjoy yourselves!*	**Si divertano!**	*Enjoy yourselves!*
Alzatevi!	*Get up!*	**Si alzino!**	*Get up!*

The pronouns are also attached in the negative imperative in the same way, as a general guideline. However, in the case of the second-person singular (**tu**) form, recall that the infinitive is the negative imperative form of the verb (see Unit 15). In this case, the pronoun may be attached or put before the verb. If attached, the final **-e** of the infinitive is dropped.

TU FORMS

AFFIRMATIVE		NEGATIVE	
Marco, **alzati!**	*Mark, get up!*	Marco, non **ti alzare!**	*Mark, don't get up!*
Maria, **alzati!**	*Mary, get up!*	Maria non **alzarti!**	*Mary, don't get up!*

The imperative of reflexive verbs is complicated, and for this reason is a constant source of blunders for learners.

ESERCIZIO
16·3

A. *Provide the affirmative imperative forms for each verb.*

	TU	LEI	NOI	VOI	LORO
1. alzarsi					
2. divertirsi					
3. lavarsi					
4. mettersi					
5. prepararsi					
6. svegliarsi					
7. vestirsi					

B. *Write an appropriate command to tell each subject given to do the indicated things.*

EXAMPLE   Tell Mark to wake up early.

_____*Marco, svegliati presto!*_____

1. Tell Mark to . . .

   a. wash his hair   _____

   b. not put on the new jacket   _____

   c. get up early   _____

   d. get dressed right away   _____

   e. enjoy himself at the party   _____

2. Tell Mrs. Verdi to . . .

   a. wash her hair   _____

   b. not put on the new dress   _____

   c. get up early   _____

   d. get dressed right away   _____

   e. enjoy herself downtown   _____

3. Tell Mark and Mary to . . .

   a. wash their hair   _____

   b. not put on new shoes   _____

   c. get up early   _____

   d. get dressed right away   _____

   e. enjoy themselves at the party _____

4. Tell Mr. Rossi and Mrs. Rossi to . . .

   a. prepare themselves to go out _____

   b. not wake up early   _____

   c. not get angry   _____

   d. not forget to call   _____

   e. enjoy themselves at the party _____

C. *Rewrite each command to tell each subject in parentheses to do the same things, making all necessary changes.*

EXAMPLE   Marco, divertiti! (Professore)

                  Professore, si diverta!

1. Claudia, alzati presto! (Signorina Bruni)

_____

2. Signor Marchi, non si arrabbi! (Marco)

_____

3. Ragazzi e ragazze, divertitevi! (Professori)

_____

4. Signore e signori, si preparino! (Ragazzi e ragazze)

_____

D. *Provide the opposite command—affirmative or negative—as required.*

EXAMPLE   Marco, alzati!
            <u>*Marco, non alzarti! (non ti alzare!)*</u>

1. Marco e Maria, non mettetevi gli stivali!

   _____

2. Signor Marchi, si alzi!

   _____

3. Sara, alzati!

   _____

4. Signorina Verdi, si preoccupi!

   _____

5. Alessandro, non dimenticarti!

   _____

E. *How do you say the following in Italian?*

1. We get up early every day.

   _____

2. It seems that he always enjoys himself in Italy.

   _____

3. She would get married if she meets the right person.

   _____

4. I always used to have fun as a child.

   _____

5. She got up late yesterday.

   _____

6. We do not speak to each other anymore.

   _____

7. They phone each other often.

   _____

8. Frank and Claudia, you haven't seen each other for many years, isn't that right?

   _____

Grammar in culture

It is interesting how different cultures classify and perceive the world. For example, a reflexive verb in one language/culture may not have a corresponding reflexive verb in another. The following Italian verbs are reflexive, but their English counterparts are not.

ITALIAN	ENGLISH
vestirsi	to dress, get dressed
rendersi conto	to realize
svegliarsi	to wake up
alzarsi	to get up

One of the most interesting Italian verbs in this regard is **chiamarsi** (*to call oneself, be named*), which is used in expressions like **Come ti chiami?** *What's your name?*

ESERCIZIO
16·4

How do you say the following in Italian?

1. I got dressed a few minutes ago.

   _____

2. She didn't realize that you (*familiar*) were here.

   _____

3. He never wakes up early.

   _____

4. She got up early this morning.

   _____

•17• Prepositions and adverbs

A preposition is a word (usually of one syllable) that comes before some part of speech, generally a noun or noun phrase, to show its relationship to some other part.

La borsa **di** Claudia è nuova. — *Claudia's purse is new.*
Lui va a scuola **in** macchina. — *He goes to school by car.*

An adverb is a word or expression modifying a verb, an adjective, or another adverb.

La borsa di Claudia è **molto** bella. — *Claudia's purse is very beautiful.*
Lui va a scuola **sempre** in macchina. — *He always goes to school by car.*

Prepositional contractions

When the following prepositions immediately precede a definite article form, they contract with it to form one word.

a	*to, at*
da	*from*
di	*of*
in	*in*
su	*on*

da + l' = dall'

Arrivano **dall'Italia** lunedì. — *They are arriving from Italy on Monday.*

di + il = del

Questo è il portatile **del fratello** di Claudia. — *This is the laptop of Claudia's brother.*

in + la = nella

Ci sono venti euro **nella scatola**. — *There are twenty euros in the box.*

The following chart summarizes the contracted forms.

	il	**i**	**lo**	**gli**	**l'**	**la**	**le**
a	al	ai	allo	agli	all'	alla	alle
da	dal	dai	dallo	dagli	dall'	dalla	dalle
di	del	dei	dello	degli	dell'	della	delle
in	nel	nei	nello	negli	nell'	nella	nelle
su	sul	sui	sullo	sugli	sull'	sulla	sulle

Contraction with the preposition **con** (*with*) is optional. In actual fact, only the forms **con + il = col** and **con + l' = coll'** are found in current day Italian with any degree of frequency.

Lui parla **col professore** domani.	*He will speak with the professor tomorrow.*
Loro arrivano **coll'Alitalia**.	*They are arriving with Alitalia.*

Other prepositions do not contract.

fra/tra	*between, among*
per	*for, through, on account of*
sopra	*above, on top*
sotto	*under, below*

L'ho messo **tra la tavola e la sedia**.	*I put it between the table and the chair.*
L'ho messo **sotto la tavola**.	*I put it under the table.*

The article is dropped in expressions that have a high degree of usage or have become idiomatic. A lot of these expressions include locations about town (home, the bank, the library, etc.) and forms of transportation (car, bus, train, etc.).

Sono **a casa**.	*I am at home.*
Vado **in macchina**.	*I'm going by car.*
Angela è **in centro**.	*Angela is downtown.*

However, if the noun in such expressions is modified in any way whatsoever, then the article must be used.

Andremo **alla casa nuova di Alessandro**.	*We will be going to Alexander's new home.*
Vado **nella macchina di Sara**.	*I'm going in Sarah's car.*

ESERCIZIO
17·1

A. *Rewrite each phrase with the contracted form of the preposition given.*

1. a

   a. la scuola _____

   b. le città _____

   c. il ragazzo _____

   d. la ragazza _____

   e. i professori _____

   f. gli avvocati _____

   g. lo zio _____

   h. l'amico _____

2. di

   a. la ragazza   _____

   b. le donne   _____

   c. il professore   _____

   d. la professoressa   _____

   e. i bambini   _____

   f. gli uomini   _____

   g. lo studente   _____

   h. l'amica   _____

3. da

   a. la scuola   _____

   b. le città   _____

   c. il Giappone   _____

   d. la Spagna   _____

   e. i medici (*doctors*)   _____

   f. gli Stati Uniti   _____

   g. lo zio   _____

   h. l'Italia   _____

4. in

   a. la città   _____

   b. le città   _____

   c. il centro   _____

   d. la scuola   _____

   e. i ristoranti   _____

   f. gli Stati Uniti   _____

   g. lo sport   _____

   h. l'anno   _____

5. su

   a. la scuola   _____

   b. le città   _____

   c. il ragazzo   _____

   d. la ragazza   _____

e. i professori   _____

f. gli avvocati   _____

g. lo zio   _____

h. l'amico   _____

B. *How do you say the following in Italian? (Note:* **guidare** *= to drive.)*

1. I put the knife between the spoon and the fork.

   _____

2. I am speaking with Mrs. Verdi this evening.

   _____

3. He is driving through (around) the city.

   _____

4. I put the key above the box.

   _____

5. It is under the box.

   _____

6. He is at home.

   _____

7. I am going in my friends' car.

   _____

Uses of the prepositions

Prepositions have many uses. All of them cannot be covered here, but these are the most common ones:

- **A** is used in front of a city name to render the idea of *in a city*.

Vivo **a Roma**.	*I live in Rome.*
Vivono **a Milwaukee**.	*They live in Milwaukee.*

- For areas larger than a city, **in** is normally used.

Vivo **in Toscana, in Italia**.	*I live in Tuscany, in Italy.*
Vivono **in (nella) Florida, negli Stati Uniti**.	*They live in Florida, in the United States.*

- **Di** is used to indicate possession or relationship.

È la macchina nuova **di Alessandro**.	*It's Alexander's new car.*
Come si chiama la figlia **del professore**?	*What's the name of the professor's daughter?*

◆ **Da** means *from* or *to* in expressions such as the following.

Vado **dal medico** domani.	*I'm going to the doctor's tomorrow.*
Vengo **dalla farmacia**.	*I'm coming from the pharmacy.*

It translates both *since* and *for* in expressions of time.

Vivo qui **dal 2004**.	*I have been living here since 2004.*
Vivo qui **da venti anni**.	*I have been living here for twenty years.*

It also translates the expression *as a . . . .*

Te lo dico **da amico**.	*I'm telling it to you as a friend.*
Da bambino, navigavo spesso in Internet.	*As a child, I used to navigate (surf) the Internet often.*

In expressions consisting of a *noun* + **da** it is translated in various ways.

una macchina **da vendere**	*a car for sale*
un abito **da sera**	*an evening dress*

◆ **Per** is used in time expressions when future duration with a definite end is implied.

Abiterò in questa città **per tre anni**. *I will live in this city for three years.*

ESERCIZIO
17·2

A. *Complete each sentence with the appropriate simple or contracted preposition, as required.*

1. I soldi sono _____ scatola (*box*).

2. Ecco i cellulari _____ amici miei.

3. Le scarpe (*shoes*) sono _____ tavola.

4. Domani mio zio andrà _____ medico.

5. Arrivano _____ dieci stasera (*tonight*).

6. Noi viaggeremo (*We will travel*) _____ Alitalia.

7. Il tappeto (*rug*) è _____ la sedia e la tavola.

8. Il gatto dorme _____ tavola, non sotto.

9. Maria rimane (*will remain*) _____ casa domani tutto il giorno.

10. Preferisco andare _____ macchina a scuola.

11. Andremo _____ casa nuova di mio fratello.

12. Andremo _____ macchina di mia sorella.

B. *How do you say the following in Italian? (Note:* **amare** = *to love.)*

1. I live in Florence.

_____

2. They live in the United States.

_____

3. There's Sarah's new car.

_____

4. What's the name of your (*familiar*) professor's daughter?

_____

5. Are they going to the doctor's tomorrow?

_____

6. I'm coming from Italy.

_____

7. They have been living in Italy for six years.

_____

8. As a child, I used to navigate the Internet often.

_____

9. She loves her evening dress.

_____

Adverbs of manner

Many of the prepositional phrases discussed above have an adverbial function. Adverbs express relations of time, place, intensity, and manner.

| Giovanni guida **lentamente**. | *John drives slowly.* |
| Questa casa è **molto** bella. | *This house is very beautiful.* |

Adverbs of manner are formed as described below. Notice that the ending **-mente** corresponds in general to the English ending *-ly*.

Change the **-o** ending of a type (1) descriptive adjective (see Unit 4) to **-a**. Then add **-mente**.

| **certo** | *certain* | **certa** + **mente** → **certamente** | *certainly* |
| **lento** | *slow* | **lenta** + **mente** → **lentamente** | *slowly* |

If the adjective is a type (2) adjective ending in **-e**, then simply add **-mente**.

| **elegante** | *elegant* | **elegantemente** | *elegantly* |
| **semplice** | *simple* | **semplicemente** | *simply* |

However, if the adjective ends in **-le** or **-re** preceded by a vowel, then the final **-e** is dropped before adding **-mente**.

facile	*easy*	**facil + mente → facilmente**	*easily*
popolare	*popular*	**popolar + mente → popolarmente**	*popularly*

Exceptions to these rules are given below.

ADJECTIVE		ADVERB	
benevolo	*benevolent*	**benevolmente**	*benevolently*
leggero	*light*	**leggermente**	*lightly*
violento	*violent*	**violentemente**	*violently*

Adjectives

Here are some adjectives that are commonly changed into adverbs.

enorme	*enormous*	**speciale**	*special*
felice	*happy*	**triste**	*sad*
preciso	*precise*	**utile**	*useful*
raro	*rare*	**vero**	*true*
regolare	*regular*		

Adverbs of manner normally follow the verb, but may begin a sentence for emphasis.

Lui scrive delle mail ai suoi amici **regolarmente**.	*He writes his friends e-mails regularly.*
Regolarmente, lui scrive delle mail ai suoi amici.	*Regularly, he writes his friends e-mails.*

ESERCIZIO
17·3

A. *Provide the adjectival or adverbial form of each word, as required.*

1. certamente   _____

2. semplice   _____

3. facilmente   _____

4. popolare   _____

5. benevolmente   _____

6. leggero   _____

7. enorme   _____

8. felicemente   _____

9. preciso   _____

10. specialmente   _____

11. utile _____

12. veramente _____

13. lento _____

14. elegantemente _____

15. regolare _____

16. tristemente _____

17. vero _____

18. simpatico _____

B. *First, indicate an adjective that expresses the opposite meaning of the one given, then provide the adverbial form. You will need to know adjectives that have been used in this and previous units. (Note:* **difficile** = *difficult;* **veloce** = *fast;* **pesante** = *heavy;* **comune** = *common.)*

EXAMPLE difficile ____*facile*____ ____*facilmente*____

1. basso _____ _____

2. triste _____ _____

3. veloce _____ _____

4. pesante _____ _____

5. vecchio _____ _____

6. comune _____ _____

Other kinds of adverbs

Adverbs cover a wide range of meanings, from time relations to quantity. Here are some very common adverbs and adverbial phrases, a number of which have been introduced in previous units. These will come in handy for the Esercizio.

allora	*then*
anche	*also, too*
ancora	*again, still, yet*
anzi	*as a matter of fact*
appena	*just, barely*
bene	*well*
di nuovo	*again, anew*
domani	*tomorrow*
finora	*until now*
fra/tra poco	*in a little while*
già	*already*
in fretta	*in a hurry*
insieme	*together*
invece	*instead*
lontano	*far*
male	*bad(ly)*
nel frattempo	*in the meantime*

oggi	*today*
oggigiorno	*nowadays*
ormai	*by now*
per caso	*by chance*
piuttosto	*rather*
poi	*after, then*
presto	*early*
prima	*first*
purtroppo	*unfortunately*
quasi	*almost*
sempre	*always*
solo	*only*
spesso	*often*
stamani	*this morning*
stasera	*this evening*
subito	*right away*
tardi	*late*
vicino	*near(by)*

Here are some examples of how they are used.

Claudia l'ha fatto **ancora** una volta.	*Claudia did it again (one more time).*
Io abito **lontano** e loro **vicino**.	*I live far and they nearby.*
Prima voglio mangiare e **poi** studierò.	*First I want to eat, and then I will study.*
Sono **quasi** le quattro.	*It's almost four o'clock.*
Noi andiamo **spesso** al cinema.	*We often go to the movies.*

In compound tenses (see Unit 11), some of these adverbs can be put between the auxiliary verb and the past participle. The ones most commonly placed is this position are **ancora**, **appena**, and **già**.

Non abbiamo **ancora** finito di lavorare.	*We haven't yet finished working.*
Ha **appena** telefonato.	*She just phoned.*
Sono **già** usciti.	*They went out already.*

The quantitative adjectives **molto**, **parecchio**, **poco**, **tanto**, and **troppo** (see Unit 9) can also be used as adverbs. But be careful! As adverbs, there is no agreement to be made.

ADJECTIVES		ADVERBS	
Lei ha **molti** soldi.	*She has a lot of money.*	Lei è **molto** intelligente.	*She is very intelligent.*
Ci sono **pochi** studenti.	*There are few students.*	Loro studiano **poco**.	*They study little.*

Tip!

To determine if a word such as **molto** is an adjective or adverb, check the word that comes after. If it is a noun, then **molto** is an adjective, agreeing with the noun. Otherwise it can be either an adverb or pronoun. In either of these cases, no agreement is required.

ESERCIZIO 17·4

A. *Choose the appropriate adverb to complete each sentence.*

1. Noi andiamo _____ al cinema.

   a. spesso   b. già

2. Lui l'ha fatto _____ una volta.

   a. ancora   b. sempre

3. Mio fratello vive _____, e mia sorella vicino.

   a. lontano   b. sempre

4. È _____ l'una.

   a. quasi   b. poi

5. Noi abbiamo _____ finito di lavorare.

   a. subito   b. appena

6. Prima voglio guardare quel programma e _____ studierò.

   a. poi   b. anzi

7. Loro mangiano _____.

   a. molti   b. molto

8. Noi invece mangiamo _____.

   a. pochi   b. poco

B. *How do you say the following in Italian?*

1. First this, then that.   _____

2. There he is, too.   _____

3. again tomorrow   _____

4. until now   _____

5. in a little while   _____

6. in a hurry   _____

7. together   _____

8. It's going well and bad.   _____

9. nowadays   _____

10. in the meantime   _____

11. by now   _____

12. by chance   _____

13. this morning, not this evening _____

14. often _____

15. rather _____

Comparison of adverbs

Adverbs are compared in the same manner as adjectives (see Unit 4).

ADVERB		COMPARATIVE/SUPERLATIVE FORMS	
lentamente	*slowly*	**più lentamente**	*more slowly*
facilmente	*easily*	**meno facilmente**	*less easily*
lontano	*far*	**il più lontano**	*the farthest*

Note the irregular comparative forms below.

ADVERB		COMPARATIVE		SUPERLATIVE	
bene	*well*	**più bene** (or) **meglio**	*better*	**il meglio**	*the best*
male	*bad(ly)*	**più male** (or) **peggio**	*worse*	**il peggio**	*the worst*

Recall the adjective forms **migliore** (*better*) and **peggiore** (*worse*). Notice that the adverb forms **meglio** and **peggio** are translated in the exact same way.

To figure out which form is the appropriate one, go back in your mind to the uncompared form in English.

> This soft drink is *good*. (*uncompared form*)
> That soft drink is *better*. (*compared form*)

Now you can see that *better* in this case corresponds to the comparative form of the adjective **buono**.

Questa bibita è **buona**.	*This soft drink is good.*
Quella bibita è **migliore**.	*That soft drink is better.*

Now, consider *better* as an adverb.

> This watch works *well*. (*uncompared form*)
> That watch works *better*. (*compared form*)

Now you can see that *better* in this case corresponds to the comparative form of the adverb **bene**.

Quest'orologio funziona **bene**.	*This watch works well.*
Quell'orologio funziona **meglio**.	*That watch works better.*

Use the exact same kind of "backward thinking" for **peggiore** and **peggio**.

Questa bibita è **cattiva**.	*This soft drink is bad.*
Quella bibita è **peggiore**.	*That soft drink is worse.*
Quest'orologio funziona **male**.	*This watch works badly.*
Quell'orologio funziona **peggio**.	*That watch works worse.*

A. *Provide the comparative and superlative forms for each adverb. The first one is done for you.*

	COMPARATIVE (MORE)	COMPARATIVE (LESS)	SUPERLATIVE (POSITIVE)
1. velocemente	*più velocemente*	*meno velocemente*	*il più velocemente*
2. vicino	_____	_____	_____
3. regolarmente	_____	_____	_____
4. presto	_____	_____	_____
5. spesso	_____	_____	_____
6. tardi	_____	_____	_____

B. *Choose the appropriate form, adjective or adverb, to complete each sentence.*

1. Quel libro è _____ di questo.

    a. migliore   b. meglio

2. Oggi va _____ di ieri.

    a. migliore   b. meglio

3. Quelle patate sono _____ di queste.

    a. migliori   b. meglio

4. Loro vivono _____ di noi.

    a. migliore   b. meglio

5. Quelle carote sono _____ di queste.

    a. peggiori   b. peggio

6. Oggi va _____ di ieri.

    a. peggiore   b. peggio

7. Quelle bibite sono _____ di queste.

    a. peggiori   b. peggio

8. In città si vive (*one lives*) _____ che in campagna (*in the country*).

    a. peggiore   b. peggio

C. *Complete each sentence with the appropriate simple or contracted preposition, as required.*

1. La borsa _____ Maria è bella.

2. Lui va _____ università _____ macchina.

3. Questo è il cellulare _____ fratello di Sara.

4. Ci sono venti dollari _____ scatola.

5. Arrivano _____ Francia lunedì.

6. L'ho messo _____ la porta e quella sedia.

7. Vivo _____ Napoli.

8. Vivono _____ Italia e precisamente _____ Italia settentrionale.

9. Domani vado _____ medico.

10. Viviamo _____ Stati Uniti _____ quarant'anni.

D. *Complete each sentence with an appropriate adverb or adverbial expression.*

1. Maria va in centro _____.

2. Questo film è _____ molto bello.

3. Noi andiamo _____ al cinema.

4. Marco l'ha fatto _____ una volta.

5. Lui vive _____ e lei _____.

6. Sono _____ le venti.

7. _____ voglio mangiare e poi vado al cinema.

8. Sono _____ usciti.

Grammar in culture

Prepositions used with types of media often show a different perspective in Italian. For example, to say *in the newspaper* in Italian, you use **su** (*on*): **sul giornale**. *On the radio* and *on TV* are rendered in Italian by **alla radio** and **alla televisione** (or sometimes, **in televisione**). The two languages coincide, however, with respect to the Internet: *on the Internet* is **su Internet**.

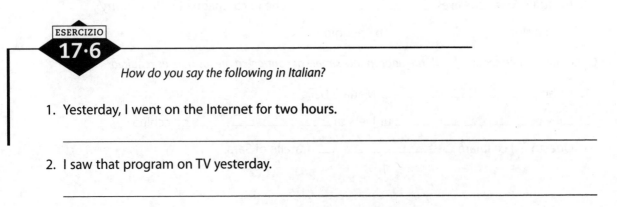

ESERCIZIO
17·6

How do you say the following in Italian?

1. Yesterday, I went on the Internet for two hours.

_____

2. I saw that program on TV yesterday.

_____

3. I heard it on the radio.

_____

4. I read it in the newspaper.

_____

·18· Sentences

A sentence is a series of words arranged into a meaningful whole. It begins with a capital letter and ends with a punctuation mark, such as a period, a question mark, or an exclamation point. It has a subject and a predicate.

Marco è italiano.	*Mark is Italian.*
È italiano Marco?	*Is Mark Italian?*
Certo, è veramente italiano!	*Certainly, he is really Italian!*

Subject and predicate

The subject is "who" or "what" the sentence is about. It is often the first element in a simple sentence. A predicate is the part of a sentence that expresses what is said about the subject. In the above sentence **Marco è italiano**, **Marco** is the subject and **è italiano** is the predicate.

Interrogative sentences

Interrogative sentences allow you to ask questions. In writing, they always have a question mark at the end.

Maria è italiana?	*Is Mary Italian?*
Maria è italiana, non è vero?	*Mary is Italian, isn't she?*
Di che nazionalità è Maria?	*Of what nationality is Mary?*

There are three main types of interrogative sentences: those that are designed to elicit a yes or no response; those that seek information of some kind; and those that simply seek consent or agreement.

The most common method of forming an interrogative sentence designed to get a yes or no response is simply to add a question mark at the end of the corresponding affirmative sentence.

Maria è italiana.	*Mary is Italian.*
È italiana?	*She's Italian?*
Sì, è italiana.	*Yes, she's Italian.*
Roberto parla molte lingue.	*Robert speaks a lot of languages.*
Lui parla francese?	*Does he speak French?*
Sì, parla francese.	*Yes, he speaks French.*
Tua sorella va in Italia quest'anno?	*Is your sister going to Italy this year?*
No, lei va in Francia.	*No, she's going to France.*

| I tuoi amici giocano a tennis? | *Do your friends play tennis?* |
| No, non giocano a tennis, giocano a calcio. | *No, they don't play tennis, they play soccer.* |

Another way to form this type of interrogative sentence is to put the entire subject at the end.

È italiana Maria?	*Is Mary Italian?*
Parla francese lui?	*Does he speak French?*
Va in Italia quest'anno tua sorella?	*Is your sister going to Italy this year?*
Giocano a tennis i tuoi amici?	*Do your friends play tennis?*

Tag questions

Tag questions are interrogative sentences designed to elicit consent or agreement of some kind. They are called *tag* because they end with an expression "tagged on." In Italian, that expression can be as follows.

vero?	*right?*
non è vero?	*isn't that correct?*
no?	*no?*
non pensi?	*don't you think?*
non credi?	*don't you believe (it)?*
non dici?	*don't you say so?*

Lui è americano, **non è vero?**	*He's American, isn't he?*
Viene anche lei, **vero?**	*She's coming, too, right?*
Prendi molto zucchero, **no?**	*You take a lot of sugar, don't you?*
L'italiano è una lingua bella, **non pensi?**	*Italian is a beautiful language, don't you think?*

ESERCIZIO
18·1

A. *Provide an alternative form of each interrogative sentence.*

EXAMPLE
Lui parla italiano?

Parla italiano lui?

1. Marco è spagnolo?

_____

2. È italiana Maria?

_____

3. Lui parla francese?

_____

4. Va in Italia quest'anno tuo fratello?

_____

5. I tuoi amici giocano a tennis?

_____

B. *Provide the question that could have produced each response.*

EXAMPLE   Sì, Claudia parla italiano.

          Claudia parla italiano? / Parla italiano Claudia?

1. Sì, Giovanni è italiano.

     _____

2. No, Maria non è francese.

     _____

3. Sì, i miei amici sono italiani.

     _____

4. No, la mia amica non va in Francia, va in Italia.

     _____

5. Sì, i miei amici giocano a calcio.

     _____

6. No, non ci sono i miei amici in questa classe.

     _____

C. *Provide the tag question that could have produced each response.*

1. Sì, prendo molto zucchero nel caffè. (*Yes, I take a lot of sugar in my coffee.*)

     _____

2. Non, non mi piace quel programma. (*No, I don't like that program.*)

     _____

3. Sì, penso che l'italiano sia una bella lingua. (*Yes, I believe that Italian is a beautiful language.*)

     _____

4. No, mio fratello non è francese. (*No, my brother is not French.*)

     _____

Question words

Interrogative sentences can also be formed with words such as *what?*, *when?*, *where?*, etc., that allow you to get information from someone. The main interrogative words are as follows:

◆ **che**   *what*

     Che libro leggi?   *What book are you reading?*
     Che leggi?   *What are you reading?*

     When used as a subject on its own, rather than as an adjective, the more appropriate form is the following one.

◆ **che cosa / cosa**   *what*

Che cosa fai?	*What are you doing?*
Cosa sono quelle cose?	*What are those things?*

◆ **chi**   *who*

Chi è quella persona?	*Who is that person?*
Chi viene alla festa?	*Who is coming to the party?*

Note the following:

di chi	*whose*
a/da (etc.) **chi**	*to/from* (etc.) *whom*
Di chi è questa rivista?	*Whose magazine is this?*
A chi hai dato la rivista?	*To whom did you give the magazine?*

◆ **come**   *how*

Maria, **come** stai?	*Mary, how are you?*
Come si chiama il tuo amico?	*What is the name of your friend?*

◆ **dove**   *where*

Dove vivono i tuoi amici?	*Where do your friends live?*
Dove vai a scuola?	*Where do you go to school?*

◆ **perché**   *why, because*

Perché dici questo?	*Why are you saying this?*
Perché non vai alla festa?	*Why aren't you going to the party?*
Non vado **perché** non ho tempo.	*I'm not going because I have no time.*

◆ **quale**   *which*

Note that with this question word the ending changes according to the gender and number of the noun it modifies.

Quale persona parla italiano?	*Which person speaks Italian?*
Quali sono gli studenti italiani?	*Which ones are the Italian students?*

◆ **quando**   *when*

Quando vai in Italia?	*When are you going to Italy?*
Quando arrivano?	*When are they arriving?*

◆ **quanto**   *how much*

Note that with this question word the ending also changes according to the gender and number of the noun it modifies.

Quanto zucchero prendi?	*How much sugar do you take?*
Quanta carne mangi?	*How much meat do you eat?*
Quanti studenti sono italiani?	*How many students are Italian?*
Quante studentesse conosci?	*How many students do you know?*

In writing, it is normal to drop the final **-e** from **come**, **dove**, and **quale** before the verb form **è** (*is*). In the case of both **come** and **dove** an apostrophe is added. But this is not the case for **quale**.

Com'è?	*How is it?*
Dov'è?	*Where is it?*
Qual è?	*Which is it?*

A. *Provide the question that could have produced each response.*

EXAMPLE   Lui si chiama Claudio.

          Come si chiama (lui)?

1. È una sedia.

   _____

2. Sono due scatole.

   _____

3. È un uomo italiano.

   _____

4. È la rivista di mia sorella.

   _____

5. Ho dato quel libro a mio fratello.

   _____

6. Sto molto bene, grazie.

   _____

7. Vivo a Chicago.

   _____

8. Non vado in centro perché non ho tempo.

   _____

9. Loro sono gli studenti d'italiano.

   _____

10. Mangio poca carne oggi.

    _____

11. Lei mangia poche carote di solito.

    _____

12. Arrivano domani.

    _____

13. La mela è buonissima!

    _____

14. È la mia, non la sua!

    _____

B. *Complete each sentence with the appropriate question word.*

1. _____ vanno quest'anno? Vanno in Italia.

2. _____ si chiama tua sorella? Si chiama Sara.

3. _____ studia matematica tuo fratello? Perché lui è molto intelligente.

4. _____ fai stasera? Vado al cinema.

5. _____ caffè vuoi, questo o quello? Voglio quel caffè.

6. _____ è quella donna? È mia cugina.

7. _____ è quel libro? È di mia mamma.

8. _____ caffè vuoi? Poco.

9. _____ studi l'italiano? Perché voglio vivere in Italia.

10. _____ è? È una macchina nuova.

Negative sentences

To make any sentence negative in Italian, just put **non** before the verb.

AFFIRMATIVE	NEGATIVE
Maria **aspetta** l'autobus.	Maria **non aspetta** l'autobus
Mary is waiting for the bus.	*Mary is not waiting for the bus.*
Il bambino **dorme**.	Il bambino **non dorme**.
The child is sleeping.	*The child is not sleeping.*

This simple rule applies as well to interrogative sentences.

INTERROGATIVE	NEGATIVE INTERROGATIVE
Maria **aspetta** l'autobus?	Maria **non aspetta** l'autobus?
Is Mary waiting for the bus?	*Isn't Mary waiting for the bus?*
Il bambino **dorme**?	Il bambino **non dorme**?
Is the child sleeping?	*The child isn't sleeping?*

Negatives

Negatives are words that allow you to deny, refuse, or oppose something.

Non conosco **nessuno** qui.	*I do not know anyone here.*
Non lo faccio **più**.	*I won't do it anymore.*

The following are some common negatives. Notice that **non** is retained.

non... affatto	*not at all*
non... mai	*never*
non... nessuno	*no one*
non... niente, nulla	*nothing*
non... più	*no more, no longer*

non... neanche/nemmeno/neppure		not even	
non... né... né		neither . . . nor	
non... mica		not really, quite	

AFFIRMATIVE		NEGATIVE	
Lui canta sempre.	*He always sings.*	Lui **non** canta **mai**.	*He never sings.*
Ci vado spesso.	*I go there a lot.*	**Non** ci vado **mai**.	*I never go there.*
Parlo e scrivo bene.	*I speak and write well.*	**Non** parlo **né** scrivo bene.	*I neither speak nor write well.*
Lui conosce tutti.	*He knows everyone.*	Lui **non** conosce **nessuno**.	*He doesn't know anyone.*

A negative can be put at the beginning of a sentence for emphasis. In this case, **non** is dropped.

Nessuno parla!	*No one is speaking!*
Mai capirò i verbi!	*Never will I understand verbs!*

ESERCIZIO
18·3

A. *Rewrite each sentence in the negative.*

1. Lui mangia sempre gli spaghetti.

   _____

2. Ieri ho mangiato la carne e le patate.

   _____

3. Marco conosce tutti in quella scuola.

   _____

4. Lui vuole qualcosa.

   _____

5. Quello è proprio vero.

   _____

B. *Answer each question negatively.*

1. Marco aspetta il suo amico?

   _____

2. Dorme Maria?

   _____

3. Conosci qualcuno qui?

   _____

4. Vai spesso in Italia?

   _____

5. Ti piace tutto, vero?

_____

6. Studi ancora?

_____

7. Ti piace anche la pizza, non è vero?

_____

8. Vuoi il caffè o il tè?

_____

9. È proprio vero, no?

_____

Objects

The predicate of sentences may or may not have an object. An object is the noun or noun phrase that receives the action of a verb, and normally follows the verb. A pronoun can also function as an object, as we saw in Units 5 and 6.

There are two types of objects: **direct** and **indirect**. These can be identified very easily as follows.

A noun or noun phrase that directly follows the verb—usually answering the question *who* or *what*—is a direct object. The noun phrase **il professore** below is a direct object.

Quella ragazza chiama **il professore** spesso.	*That girl calls the professor often.*

A noun or noun phrase that follows the verb, but is introduced by a preposition—often **a**—is an indirect object. The noun phrase **al professore** below is an indirect object.

Quella ragazza scrive **al professore** spesso.	*That girl writes to the professor often.*

Whether an object is direct or indirect depends on the verb. Some verbs must be followed only by one type of object or the other. Fortunately, most verbs in Italian match their English equivalents when it comes to whether or not a direct or indirect object should follow. **Mangiare** (*to eat*) takes a direct object in both languages and **andare** (*to go*) takes an indirect object in both.

Mio fratello mangia sempre **la pizza**.	*My bother always eats pizza.*
Mio fratello va spesso **alla pizzeria**.	*My brother goes often to the pizza parlor.*

However, there are some differences! Here are the most important ones.

Verbs requiring a direct object

ascoltare   *to listen (to)*

    Mia madre ascolta la radio ogni sera.   *My mother listens to the radio every evening.*

aspettare   *to wait (for)*

    Maria sta aspettando l'autobus.   *Mary is waiting for the bus.*

cercare   *to look (for)*

    Lei sta cercando la sua borsa.   *She is looking for her purse.*

Verbs requiring an indirect object

chiedere (a)   *to ask (someone)*

    Marco chiede al professore di venire.   *Mark asks the professor to come.*

telefonare (a)   *to phone, call (by phone)*

    Daniela telefona spesso a sua madre.   *Danielle phones her mother often.*

rispondere (a)   *to answer*

    La studentessa risponde sempre alle domande.   *The student always answers the questions.*

ESERCIZIO
18·4

A. *Answer each question affirmatively with the nouns or noun phrases in parentheses. To facilitate this exercise, the other parts of the answer are given to you.*

EXAMPLE 1   Cosa mangi? (pizza)

         Mangio la pizza.

EXAMPLE 2   Dove vai? (centro)

         Vado in centro.

1. A che cosa risponde sempre la professoressa? (domande)

   La professoressa risponde sempre _____.

2. A chi telefoni ogni sera, Maria? (la mia amica)

   Ogni sera telefono _____.

3. A chi hai chiesto quella cosa? (Marco)

   Ho chiesto quella cosa _____.

4. Che cosa cerchi? (una nuova macchina)

   Cerco _____.

5. Chi aspettano Alessandro e Giovanni? (la loro sorella)

   Alessandro e Giovanni aspettano _____.

B. *Now answer each question by using the indicated nouns or noun phrases in parentheses as objects.*

1. Dove vai spesso? (centro)

   _____

2. Che cosa mangi spesso? (la pasta)

   _____

3. Che cosa ascolti ogni sera? (la radio)

   _____

4. Chi chiami spesso? (mia sorella)

   _____

5. Che cosa aspetti? (l'autobus)

   _____

Conjunctions and relative pronouns

A sentence can have more than one subject or predicate. In such cases the different subject and predicate structures are called clauses. Clauses are united by forms such as conjunctions and relative pronouns.

To join two sentences, two clauses, two words, etc., the conjunctions **e** (*and*), **o** (*or*), and **ma** (*but*) are often used.

Lei studia **e** suo fratello guarda la TV.	*She is studying and her brother is watching TV.*
Vengo in macchina **o** a piedi.	*I'm coming by car or on foot.*
Mi piace la matematica, **ma** studio l'italiano.	*I like math, but I am studying Italian.*

(In Unit 10 we discussed conjunctions that require the subjunctive in the clauses they introduce.)

Clauses that are used as objects are called subordinate clauses. Consider the following sentence that is made up of a main clause and a subordinate clause connected by **che**. This connector word is called a relative pronoun.

Maria dice **che** il francese è una bella lingua.	*Mary says that French is a beautiful language.*

Main clause	=	**Maria dice**
Relative pronoun	=	**che**
Subordinate clause	=	**il francese è una bella lingua**

As you can see, a clause is a group of related words that contains a subject and predicate and is part of the main sentence.

There are two main types of subordinate clauses. First, a relative clause is a subordinate clause introduced by a relative pronoun, as we have just seen. Note that in English the relative pronoun can often be omitted. This is not the case in Italian.

The relative pronouns in Italian are as follows.

che	*that, which, who*
cui (*used after a preposition*)	*which, of whom, to whom, etc.*
chi	*whoever (he who, she who, they who)*
ciò che, quel che, quello che	*that which*

Here are some examples of their uses.

La donna **che** legge il giornale è mia sorella.	*The woman who is reading the newspaper is my sister.*
Il ragazzo **a cui** ho dato il libro è mio cugino.	*The boy to whom I gave the book is my cousin.*
Non trovo lo zaino **in cui** ho messo il tuo libro.	*I can't find the backpack in which I put your book.*
Ecco la rivista **di cui** ho parlato.	*Here is the magazine of which I spoke.*
Chi va in Italia si divertirà.	*Whoever goes to Italy will enjoy himself/herself.*
Ciò che dici non ha senso.	*What you are saying makes no sense.*
Non sai **quel che** dici.	*You don't know what you are saying.*
Quello che dici è vero.	*What (That which) you are saying is true.*

Both **che** and **cui** can be replaced by the *definite article* + **quale**, if there is an antecedent (the noun or noun phrase to which **quale** refers). **Quale** changes in form according to the number of the antecedent and is always preceded by the definite article (which must also indicate the gender and number of the antecedent).

L'uomo che legge il giornale è italiano.	*The man who is reading the newspaper is Italian.*

(or)

L'uomo **il quale** legge il giornale è italiano.	*The man who is reading the newspaper is Italian.*
Gli uomini che leggono il giornale sono italiani.	*The men who are reading the newspaper are Italian.*

(or)

Gli uomini **i quali** leggono il giornale sono italiani.	*The men who are reading the newspaper are Italian.*
La donna che legge il giornale è italiana.	*The woman who is reading the newspaper is Italian.*

(or)

La donna **la quale** legge il giornale è italiana.	*The woman who is reading the newspaper is Italian.*
Le donne che leggono il giornale sono italiane.	*The women who are reading the newspapers are Italian.*

(or)

Le donne **le quali** leggono il giornale sono italiane.	*The women who are reading the newspaper are Italian.*

The form **il cui** is used to convey possession: *whose*. The article varies according to the gender and number of the noun modified.

Ecco il ragazzo **il cui** padre è professore.	Here is the boy whose father is a professor.
Ecco gli scrittori **i cui** romanzi sono celebri.	Here are the writers whose novels are famous.
Ecco la ragazza **la cui** intelligenza è straordinaria.	Here is the girl whose intelligence is extraordinary.
Ecco la ragazza **le cui** amiche sono italiane.	Here is the girl whose friends are Italian.

A temporal clause is a subordinate clause introduced by conjunctions that indicate time relations.

appena	*as soon as*
dopo (che)	*after*
mentre	*while*
quando	*when*

| Andremo al cinema, **dopo che** avremo finito di mangiare. | *We will go to the movies, after (having finished) eating.* |
| **Quando** arriveranno, cominceremo a mangiare. | *When they arrive, we'll begin eating.* |

ESERCIZIO

18·5

A. *Choose the conjoining structure (conjunction or relative pronoun) that best introduces each clause.*

1. _____ Giacomo arriva, andremo al negozio (*store*).

   a. Quando   b. Che

2. _____ arriva la madre, ci metteremo a (*we will start to*) studiare.

   a. Quel che   b. Appena

3. _____ che sei uscito, è arrivata Sandra.

   a. Quando   b. Dopo

4. _____ tu studi, io leggo il giornale.

   a. Mentre   b. Dopo che

5. La persona _____ legge il giornale è una mia amica.

   a. che   b. cui

6. Le scarpe (*shoes*) _____ hai comprato ieri sono molto belle.

   a. le cui   b. le quali

7. La persona _____ hai dato il libro è un mio amico.

   a. a cui   b. al quale

8. _____ va a Roma, si divertirà.

   a. Ciò che   b. Chi

9. Ecco il ragazzo _____ sorella vuole essere medico.

   a. il cui   b. la cui

B. *Rewrite the two sentences as one with an appropriate conjoining structure.*

1. Sara sta studiando. Suo fratello guarda la TV.

   _____

2. La ragazza ha i capelli biondi (*blond hair*). La ragazza parla italiano molto bene.

   _____

3. Paolo parla italiano. Franca parla italiano.

   _____

4. Mi piace il libro. Maria sta leggendo (*is reading*) il libro.

   _____

5. Non trovo (*I can't find*) lo zaino. Nello zaino ho messo il tuo libro.

   _____

C. *Provide the question that could have produced each response.*

1. Sì, Maria è italiana.

   _____

2. No, loro non prendono zucchero.

   _____

3. Sì, Marco parla italiano molto bene.

   _____

4. No, lui non è andato al cinema ieri.

   _____

D. *Provide the question that could have produced each response.*

1. Leggo una rivista.

   _____

2. È un amico.

   _____

3. È la mia penna.

   _____

4. Il mio amico si chiama Alessandro.

   _____

5. I miei amici vivono negli Stati Uniti.

   _____

6. Non vado alla festa perché sono stanco.

   _____

7. Mi piace questa rivista, non quella.

_____

8. Vado a Roma domani.

_____

9. Prendo tanto zucchero.

_____

E. *Complete each sentence with an appropriate conjoining structure.*

1. Marco studia _____ sua sorella guarda la TV.

2. Lui viene in autobus _____ a piedi.

3. Studio la matematica, _____ mi piace l'italiano.

4. La persona _____ legge quella rivista è mia sorella.

5. Il ragazzo a _____ ho dato il libro è mio fratello.

6. Non trovo la borsa in _____ ho messo la mia chiave.

7. Ecco la rivista di _____ ho parlato.

8. _____ va in Italia si divertirà.

9. _____ dici non è affatto vero.

10. Ecco l'uomo la _____ sorella è medico.

11. Ecco la persona alla _____ ho dato il mio portatile.

12. Ecco le persone delle _____ ho parlato ieri.

Grammar in culture

Digital communications are changing how Italian sentences are written, especially in text messages and social media. Sentences are shorter and contain numerous abbreviations and acronyms. Here is an example.

Ciao Maria, tvb
Bye Maria, ilu

Ciao Maria, ti voglio bene.
Bye, Maria, I love you.

Try to figure out what the following abbreviations and acronyms stand for in Italian. Good luck!

1. c6? _____

2. ×ké _____

3. qnd _____

4. tvtb _____

Numbers

As you know, number words replace digits and other mathematical symbols to specify how many people, things, events, etc., there are. They are divided into cardinal numbers and ordinal numbers. The former are the counting numbers; the latter are used to indicate the order of something (*first, second,* etc.).

Cardinal

Quanti bambini ci sono nella famiglia?	*How many children are there in the family?*
Ci sono **due** bambini nella famiglia.	*There are two children in the family.*

Ordinal

Come si chiama **il primo** nato?	*What's the name of the first born?*
Si chiama Alessandro.	*His name is Alexander.*

The cardinal numbers

The first twenty counting numbers are given below.

0	**zero**	11	**undici**
1	**uno**	12	**dodici**
2	**due**	13	**tredici**
3	**tre**	14	**quattordici**
4	**quattro**	15	**quindici**
5	**cinque**	16	**sedici**
6	**sei**	17	**diciassette**
7	**sette**	18	**diciotto**
8	**otto**	19	**diciannove**
9	**nove**	20	**venti**
10	**dieci**		

As in English, the number words from twenty on are formed by combining number words logically as shown below.

$$22 \rightarrow \text{venti} + \text{due} = \text{ventidue}$$
$$89 \rightarrow \text{ottanta} + \text{nove} = \text{ottantanove}$$
$$112 \rightarrow \text{cento} + \text{dodici} = \text{centododici (or) cento dodici}$$
$$1234 \rightarrow \text{mille} + \text{duecento} + \text{trentaquattro} = \text{milleduecentotrentaquattro}$$
$$\text{(or) mille duecento trentaquattro}$$

There are a few adjustments to be made.

When **uno** and **otto** are used in numbers greater than twenty, the final vowel of the number word to which they are attached is dropped.

$$21 \rightarrow \text{venti} + \text{uno} = \text{ventuno}$$
$$48 \rightarrow \text{quaranta} + \text{otto} = \text{quarantotto}$$

When **tre** is added on, it must be written with an accent (to show that the stress is on the final vowel).

$$33 \rightarrow \text{trenta} + \text{tre} = \text{trentatré}$$
$$53 \rightarrow \text{cinquanta} + \text{tre} = \text{cinquantatré}$$

Here are the number words from 20 to 100.

20	venti	21, 22, 23, etc.	**ventuno, ventidue, ventitré,** etc.
30	trenta	31, 32, 33, etc.	**trentuno, trentadue, trentatré,** etc.
40	quaranta	41, 42, 43, etc.	**quarantuno, quarantadue, quarantatré,** etc.
50	cinquanta	51, 52, 53, etc.	**cinquantuno, cinquantadue, cinquantatré,** etc.
60	sessanta	61, 62, 63, etc.	**sessantuno, sessantadue, sessantatré,** etc.
70	settanta	71, 72, 73, etc.	**settantuno, settantadue, settantatré,** etc.
80	ottanta	81, 82, 83, etc.	**ottantuno, ottantadue, ottantatré,** etc.
90	novanta	91, 92, 93, etc.	**novantuno, novantadue, novantatré,** etc.
100	cento	101, 102, 103, etc.	**centuno, centodue, centotré,** etc.

To form the number words for 200, 300, etc., simply add **cento**, as shown below:

200	**duecento**
300	**trecento**
400	**quattrocento**
500	**cinquecento**
600	**seicento**
700	**settecento**
800	**ottocento**
900	**novecento**
1000	**mille**

The words for the higher numbers are constructed in the same way. Here are some examples. Note that, when written out, larger numbers can remain separate words or be joined together to form one single (long) word.

201	**duecentuno**
302	**trecentodue**
403	**quattrocentotré**
524	**cinquecento ventiquattro** (or) **cinquecentoventiquattro**
635	**seicento trentacinque** (or) **seicentotrentacinque**
1000	**mille**
1001	**milleuno**
1002	**milledue**
1234	**mille duecento trentaquattro** (or) **milleduecentotrentaquattro**

The plural of **mille** is **mila**.

2000	**duemila**
3000	**tremila**
40.574	**quarantamila cinquecento settantaquattro**
100.000	**centomila**
200.000	**duecentomila**

The plural of **milione** is **milioni**.

1.000.000	**un milione**
2.000.000	**due milioni**
3.000.000	**tre milioni**

Milione is always followed by **di** when used before a noun.

un milione di dollari	*a million dollars*
due milioni di euro	*two million euros*

Note that **euro** is invariable.

Remember, cardinal numbers may be written as one word. But for large numbers, it is often better to separate them logically, so that they can be read easily.

Italians use periods where Americans use commas, and vice versa. (Note: **virgola** = *comma*.)

ITALIAN	AMERICAN	
30.256	30,256	**trentamila duecento cinquantasei**
2,54	2.54	**due virgola cinquantaquattro**

When the number **uno** (or any number constructed with it, such as **ventuno**, **trentuno**, etc.) is used with a noun, it is treated like the indefinite article, with the final vowel changing according to the initial letter(s) of the noun that follows.

uno zio	*one uncle*
ventun anni	*twenty-one years*
trentuna ragazze	*thirty-one girls*
ventuno zaini	*twenty-one backpacks*

Note: The word **nessuno** has a negative meaning in the sense of *none, no one,* or *not one.* It is made up of **ness** + **uno**, and is thus treated like the indefinite article when used with a noun (see Unit 3). Note that the noun is always in the singular, even if its meaning is plural. In sum:

uno	→	**nessuno**
un	→	**nessun**
una	→	**nessuna**
un'	→	**nessun'**

nessuno zio	*no uncle/uncles*
nessun amico	*no friend/friends (m.)*
nessuna zia	*no aunt/aunts*
nessun'amica	*no friend/friends (f.)*

The indefinite article us used in front of **altro** (*other*) to produce the word *another.* Its two forms are: **un altro** (*m.*) and **un'altra** (*f.*).

un altro zio	*another uncle*
un'altra ragazza	*another girl*

Coffee and other drinks!

This vocabulary will come in handy for doing the Esercizio that follows.

aranciata	*orange drink*	**limonata**	*lemonade*
bibita	*soft drink*	**(caffè) lungo**	*long/mild coffee*
bicchiere (*m.*)	*glass*	**(caffè) macchiato**	*coffee with a drop of milk*
caffellatte (*m.*)	*coffee with milk (a "latte")*	**(caffè) ristretto**	*short/strong coffee*
cappuccino	*cappuccino*	**succo di frutta**	*fruit juice*
(caffè) corretto	*coffee with a drop of alcohol*	**tè** (*m.*)	*tea*
espresso	*espresso*	**zabaione** (*m.*)	*egg custard*
latte (*m.*)	*milk*		

ESERCIZIO 19·1

A. *Write out all the number words (up to 99) that end with the given digit. Follow the example.*

EXAMPLE   3 (= 3, 13, 23, 33, 43, 53, 63, 73, 83, 93)

tre, tredici, ventitré, trentatré, quarantatré, cinquantatré, sessantatré, settantatré, ottantatré, novantatré

1. 2 _____

_____

2. 4 _____

_____

3. 9 _____

_____

4. 8 _____

_____

5. 7 _____

_____

6. 1 _____

_____

7. 5 _____

_____

8. 6 _____

_____

9. 0 _____

_____

B. *Translate each phrase, providing the appropriate number word for each digit. (Note:* **centimetro** *= centimeter;* **metro** *= meter.)*

EXAMPLE   334 children

           trecento trentaquattro bambini

1. 701 men _____

2. 291 women _____

3. 1.568 students _____

4. 45.553 cell phones _____

5. 789.278 dollars _____

6. 2.456.233 euros _____

7. 18 waiters _____

8. 8.000.000 euros _____

9. 122 cars _____

10. 991 dollars _____

11. 3,58 centimeters _____

12. 0,56 meters _____

C. *Provide the appropriate translations of* another *and* none *for each phrase. The first one is done for you.*

NOUN	ANOTHER	NONE
1. caffè	*un altro caffè*	*nessun caffè*
2. espresso		
3. tè		
4. caffè ristretto		
5. caffè lungo		
6. caffè corretto		
7. zabaione		
8. bibita		
9. bicchiere di vino		
10. bicchiere di latte		

11. caffellatte   _____   _____

12. cappuccino   _____   _____

13. aranciata   _____   _____

14. limonata   _____   _____

15. succo di frutta   _____   _____

Telling time

Perhaps the most common of all the communicative functions associated with numbers is telling time. Here's how to tell time in Italian.

Che ora è?	*What time is it?* (literally: *What hour is it?*)

(or)

Che ore sono?	*What time is it?* (literally: *What hours are they?*)

The hours are feminine in gender. Therefore, they are preceded by the feminine forms of the definite article.

l'una	*one o'clock* (Note: This is the only singular form.)
le due	*two o'clock*
le tre	*three o'clock*
le quattro	*four o'clock*

Useful vocabulary

la mattina	*morning*
il pomeriggio	*afternoon*
la sera	*evening*
la notte	*night*

Useful expressions

Buongiorno!	*Good morning!, Good day!*
Buon pomeriggio!	*Good afternoon!*
Buonasera!	*Good evening!*
Buonanotte!	*Good night!*

In ordinary conversation, the morning, afternoon, and evening hours are distinguished by the following expressions.

di/della mattina (del mattino)	*in the morning*
di/del pomeriggio	*in the afternoon*
di/della sera	*in the evening*
di/della notte	*in the night / at night*
Sono le otto di mattina.	*It's eight o'clock in the morning.*
Sono le nove di sera.	*It's nine o'clock in the evening.*

Officially, however, telling time in Italian is carried out on the basis of the twenty-four-hour clock. Thus, after the noon hour, continue sequentially with the numbers.

le tredici	*1:00 P.M. (thirteen hundred hours)*
le quattordici	*2:00 P.M. (fourteen hundred hours)*
le quindici	*3:00 P.M. (fifteen hundred hours)*

le sedici	4:00 P.M. (sixteen hundred hours)
Sono le quindici.	It's 3:00 P.M.
Sono le venti.	It's 8:00 P.M.
Sono le ventiquattro.	It's (twelve) midnight.

Minutes are simply added to the hour with the conjunction **e.**

Sono le tre e venti.	It's three-twenty.
È l'una e quaranta.	It's one-forty.
Sono le sedici e cinquanta.	It's 4:50 P.M.
Sono le ventidue e cinque.	It's 10:05 P.M.

As the next hour approaches, an alternative way of expressing the time is: *the next hour* — (**meno**) *the number of minutes left.*

8.58	**le otto e cinquantotto** (or) **le nove meno due**
10.50	**le dieci e cinquanta** (or) **le undici meno dieci**

Note that where the colon is used with telling time in English, the period is generally used in Italian.

The expressions **un quarto** (*a quarter*) and **mezzo** or **mezza** (*half*) can be used for the quarter and half hour.

3.15	**le tre e quindici** (or) **le tre e un quarto**
4.30	**le quattro e trenta** (or) **le quattro e mezzo/mezza**
5.45	**le cinque e quaranta cinque** (or) **le sei meno un quarto** (or) **le cinque e tre quarti** (*three quarters*)

Noon and midnight can also be expressed by **il mezzogiorno** and **la mezzanotte,** respectively.

Sono le dodici.	(or)	**È mezzogiorno.**	It's noon.
Sono le ventiquattro.	(or)	**È mezzanotte.**	It's midnight.

Note: The following expressions are used in everyday conversation.

preciso	*exactly*
È l'una precisa.	*It's exactly one o'clock.*
Sono le otto precise.	*It's exactly eight o'clock.*
in punto	*on the dot*
È l'una in punto.	*It's one o'clock on the dot.*
Sono le otto in punto.	*It's eight o'clock on the dot.*

Time!

The word **ora** means *time* in the sense of *hour.* The abstract concept of *time* is expressed by **il tempo.**

Come passa il tempo!	*How time flies!*

And the concept of *time* to indicate a particular moment or occurrence is expressed by **la volta.**

una volta	*once, one time*
due volte	*twice*
tre volte	*three times*

A. *Write out the time in Italian using the twenty-four-hour clock.*

EXAMPLE   3:42 P.M.

          Sono le quindici e quarantadue.

1. 2:20 P.M. _____

2. 8:35 A.M. _____

3. 4:50 P.M. _____

4. 9:14 A.M. _____

5. 5:12 P.M. _____

6. 10:42 A.M. _____

7. 1:05 A.M. _____

8. 11:28 A.M. _____

9. 7:18 P.M. _____

10. 8:29 P.M. _____

11. 10:30 P.M. _____

12. 11:38 P.M. _____

B. *Provide an equivalent way of telling the time. Do not use the twenty-four-hour clock in this Esercizio. Follow the time with an expression that fits it best.*

EXAMPLE 1   2:20 P.M.

        Sono le due e venti del pomeriggio.

        Buon pomeriggio!

EXAMPLE 2   8:45 A.M.

        Sono le otto e quarantacinque (della mattina/del mattino).

        Sono le nove meno quindici. / Sono le nove meno un quarto.

        Buongiorno!

1. 6:15 A.M. _____

_____

2. 7:30 P.M. _____

_____

3. 9:45 A.M. _____

_____

4. 8:30 P.M. _____

_____

5. 9:58 A.M. _____

_____

6. 12:00 A.M. _____

_____

7. 12:00 P.M. _____

_____

8. 1:00 P.M. _____

_____

9. 8:00 A.M. _____

_____

C. *How do you say the following in Italian? (Note:* **fare qualcosa** = *to do something.)*

1. Time flies!

_____

2. I always do something two or three times.

_____

3. What time is it?

_____

The ordinal numbers

The first ten ordinal numbers are as follows.

first (1st)	**primo (1º)**
second (2nd)	**secondo (2º)**
third (3rd)	**terzo (3º)**
fourth (4th)	**quarto (4º)**
fifth (5th)	**quinto (5º)**
sixth (6th)	**sesto (6º)**
seventh (7th)	**settimo (7º)**
eighth (8th)	**ottavo (8º)**
ninth (9th)	**nono (9º)**
tenth (10th)	**decimo (10º)**

The remaining ordinals are easily constructed in the following manner.
Take the corresponding cardinal number, drop its vowel ending, and add **-esimo**.

eleventh/11th	**undici + -esimo**	= **undicesimo/11º**
forty-second/42nd	**quaranta due + -esimo**	= **quarantaduesimo/42º**

If the cardinal number ends in **-tré**, remove the accent mark but retain the **e**.

twenty-third/23rd	**ventitré** + **-esimo**	= **ventitreesimo/23º**
thirty-third/33rd	**trentatré** + **-esimo**	= **trentatreesimo/33º**

If the cardinal number ends in **-sei**, do not drop the final **i**.

twenty-sixth/26th	**ventisei** + **-esimo**	= **ventiseiesimo/26º**

Unlike the cardinal numbers, ordinal numbers are adjectives. Therefore, they agree with the noun they modify in gender and number. (Note: The superscript letter which accompanies the ordinal digit in Italian must also change to indicate gender and number.)

il primo (1º) giorno	*the first (1st) day*
la ventesima (20ª) volta	*the twentieth (20th) time*
tutti gli ottavi (8ⁱ) capitoli	*all the eighth (8th) chapters*

Like any adjective, an ordinal can be easily transformed into a pronoun.

(Lui) È **il terzo** in fila.	*He is the third in line.*
Sono tra **i primi** della classe.	*They are among the first of their class.*

Unlike English usage, in Italian the definite article is not used when the ordinals are used with a proper name.

Elisabetta II	*Elizabeth (the) II (Elizabeth the Second)*
Papa Giovanni XXIII (Ventitreesimo)	*Pope John (the) XXIII*
Luigi XIV (Quattordicesimo)	*Louis (the) XIV*

Note: As in English, cardinals are used to express the numerator and ordinals the denominator of fractions. Note that if the numerator is greater than *1*, the denominator, being an ordinal adjective, must be in the plural.

$\frac{1}{17}$	**un diciasettesimo**
$\frac{3}{4}$	**tre quarti**
$\frac{5}{9}$	**cinque noni**

Be careful!

The fraction ½ is different.

½
mezzo (*adjective*)	**un mezzo litro**	*a half liter*
metà (*noun*)	**la metà di tutto**	*half of everything*

ESERCIZIO
19·3

A. *Translate each phrase, providing the appropriate ordinal number word. (Note:* **piano** *= floor [of a building].)*

1. 1st time and 11th time _____

2. 2nd time and 22nd time _____

3. 3rd floor and 33rd floor _____

4. 4th chapter and 44th day _____

5. 5th soft drink and 55th espresso _____

6. 6th photograph and 66th week _____

7. 7th glass of milk and 77th month _____

8. 8th cappuccino and 88th year _____

9. 9th lemonade and 99th time _____

10. 10th student (*f.*) and 100th class _____

11. ⅛ and ⁵⁄₇ _____

12. ⅔ and ½ of everything _____

13. ½ liter _____

B. *How do you say the following in Italian?*

1. Pope John the XXIII _____

2. She is the first of the class. _____

3. He is the eighth in line. _____

Numerical expressions

Note the following useful expressions.

= **fa**		*equals*
+ **più**		*plus*
23 + 36 = 59		**ventitré più trentasei fa cinquantanove**
− **meno**		*minus*
8 − 3 = 5		**otto meno tre fa cinque**
× **per**		*times*
7 × 2 = 14		**sette per due fa quattordici**
÷ **diviso**		*divided*
16 ÷ 2 = 8		**sedici diviso per due fa otto**

The following expression is used to ask someone's age. It translates literally as *How many years do you have?*

Quanti anni ha?	*How old are you? (pol., sing.)*
Quanti anni hai?	*How old are you? (fam., sing.)*
Ho ventidue anni.	*I am twenty-two years old.*
Ho ottantotto anni.	*I am eighty-eight years old.*

Note two other useful numerical expressions.

il doppio	*double*
una dozzina	*a dozen*

Dates

Dates are expressed by the following formula.

Che giorno è?	*What's today's date? / What day is it?*
È il quindici settembre.	*It's September 15th.* (**literally:** *the fifteen September*)
È il ventun settembre.	*It's September 21st.* (literally: *the twenty-one September*)

The exception to this formula is the first day of every month, for which you must use the ordinal number **primo**.

Che giorno è?	*What's today's date?*
È il primo ottobre.	*It's October 1st.*
È il primo giugno.	*It's June 1st.*

Years are always preceded by the definite article.

È il 2010.	*It's 2010.*
Quando sei nato (-a)?	*When were you born?*
Sono nato (-a) il due marzo del 1994.	*I was born on March 2, 1994.*

Months

gennaio	*January*	**luglio**	*July*
febbraio	*February*	**agosto**	*August*
marzo	*March*	**settembre**	*September*
aprile	*April*	**ottobre**	*October*
maggio	*May*	**novembre**	*November*
giugno	*June*	**dicembre**	*December*

ESERCIZIO
19·4

A. *Express the date in Italian. Write out all numbers.*

1. January 23 _____

2. February 14 _____

3. March 7 _____

4. April 4 _____

5. May 3 _____

6. June 30 _____

7. July 31 _____

8. August 1 _____

9. September 8 _____

10. October 27 _____

11. November 18 _____

12. December 25 _____

B. *Answer each question with the information in parentheses or provide the answer if no information is given. Write out all numbers except years.*

EXAMPLE   Che giorno è? (*September 15, 2012*)

         È il quindici settembre, 2012.

1. Che giorno è? (*December 21, 2014*)

_____

2. Quando sei nato (-a)?

_____

3. Quanto caffè vuoi? (*double*)

_____

4. Quanti studenti ci sono in classe? (*a dozen*)

_____

5. Quanto fa due più otto?

_____

6. Quanto fa otto meno tre?

_____

7. Quanto fa quattro per ventidue?

_____

8. Quanto fa venti diviso per quattro?

_____

9. Quanti anni hai? (*provide your age*)

_____

C. *Write out the cardinal and then the ordinal for each number.*

		CARDINAL	ORDINAL
1.	7(th)	_____	_____
2.	12(th)	_____	_____
3.	17(th)	_____	_____
4.	18(th)	_____	_____
5.	19(th)	_____	_____
6.	24(th)	_____	_____
7.	31(st)	_____	_____
8.	43(rd)	_____	_____
9.	58(th)	_____	_____
10.	398(th)	_____	_____
11.	2,012(th)	_____	_____
12.	34,599(th)	_____	_____

D. *How do you say the following in Italian?*

1. four thousand euros _____

2. five million dollars _____

3. twenty-one girls _____

4. I am thirty-three years old. _____

5. no uncles _____

6. no aunts _____

7. another boy _____

8. another girl _____

9. a half liter _____

10. 16 divided by 4 equals 4. _____

11. It's Monday, July 12. _____

12. I was born on June 23. _____

13. What's today's date? _____

Grammar in culture

In Italy, the 24-hour clock is commonly used, even in conversation. Although you may, of course, use time expressions based on the 12-hour clock, it is important to get used to the 24-hour clock.

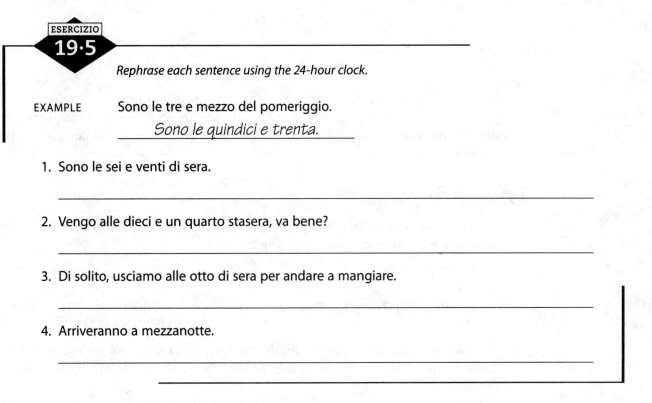

ESERCIZIO
19·5

Rephrase each sentence using the 24-hour clock.

EXAMPLE   Sono le tre e mezzo del pomeriggio.
           Sono le quindici e trenta.

1. Sono le sei e venti di sera.

   _____

2. Vengo alle dieci e un quarto stasera, va bene?

   _____

3. Di solito, usciamo alle otto di sera per andare a mangiare.

   _____

4. Arriveranno a mezzanotte.

   _____

Miscellaneous topics

In this final unit we will review topics that have special grammatical characteristics or require only a quick refreshing. The main topics to be discussed here are the verb **piacere**, the **passive voice** of verbs, and the two verbs that correspond to *to know*.

The verb **piacere**

The verb **piacere** is used for expressing likes and dislikes. But it is a tricky verb because it literally means *to be pleasing to*.

Mi **piace** la pizza.	*I like pizza. (Pizza is pleasing to me.)*
Non gli è **piaciuta** la pizza.	*He didn't like the pizza. (The pizza was not pleasing to him.)*

Needless to say, because of this difference **piacere** is a constant source of difficulties and errors for learners. It is regular in all tenses, except the following three.

Present indicative

piaccio   piaci   piace   piacciamo   piacete   piacciono

Past absolute

piacqui   piacesti   piacque   piacemmo   piaceste   piacquero

Present subjunctive

(io) piaccia, (tu) piaccia, (lui/lei; Lei) piaccia, (noi) piacciamo, (voi) piacciate, (loro; Loro) piacciano

It is conjugated with **essere** in compound tenses.

Non mi **è piaciuta** la pasta.	*I didn't like the pasta.*
Non gli **sono piaciuti** gli spaghetti.	*He didn't like the spaghetti.*

When saying that you or someone else likes something, translate the English expression into your mind as *to be pleasing to* and then follow the word order in the formula below.

EXPRESSION	TRANSLATE TO	ITALIAN EXPRESSION
I like that book.	*That book is pleasing to me.*	Mi **piace** quel libro. (Quel libro **piace** a me.)
We like those books.	*Those books are pleasing to us.*	Ci **piacciono** quei libri.
She likes her brothers.	*Her brothers are pleasing to her.*	Le **piacciono** i suoi fratelli.
The brothers like her.	*She is pleasing to her brothers.*	Lei **piace** ai suoi fratelli.

If you think of the verb **piacere** in this way, you will always be correct. Notice that the real subject is the thing or person that is liked (that is pleasing) and usually comes after the verb (although this is not necessary).

Mary likes John.	*John is pleasing to Mary.*	A Maria **piace** Giovanni. (or) Giovanni **piace** a Maria.

In compound tenses the past participle agrees with the subject.

I didn't like her.	*She was not pleasing to me.*	(Lei) non mi **è piaciuta**.
She didn't like us.	*We were not pleasing to her.*	(Noi) non le **siamo piaciuti**.

You might need to use stressed pronouns for reasons of emphasis or clarity (see Unit 5).

La musica **piace a me**, non **a te**!	*I like the music, not you! (The music is pleasing to me, not to you!)*

A handy rule of thumb

Since the verb is often used with indirect object pronouns, think of these pronouns as corresponding to the subject of the verb in English: *I like* = **mi piace/piacciono**. Then make the verb agree with the predicate (the thing or things liked).

Mi **piace** la pizza.	*I like (the) pizza. ([The] Pizza is pleasing to me.)*
Ti **piacciono** gli spaghetti.	*You like (the) spaghetti. ([The] Spaghetti are pleasing to you.)*
Gli **piace** la pizza.	*He likes (the) pizza. ([The] Pizza is pleasing to him.)*
Le **piacciono** gli spaghetti.	*She likes (the) spaghetti. ([The] Spaghetti are pleasing to her.)*
Ci **piace** la pizza.	*We like (the) pizza. ([The] Pizza is pleasing to us.)*
Vi **piacciono** gli spaghetti.	*You like (the) spaghetti. ([The] Spaghetti are pleasing to you.)*
Gli **piace** la pizza.	*They like (the) pizza. ([The] Pizza is pleasing to them.)*

This is merely a rule of thumb. If you are unsure, go through the procedure described above.

Note

To say that you like to do something, use the infinitive of the verb (of the activity you like to do) and the third-person singular form of **piacere**.

Mi **piace ascoltare** la musica.	*I like listening to music.*
A Laura **piace correre** la mattina.	*Laura likes to run (running) in the morning.*

A. *Choose the correct form of the verb to complete each sentence.*

1. Claudia, ti _____ quel film?

   a. piace   b. piaccio

2. Marco, io ti _____?

   a. piace   b. piaccio

3. A mio fratello non _____ quei libri.

   a. piacerà   b. piaceranno

4. A mia sorella non sono _____ gli spaghetti.

   a. piaciuta   b. piaciuti

5. Da bambini, ci _____ guardare spesso la TV.

   a. piaceva   b. piacevano

6. Noi non siamo _____ a tua madre.

   a. piaciuta   b. piaciuti

7. A chi _____ quelle riviste?

   a. piace   b. piacciono

B. *How do you say the following in Italian?*

1. We like that book.

   _____

2. But we don't like those other books.

   _____

3. She likes him.

   _____

4. And he likes her.

   _____

5. Mary likes me.

   _____

6. I didn't like them.

   _____

7. He didn't like us.

_____

8. He likes that music, not her.

_____

The passive and the impersonal **si**

Verbs are marked not only for mood and tense, as we have seen in previous units, but also for voice, which can be active or passive. In an active sentence the subject acts upon the object.

Il bambino **ha mangiato** la pizza.   *The boy ate the pizza.*

Many (non-reflexive) verbs also have a passive form, whereby the subject is acted upon by the object (so to speak).

La pizza **è mangiata** dal bambino.   *The pizza is eaten by the boy.*

An active sentence can be turned into a corresponding passive sentence according to the following three rules.

1. Change the order of the subject and the object

   Il bambino mangia **la mela**.   *The boy eats the apple.*
   → **La mela** (mangia) **il bambino**.

2. Change the verb into the passive form by introducing the auxiliary verb **essere** in the same tense and mood and by changing the verb into the past participle. Recall that the past participle of a verb conjugated with **essere** agrees with the subject (which is now **la mela**).

   La mela (**mangia**) il bambino.
   → **La mela** è mangia**ta** (il bambino).   *The apple is eaten (the boy).*

3. Put **da** (*by*) before **il bambino**. Remember to use the contracted form of the preposition when necessary.

   La mela è mangiata **dal** bambino.   *The apple is eaten by the boy.*

The following are some examples of corresponding active and passive forms of sentences. Note that the tense and mood is retained in the auxiliary of the passive—that is, if the verb in the active is the present indicative, then **essere** must be in the present indicative followed by the past participle; if the verb in the active is the future, then **essere** must be in the future followed by the past participle; and so on.

ACTIVE	PASSIVE
PRESENT PERFECT	PRESENT PERFECT + PAST PARTICIPLE
La donna **ha letto** quel libro.	Quel libro **è stato letto** dalla donna.
The woman read that book.	*That book was read by the woman.*

FUTURE	FUTURE + PAST PARTICIPLE
Quell'uomo **comprerà** quelle scarpe.	Quelle scarpe **saranno comprate** da quell'uomo.
That man will buy those shoes.	*Those shoes will be bought by that man.*

PAST ABSOLUTE	PAST ABSOLUTE + PAST PARTICIPLE
Io **scrissi** quell'e-mail.	Quell'e-mail **fu scritta** da me.
I wrote that e-mail.	*That e-mail was written by me.*

Remember that **io** becomes an object pronoun, **me**, after a preposition (see Unit 5).

The passive form of the verb is used to express ideas and situations that are communicated more appropriately in this form.

La lezione **è finita** alle sei.	*The class finished at six.*
I negozi **sono chiusi** a quest'ora.	*Stores are closed at this hour.*

The impersonal si

A similar general form of expression involves the use of the impersonal **si**, which means *one* (in general), *we*, *they*, and so on. It has the following peculiar characteristics.

The verb appears to agree with what seems to be the predicate, not the subject, because, as you can see below, the construction is really a type of passive form.

Si beve quel caffè solo in Italia.	*One drinks that coffee only in Italy.*
Quel caffè è bevuto solo in Italia.	*That coffee is drunk only in Italy.*
Si bevono quei vini solo in Italia.	*One drinks those wines only in Italy.*
Quei vini sono bevuti solo in Italia.	*Those wines are drunk only in Italy.*

In compound tenses, the auxiliary verb is **essere**.

Si è venduta quella macchina solo in Italia.	*One sold that car only in Italy.*
Quella macchina è stata venduta solo in Italia.	*That car was sold only in Italy.*
Si sono vendute quelle macchine solo in Italia.	*One sold those cars only in Italy.*
Quelle macchine sono state vendute solo in Italia.	*Those cars were sold only in Italy.*

When followed by a predicate adjective, the adjective is always in the plural.

Sì è **felici** in Italia.	*One is happy in Italy.*
Si è molto **simpatici** in Italia.	*One is very nice in Italy.*

Direct object pronouns are placed before the impersonal **si**.

Si deve dire sempre la verità.	*One must always tell the truth.*
La si deve dire sempre.	*One must always tell it.*

In front of the reflexive pronoun **si**, the impersonal **si** is changed to **ci**, to avoid using the same pronoun twice.

Una persona **si** diverte in Italia.	*A person enjoys himself/herself in Italy.*
Ci si diverte in Italia.	*One enjoys oneself in Italy.*
Ci si annoia spesso al cinema oggigiorno.	*One gets bored often at the movies nowadays.*

A. *Rewrite each sentence in its active or passive form, as required.*

1. Mia sorella non ha mangiato la pizza ieri.

   _____

2. Gli spaghetti sono mangiati solo da mio fratello.

   _____

3. Alessandro mangia sempre le patate a cena.

   _____

4. Quel libro è letto da tutti.

   _____

5. Quella donna comprerà la macchina giapponese.

   _____

6. Quell'e-mail fu scritta dal mio amico tempo fa.

   _____

7. Maria ha comprato quella giacca.

   _____

8. Quella casa è stata comprata dai miei genitori.

   _____

9. Gli studenti studieranno quella lezione per domani.

   _____

B. *How do you say the following in Italian? (Note:* **negozio** = *store.)*

1. The class began at nine.

   _____

2. Stores are open at this hour.

   _____

3. One drinks that coffee only in Italy.

   _____

4. One eats those potatoes only in Italy.

   _____

5. One saw that thing only in Italy.

   _____

6. One is happy in Italy.

_____

7. One always enjoys oneself in Italy.

_____

Other topics

Fare

The verb **fare** can be used in causative constructions (*to have someone do something*). The form of **fare** is followed by a verb in the infinitive, and the preposition **a** precedes the person who is being made to do something.

Sara **fa lavare** i piatti **a suo fratello**.	*Sarah has her brother wash the dishes.*
Sara li **fa lavare a lui**.	*Sarah has him wash them.*

In the present conditional, the modal verbs (**potere**, **volere**, **dovere**) are translated in English as *could*, *would*, and *should*, and in the past conditional as *could have*, *would have*, and *should have*.

Lo **potrei** fare.	*I could do it.*
Lo **avrei potuto** fare.	*I could have done it.*
Lo **vorrei** fare	*I would want/like to do it.*
Lo **avrei voluto** fare.	*I would have wanted/liked to do it.*
Lo **dovrei** fare.	*I should do it.*
Lo **avrei dovuto** fare.	*I should have done it.*

Note that a modal is followed directly by an infinitive. As we have seen in previous units, some verbs are followed by the preposition **a** before an infinitive.

Cominciano **a capire**.	*They are starting to understand.*
Devo imparare **a usare** Internet.	*I must learn how to use the Internet.*

Others are followed instead by **di**.

Finiranno **di lavorare** alle sei.	*They will finish working at six o'clock.*
Cercheremo **di rientrare** presto.	*We will try to get back home early.*

Others still are not followed by any preposition.

Desiderano **andare** in Italia.	*They want to go to Italy.*
Preferisco **rimanere** a casa stasera.	*I prefer staying home tonight.*

The only sure way to learn which preposition (if any) is used after a certain verb is to consult a good dictionary!

To know: sapere and conoscere

The main uses and features of the verbs **sapere** and **conoscere** can be summarized as follows.

    Sapere is used:

- To indicate that you or others *know something* (*a fact* or *piece of information*)

Marco **sa** il tuo indirizzo.	*Mark knows your address.*
Io non **so** il tuo nome.	*I don't know your name.*

- To indicate that you or others *know that . . .*

So che lui è felice.	*I know that he is happy.*
Loro non **sanno** che io sono qui.	*They do not know that I am here.*

- To indicate that you or others *know how to do something*

Maria **sa suonare** il pianoforte.	*Mary knows how to play the piano.*
Io non **so parlare** il francese.	*I do not know how to speak French.*

    Conoscere is used:

- To indicate that you or others *know someone*

Claudia, **conosci** un buon medico?	*Claudia, do you know a good doctor?*
Noi non **conosciamo** tuo zio.	*We do not know your uncle.*

- To indicate that you or others *are familiar with something* (*a place*, etc.):

Conosci Milano?	*Are you familiar with Milan?*
Conosco un buon ristorante qui vicino.	*I know a good restaurant near here.*

ESERCIZIO 20·3

    A. *Choose the appropriate verb to complete each sentence.*

1. Mio cugino _____ parlare francese molto bene.

    a. sa   b. conosce

2. Io non _____ tanta gente qui.

    a. so   b. conosco

3. Signor Verdi, Lei _____ dov'è via Nazionale?

    a. sa   b. conosce

4. Noi _____ un buon ristorante in Piazza della Repubblica.

    a. sappiamo   b. conosciamo

5. I tuoi amici non _____ il mio indirizzo di casa.

    a. sanno   b. conoscono

6. Tu _____ mio fratello?

    a. sai   b. conosci

7. Chi _____ la città di Napoli?

    a. sa   b. conosce

8. Io non _____ nessuno in questa città.

    a. so   b. conosco

B. *How do you say the following in Italian?*

1. Mary has her sister wash the dishes.

    _____

2. Mary has her wash them.

    _____

3. I could do it, but I won't do it.

    _____

4. They are starting to speak Italian well.

    _____

5. Mark, you must learn how to use the Internet.

    _____

6. They always finish working at six o'clock.

    _____

7. We will try to get back home early.

    _____

8. They have always wanted to go to Italy.

    _____

C. *Choose the correct form of the verb to complete each sentence.*

1. Maria, ti _____ quel film?

    a. è piaciuto   b. è piaciuta

2. Professoressa Verdi, io Le _____?

    a. piace   b. piaccio

3. A mio fratello non _____ quel film.

    a. piacerà   b. piaceranno

4. A mia sorella non _____ quegli spaghetti.

    a. piacerà   b. piaceranno

5. Da bambini, ci _____ andare spesso in Italia.

    a. piaceva   b. piacevano

6. Loro _____ un buon ristorante in centro.

    a. sanno   b. conoscono

7. Io non _____ il tuo indirizzo di casa.

    a. so   b. conosco

8. Tu _____ mia sorella?

    a. sai   b. conosci

D. *How do you say the following in Italian?*

1. I could have done it earlier.

   _____

2. I would want to do it, but I can't.

   _____

3. I would have wanted to do it.

   _____

4. I should do it.

   _____

5. I should have done it.

   _____

6. My sister had me wash the dishes.

   _____

7. I wanted to go out tonight, but I can't because I have to study.

   _____

8. One can do many interesting things in Italy.

   _____

Grammar in culture

Piacere represents a different perspective on *liking*. In a way, it is a kind of passive: In Italian, something is pleasing to someone.

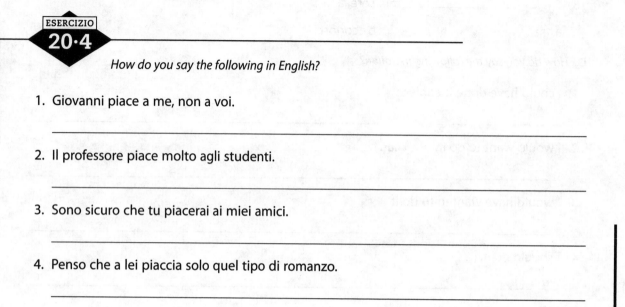

ESERCIZIO
20·4

How do you say the following in English?

1. Giovanni piace a me, non a voi.

   _____

2. Il professore piace molto agli studenti.

   _____

3. Sono sicuro che tu piacerai ai miei amici.

   _____

4. Penso che a lei piaccia solo quel tipo di romanzo.

   _____

Irregular verb tables

The following verbs are irregular in one or more tenses as shown. Verbs conjugated with **essere** in compound tenses are indicated by a notation in parentheses.

andare (essere)   *to go*

	PRESENT INDICATIVE	FUTURE	IMPERATIVE	CONDITIONAL	PRESENT SUBJUNCTIVE
IO	vado	andrò	—	andrei	vada
TU	vai	andrai	va'	andresti	vada
LUI/LEI	va	andrà	—	andrebbe	vada
LEI	va	andrà	vada	andrebbe	vada
NOI	andiamo	andremo	andiamo	andremmo	andiamo
VOI	andate	andrete	andate	andreste	andiate
LORO; LORO	vanno	andranno	vadano	andrebbero	vadano

aprire   *to open*
Past participle: aperto

avere   *to have*

	PRESENT INDICATIVE	PAST ABSOLUTE	FUTURE	IMPERATIVE	CONDITIONAL	PRESENT SUBJUNCTIVE
IO	ho	ebbi	avrò	—	avrei	abbia
TU	hai	avesti	avrai	abbi	avresti	abbia
LUI/LEI	ha	ebbe	avrà	—	avrebbe	abbia
LEI	ha	ebbe	avrà	abbia	avrebbe	abbia
NOI	abbiamo	avemmo	avremo	abbiamo	avremmo	abbiamo
VOI	avete	aveste	avrete	abbiate	avreste	abbiate
LORO; LORO	hanno	ebbero	avranno	abbiano	avrebbero	abbiano

bere *to drink*
Past participle: bevuto

	PRESENT INDICATIVE	IMPERFECT	PAST ABSOLUTE	FUTURE	IMPERATIVE	CONDITIONAL	PRESENT SUBJUNCTIVE	IMPERFECT SUBJUNCTIVE
IO	bevo	bevevo	bevvi (bevetti)	berrò	—	berrei	beva	
TU	bevi	bevevi	bevesti	berrai	bevi	berresti	beva	
LUI/LEI	beve	beveva	bevve (bevette)	berrà	—	berrebbe	beva	
LEI	beve	beveva	bevve (bevette)	berrà	beva	berrebbe	beva	
NOI	beviamo	bevevamo	bevemmo	berremo	beviamo	berremmo	beviamo	
VOI	bevete	bevevate	beveste	berrete	bevete	berreste	beviate	
LORO; LORO	bevono	bevevano	bevvero (bevettero)	berranno	bevano	berrebbero	bevano	

Gerund: bevendo

cadere (essere) *to fall*

	PRESENT INDICATIVE	IMPERFECT	PAST ABSOLUTE	FUTURE	IMPERATIVE	CONDITIONAL	PRESENT SUBJUNCTIVE	IMPERFECT SUBJUNCTIVE
IO			caddi	cadrò		cadrei	cada	
TU			cadesti	cadrai		cadresti	cada	
LUI/LEI			cadde	cadrà		cadrebbe	cada	
LEI			cadde	cadrà		cadrebbe	cada	
NOI			cademmo	cadremo		cadremmo	cadiamo	
VOI			cadeste	cadrete		cadreste	cadiate	
LORO; LORO			caddero	cadranno		cadrebbero	cadano	

chiedere *to ask for*
Past participle: chiesto

	PRESENT INDICATIVE	IMPERFECT	PAST ABSOLUTE	FUTURE	IMPERATIVE	CONDITIONAL	PRESENT SUBJUNCTIVE	IMPERFECT SUBJUNCTIVE
IO			chiesi					
TU			chiedesti					
LUI/LEI			chiese					
LEI			chiese					
NOI			chiedemmo					
VOI			chiedeste					
LORO; LORO			chiesero					

chiudere *to close*
Past participle: chiuso

	PRESENT INDICATIVE	IMPERFECT	PAST ABSOLUTE	FUTURE	IMPERATIVE	CONDITIONAL	PRESENT SUBJUNCTIVE	IMPERFECT SUBJUNCTIVE
IO			chiusi					
TU			chiudesti					
LUI/LEI			chiuse					
LEI			chiuse					
NOI			chiudemmo					
VOI			chiudeste					
LORO; LORO			chiusero					

conoscere *to know*

	PRESENT INDICATIVE	IMPERFECT	PAST ABSOLUTE	FUTURE	IMPERATIVE	CONDITIONAL	PRESENT SUBJUNCTIVE	IMPERFECT SUBJUNCTIVE
IO			conobbi					
TU			conoscesti					
LUI/LEI			conobbe					
LEI			conobbe					
NOI			conoscemmo					
VOI			conosceste					
LORO; LORO			conobbero					

dare *to give*
Past participle: dato

	PRESENT INDICIATIVE	IMPERFECT	PAST ABSOLUTE	FUTURE	IMPERATIVE	CONDITIONAL	PRESENT SUBJUNCTIVE	IMPERFECT SUBJUNCTIVE
IO	do	davo	diedi	darò	—		dia	dessi
TU	dai	davi	desti	darai	da'		dia	dessi
LUI/LEI	dà	dava	diede	darà	—		dia	desse
LEI	dà	dava	diede	darà	dia		dia	desse
NOI	diamo	davamo	demmo	daremo	diamo		diamo	dessimo
VOI	date	davate	deste	darete	date		diate	deste
LORO; LORO	danno	davano	diedero	daranno	diano		diano	dessero

Gerund: dando

decidere *to decide*
Past participle: deciso

	PRESENT INDICATIVE	IMPERFECT	PAST ABSOLUTE	FUTURE	IMPERATIVE	CONDITIONAL	PRESENT SUBJUNCTIVE	IMPERFECT SUBJUNCTIVE
IO			decisi					
TU			decidesti					
LUI/LEI			decise					
LEI			decise					
NOI			decidemmo					
VOI			decideste					
LORO; LORO			decisero					

dire *to say, tell*
Past participle: detto

	PRESENT INDICATIVE	IMPERFECT	PAST ABSOLUTE	FUTURE	IMPERATIVE	CONDITIONAL	PRESENT SUBJUNCTIVE	IMPERFECT SUBJUNCTIVE
IO	dico	dicevo	dissi	dirò	—	direi	dica	dicessi
TU	dici	dicevi	dicesti	dirai	di'	diresti	dica	dicessi
LUI/LEI	dice	diceva	disse	dirà	—	direbbe	dica	dicesse
LEI	dice	diceva	disse	dirà	dica	direbbe	dica	dicesse
NOI	diciamo	dicevamo	dicemmo	diremo	diciamo	diremmo	diciamo	dicessimo
VOI	dite	dicevate	diceste	direte	dite	direste	diciate	diceste
LORO; LORO	dicono	dicevano	dissero	diranno	dicano	direbbero	dicano	dicessero

Gerund: dicendo

dovere *to have to*

	PRESENT INDICATIVE	IMPERFECT	PAST ABSOLUTE	FUTURE	IMPERATIVE	CONDITIONAL	PRESENT SUBJUNCTIVE	IMPERFECT SUBJUNCTIVE
IO	devo			dovrò		dovrei	deva (debba)	
TU	devi			dovrai		dovresti	deva (debba)	
LUI/LEI	deve			dovrà		dovrebbe	deva (debba)	
LEI	deve			dovrà		dovrebbe	deva (debba)	
NOI	dobbiamo			dovremo		dovremmo	dobbiamo	
VOI	dovete			dovrete		dovreste	dobbiate	
LORO; LORO	devono			dovranno		dovrebbero	devano (debbano)	

essere (essere) *to be*
Past participle: stato

	PRESENT INDICATIVE	IMPERFECT	PAST ABSOLUTE	FUTURE	IMPERATIVE	CONDITIONAL	PRESENT SUBJUNCTIVE	IMPERFECT SUBJUNCTIVE
IO	sono	ero	fui	sarò	—	sarei	sia	fossi
TU	sei	eri	fosti	sarai	sii	saresti	sia	fossi
LUI/LEI	è	era	fu	sarà	—	sarebbe	sia	fosse
LEI	è	era	fu	sarà	sia	sarebbe	sia	fosse
NOI	siamo	eravamo	fummo	saremo	siamo	saremmo	siamo	fossimo
VOI	siete	eravate	foste	sarete	siate	sareste	siate	foste
LORO; LORO	sono	erano	furono	saranno	siano	sarebbero	siano	fossero

fare *to do, make*
Past participle: fatto

	PRESENT INDICATIVE	IMPERFECT	PAST ABSOLUTE	FUTURE	IMPERATIVE	CONDITIONAL	PRESENT SUBJUNCTIVE	IMPERFECT SUBJUNCTIVE
IO	faccio	facevo	feci	farò	—	farei	faccia	facessi
TU	fai	facevi	facesti	farai	fa'	faresti	faccia	facessi
LUI/LEI	fa	faceva	fece	farà	—	farebbe	faccia	facesse
LEI	fa	faceva	fece	farà	faccia	farebbe	faccia	facesse
NOI	facciamo	facevamo	facemmo	faremo	facciamo	faremmo	facciamo	facessimo
VOI	fate	facevate	faceste	farete	fate	fareste	facciate	faceste
LORO; LORO	fanno	facevano	fecero	faranno	facciano	farebbero	facciano	facessero

Gerund: facendo

leggere *to read*
Past participle: letto

	PRESENT INDICATIVE	IMPERFECT	PAST ABSOLUTE	FUTURE	IMPERATIVE	CONDITIONAL	PRESENT SUBJUNCTIVE	IMPERFECT SUBJUNCTIVE
IO			lessi					
TU			leggesti					
LUI/LEI			lesse					
LEI			lesse					
NOI			leggemmo					
VOI			leggeste					
LORO; LORO			lessero					

mettere *to put*
Past participle: messo

	PRESENT INDICATIVE	IMPERFECT	PAST ABSOLUTE	FUTURE	IMPERATIVE	CONDITIONAL	PRESENT SUBJUNCTIVE	IMPERFECT SUBJUNCTIVE
IO			misi					
TU			mettesti					
LUI/LEI			mise					
LEI			mise					
NOI			mettemmo					
VOI			metteste					
LORO/LORO			misero					

nascere (essere) *to be born*
Past participle: nato

	PRESENT INDICATIVE	IMPERFECT	PAST ABSOLUTE	FUTURE	IMPERATIVE	CONDITIONAL	PRESENT SUBJUNCTIVE	IMPERFECT SUBJUNCTIVE
IO			nacqui					
TU			nascesti					
LUI/LEI			nacque					
LEI			nacque					
NOI			nascemmo					
VIO			nasceste					
LORO; LORO			nacquero					

perdere *to lose*
Past participle: perso

	PRESENT INDICATIVE	IMPERFECT	PAST ABSOLUTE	FUTURE	IMPERATIVE	CONDITIONAL	PRESENT SUBJUNCTIVE	IMPERFECT SUBJUNCTIVE
IO			persi					
TU			perdesti					
LUI/LEI			perse					
LEI			perse					
NOI			perdemmo					
VOI			perdeste					
LORO; LORO			persero					

piacere (essere) *to like, be pleasing to*
Past participle: piaciuto

	PRESENT INDICATIVE	IMPERFECT	PAST ABSOLUTE	FUTURE	IMPERATIVE	CONDITIONAL	PRESENT SUBJUNCTIVE	IMPERFECT SUBJUNCTIVE
IO	piaccio		piacqui				piaccia	
TU	piaci		piacesti				piaccia	
LUI/LEI	piace		piacque				piaccia	
LEI	piace		piacque				piaccia	
NOI	piacciamo		piacemmo				piacciamo	
VOI	piacete		piaceste				piacciate	
LORO; LORO	piacciono		piacquero				piacciano	

potere *to be able to*

	PRESENT INDICATIVE	IMPERFECT	PAST ABSOLUTE	FUTURE	IMPERATIVE	CONDITIONAL	PRESENT SUBJUNCTIVE	IMPERFECT SUBJUNCTIVE
IO	posso			potrò		potrei	possa	
TU	puoi			potrai		potresti	possa	
LUI/LEI	può			potrà		potrebbe	possa	
LEI	può			potrà		potrebbe	possa	
NOI	possiamo			potremo		potremmo	possiamo	
VOI	potete			potrete		potreste	possiate	
LORO; LORO	possono			potranno		potrebbero	possano	

prendere *to take*
Past participle: preso

	PRESENT INDICATIVE	IMPERFECT	PAST ABSOLUTE	FUTURE	IMPERATIVE	CONDITIONAL	PRESENT SUBJUNCTIVE	IMPERFECT SUBJUNCTIVE
IO			presi					
TU			prendesti					
LUI/LEI			prese					
LEI			prese					
NOI			prendemmo					
VOI			prendeste					
LORO; LORO			presero					

salire (essere) *to go up*

	PRESENT INDICATIVE	IMPERFECT	PAST ABSOLUTE	FUTURE	IMPERATIVE	CONDITIONAL	PRESENT SUBJUNCTIVE	IMPERFECT SUBJUNCTIVE
IO	salgo				—		salga	
TU	sali				sali		salga	
LUI/LEI	sale				—		salga	
LEI	sale				salga		salga	
NOI	saliamo				saliamo		saliamo	
VOI	salite				salite		saliate	
LORO; LORO	salgano				salgono		salgano	

sapere *to know*

	PRESENT INDICATIVE	IMPERFECT	PAST ABSOLUTE	FUTURE	IMPERATIVE	CONDITIONAL	PRESENT SUBJUNCTIVE	IMPERFECT SUBJUNCTIVE
IO	so		seppi	saprò	—	saprei	sappia	
TU	sai		sapesti	saprai	sappi	sapresti	sappia	
LUI/LEI	sa		seppe	saprà	—	saprebbe	sappia	
LEI	sa		seppe	saprà	sappia	saprebbe	sappia	
NOI	sappiamo		sapemmo	sapremo	sappiamo	sapremmo	sappiamo	
VOI	sapete		sapeste	saprete	sappiate	sapreste	sappiate	
LORO; LORO	sanno		seppero	sapranno	sappiano	saprebbero	sappiano	

scegliere *to choose, select*
Past participle: scelto

	PRESENT INDICATIVE	IMPERFECT	PAST ABSOLUTE	FUTURE	IMPERATIVE	CONDITIONAL	PRESENT SUBJUNCTIVE	IMPERFECT SUBJUNCTIVE
IO	scelgo		scelsi		—		scelga	
TU	scegli		scegliesti		scegli		scelga	
LUI/LEI	sceglie		scelse		—		scelga	
LEI	sceglie		scelse		scelga		scelga	
NOI	scegliamo		scegliemmo		scegliamo		scegliamo	
VOI	scegliete		sceglieste		scegliete		scegliate	
LORO; LORO	scelgono		scelsero		scelgano		scelgano	

scendere *to descend, go down*
Past participle: sceso

	PRESENT INDICATIVE	IMPERFECT	PAST ABSOLUTE	FUTURE	IMPERATIVE	CONDITIONAL	PRESENT SUBJUNCTIVE	IMPERFECT SUBJUNCTIVE
IO			scesi					
TU			scendesti					
LUI/LEI			scese					
LEI			scese					
NOI			scendemmo					
VOI			scendeste					
LORO; LORO			scesero					

scrivere *to write*
Past participle: scritto

	PRESENT INDICATIVE	IMPERFECT	PAST ABSOLUTE	FUTURE	IMPERATIVE	CONDITIONAL	PRESENT SUBJUNCTIVE	IMPERFECT SUBJUNCTIVE
IO			scrissi					
TU			scrivesti					
LUI/LEI			scrisse					
LEI			scrisse					
NOI			scrivemmo					
VOI			scriveste					
LORO; LORO			scrissero					

stare (essere) *to stay*
Past participle: stato

	PRESENT INDICATIVE	IMPERFECT	PAST ABSOLUTE	FUTURE	IMPERATIVE	CONDITIONAL	PRESENT SUBJUNCTIVE	IMPERFECT SUBJUNCTIVE
IO	sto	stavo	stetti	starò	—	starei	stia	stessi
TU	stai	stavi	stesti	starai	sta'	staresti	stia	stessi
LUI/LEI	sta	stava	stette	starà	—	starebbe	stia	stesse
LEI	sta	stava	stette	starà	stia	starebbe	stia	stesse
NOI	stiamo	stavamo	stemmo	staremo	stiamo	staremmo	stiamo	stessimo
VOI	state	stavate	steste	starete	state	stareste	stiate	steste
LORO; LORO	stanno	stavano	stettero	staranno	stiano	starebbero	stiano	stessero

Gerund: stando

tenere *to hold, keep*

	PRESENT INDICATIVE	IMPERFECT	PAST ABSOLUTE	FUTURE	IMPERATIVE	CONDITIONAL	PRESENT SUBJUNCTIVE	IMPERFECT SUBJUNCTIVE
IO	tengo		tenni	terrò	—	terrei	tenga	
TU	tieni		tenesti	terrai	tieni	terresti	tenga	
LUI/LEI	tiene		tenne	terrà	—	terrebbe	tenga	
LEI	tiene		tenne	terrà	tenga	terrebbe	tenga	
NOI	teniamo		tenemmo	terremo	teniamo	terremmo	teniamo	
VOI	tenete		teneste	terrete	tenete	terreste	teniate	
LORO; LORO	tengono		tennero	terranno	tengano	terrebbero	tengano	

uscire (essere) *to go out*

	PRESENT INDICATIVE	IMPERFECT	PAST ABSOLUTE	FUTURE	IMPERATIVE	CONDITIONAL	PRESENT SUBJUNCTIVE	IMPERFECT SUBJUNCTIVE
IO	esco						esca	
TU	esci				esci		esca	
LUI/LEI	esce				—		esca	
LEI	esce				esca		esca	
NOI	usciamo				usciamo		usciamo	
VOI	uscite				uscite		usciate	
LORO; LORO	escono				escano		escano	

vedere *to see*
Past participle: visto

	PRESENT INDICATIVE	IMPERFECT	PAST ABSOLUTE	FUTURE	IMPERATIVE	CONDITIONAL	PRESENT SUBJUNCTIVE	IMPERFECT SUBJUNCTIVE
IO			vidi	vedrò		vedrei		
TU			vedesti	vedrai		vedresti		
LUI/LEI			vide	vedrà		vedrebbe		
LEI			vide	vedrà		vedrebbe		
NOI			vedemmo	vedremo		vedremmo		
VOI			vedeste	vedrete		vedreste		
LORO; LORO			videro	vedranno		vedrebbero		

venire (essere)   *to come*
Past participle: venuto

	PRESENT INDICATIVE	IMPERFECT	PAST ABSOLUTE	FUTURE	IMPERATIVE	CONDITIONAL	PRESENT SUBJUNCTIVE	IMPERFECT SUBJUNCTIVE
IO	vengo		venni	verrò	—	verrei	venga	
TU	vieni		venisti	verrai	vieni	verresti	venga	
LUI/LEI	viene		venne	verrà	—	verrebbe	venga	
LEI	viene		venne	verrà	venga	verrebbe	venga	
NOI	veniamo		venimmo	verremo	veniamo	verremmo	veniamo	
VOI	venite		veniste	verrete	venite	verreste	veniate	
LORO; LORO	vengono		vennero	verranno	vengano	verrebbero	vengano	

vincere   *to win*
Past participle: vinto

	PRESENT INDICATIVE	IMPERFECT	PAST ABSOLUTE	FUTURE	IMPERATIVE	CONDITIONAL	PRESENT SUBJUNCTIVE	IMPERFECT SUBJUNCTIVE
IO			vinsi					
TU			vincesti					
LUI/LEI			vinse					
LEI			vinse					
NOI			vincemmo					
VOI			vinceste					
LORO; LORO			vinsero					

volere   *to want*

	PRESENT INDICATIVE	IMPERFECT	PAST ABSOLUTE	FUTURE	IMPERATIVE	CONDITIONAL	PRESENT SUBJUNCTIVE	IMPERFECT SUBJUNCTIVE
IO	voglio		volli	vorrò		vorrei	voglia	
TU	vuoi		volesti	vorrai		vorresti	voglia	
LUI/LEI	vuole		volle	vorrà		vorrebbe	voglia	
LEI	vuole		volle	vorrà		vorrebbe	voglia	
NOI	vogliamo		volemmo	vorremo		vorremmo	vogliamo	
VOI	volete		voleste	vorrete		vorreste	vogliate	
LORO; LORO	vogliono		vollero	vorranno		vorrebbero	vogliano	

Italian-English glossary

A

a to, at, in
a meno che unless
abbastanza enough
acqua water
adesso now
affare (*m.*) business transaction
affatto not at all
affinché so that
agosto August
albero tree
alcuni (*m.*) / **alcune** (*f.*) some, several
allegare to attach
allora then
alto tall
altro other
alzarsi to get up
americano American
amico (*m.*) / **amica** (*f.*) friend
analisi (*f.*) analysis
anche also, too
ancora again, still, yet
andare (essere) to go
andare via to go away
anno year
annoiarsi to become bored
antropologo anthropologist
anzi as a matter of fact
appena just, barely
aprile April
aprire to open
arancia (noun) orange
aranciata orange drink
arancio orange tree
arancione (adjective) orange
architetto (*m./f.*) architect
arcobaleno rainbow
arrabbiarsi to become angry
arrivare (essere) to arrive
ascoltare to listen (to)
asino donkey
aspettare to wait (for)

assai quite, enough
attore (*m.*) / **attrice** (*f.*) actor/actress
autobus (*m.*) bus
automobile (*f.*) automobile
autore (*m.*) / **autrice** (*f.*) author
avere to have
avvocato (*m./f.*) lawyer
azzurro blue

B

babbo dad
baciare to kiss
bacio kiss
baffi (*m., pl.*) mustache
bagno bathroom
bambino child
banca bank
basso short
bello beautiful, handsome, nice
benché although
bene well
benevolo benevolent
bere to drink
bianco white
bibita soft drink
bicchiere (*m.*) glass
biglietto ticket
biologia biology
biologo biologist
biondo blond
bisognare to be necessary
blu dark blue
borsa purse
bottiglia bottle
braccio arm
bravo good, good at something
brindisi (*m.*) drinking toast
brutto ugly
bue (*m.*) ox
bugia lie
Buon pomeriggio! Good afternoon!
Buonanotte! Good night!

Buonasera! Good evening!
Buongiorno! Good morning! Good day!
buono good

C

cacciavite (*m.*) screwdriver
cadere (essere) to fall
caffè (*m.*) coffee
caffellatte (*m.*) coffee with milk (a "latte")
calcio soccer
caldo hot
camera bedroom
cameriere (*m.*) / **cameriera** (*f.*) waiter/waitress
camicia shirt
cane (*m.*) dog
cantante (*m./f.*) singer
cantare to sing
capelli (*m., pl.*) hair (on the head)
capire (*type 2*) to understand
capoluogo capital of a region
caporeparto head of a department
cappotto coat
cappuccino cappuccino
carne (*f.*) meat
caro dear
carota carrot
casa house
cassaforte (*f.*) safe (for valuables)
cattivo bad
celeste sky blue
cellulare (*m.*) cell phone
centimetro centimeter
centrale central
centro downtown, center of town
cercare to look, search for
certo certain
che what, that, which, who
che cosa what
chi who, whoever
chiamare to call
chiamarsi to be called, named
chiave (*f.*) key
chiedere to ask
chimica chemistry
chiudere to close
chiunque whoever
ciao hi, bye
ciliegia cherry
ciliegio cherry tree
cinematografo (il cinema) movie theater
città (*f.*) city
clacson (*m.*) car horn
cognata sister-in-law
cognato brother-in-law
cognome (*m.*) surname, family name
coltello knife
come as, like, how

come se as if
cominciare to begin
compito task, homework assignment
comprare to buy
computer (*m.*) computer
comune common
con with
conoscere to know, be familiar with
conto bill, check
copione (*m.*) script
cordone (*m.*) rope
corpo body
corretto correct; coffee with a drop of alcohol
cosa thing
così as, so
costare (essere) to cost
costoso costly, expensive
cravatta necktie
credere to believe
crisi (*f.*) crisis
cucchiaino teaspoon
cucchiaio spoon
cucina kitchen
cugino (*m.*) / **cugina** (*f.*) cousin
cui which, whom

D

da from, at
dare to give
data date
decidere to decide
decimo tenth
dentista (*m./f.*) dentist
desiderare to desire
destra right (direction)
di of, about
di nuovo again, anew
di solito usually
diagramma (*m.*) diagram
dicembre December
difficile difficult
dimenticarsi to forget
dire to say, tell
dito finger
diventare (essere) to become
divertirsi to enjoy oneself, have fun
dolce sweet
dollaro dollar
domani tomorrow
domenica Sunday
donna woman
dopo after
doppio double
dormire to sleep
dottore (*m.*) / **dottoressa** (*f.*) doctor, university graduate
dove where
dovere to have to

dovunque wherever
dozzina dozen
dramma (*m.*) drama
dubitare to doubt
durare (**essere**) to last

E

e and
ecco here is, here are, there is, there are
egli he
elefante (*m.*) / **elefantessa** (*f.*) elephant
elegante elegant
ella she
enorme enormous
entrare (**essere**) to enter
esame (*m.*) exam
espresso espresso coffee
esserci to be there
essere (**essere**) to be
esso it
euro (*inv.*) euro

F

fa ago
faccia face
facile easy
fagiolino string bean
fagiolo bean
fame (*f.*) hunger
fare to do, make
farmacia pharmacy
farmacista (*m./f.*) pharmacist
favore (*m.*) favor
febbraio February
felice happy
ferrovia railroad
festa party
fico fig, fig tree
figlia daughter
figlio son
film (*m.*) movie, film
finestra window
finire (*type 2*) to finish
finora until now
fisica physics
forbici (*f., pl.*) scissors
forchetta fork
forse maybe
fotografia photograph, **foto** photo
fra between, among
francese (*m./f.*) French
francobollo postage stamp
fratello brother
freddo cold
frutta fruit

G

gallo rooster
gatto cat
gelato ice cream
genero son-in-law
genitore (*m.*) parent
gennaio January
gente (*f.*) people
geografia geography
geometra (*m./f.*) draftsperson
già already
giacca jacket
giallo yellow
ginocchio knee
giocare to play (a sport)
gioco game
giornale (*m.*) newspaper
giorno day
giovane young
giovedì (*m.*) Thursday
gioventù (*f.*) youth
giugno June
giusto right (correctness), just
gnocco dumpling
gonna skirt
grande big, large, important, great
grasso fat
grazie thank you
greco Greek
grigio gray
guardare to watch, look at
guardia guard
guarire (*type 2*) to get better, heal, cure
guidare to drive

I

ieri yesterday
immaginare to imagine
imparare to learn
impermeabile (*m.*) raincoat
importante important
in in
in fretta in a hurry
in punto on the dot
incontrare to meet, run into
indicare to indicate
indirizzo address
infermiere (*m.*) / **infermiera** (*f.*) nurse
inglese (*m./f.*) English
insalata salad
insieme together
intelligente intelligent
interessante interesting
invece instead
inventare to invent
io I
ipotesi (*f.*) hypothesis

isola island
italiano Italian

L

là over there
labbro lip
lago lake
lamentarsi to complain
latte (*m.*) milk
lavarsi to wash oneself
lavorare to work
leggere to read
leggero light
lei she
Lei (*pol.*, *sing.*) you
lento slow
leone (*m.*) / **leonessa** (*f.*) the lion
lì there
libretto opera libretto, bankbook
libricino little book
libro book
limonata lemonade
limone (*m.*) lemon, lemon tree
lingua language
lontano far
Loro (*pol.*, *pl.*) your
loro they, their
luglio July
lui he
lunedì (*m.*) Monday
lungo long
luogo place

M

ma but
macchiato coffee with a drop of milk
macchina car
madre (*f.*) mother
maggio May
maggiore bigger, greater, major, older
magro skinny
mai ever, never
mail (*f.*) e-mail
mal di denti toothache
mal di gola sore throat
mal di stomaco stomachache
mal di testa headache
male bad(ly)
mamma mom
mandare to send
mandarino mandarin, mandarin tree
mangiare to eat
mano (*f.*) hand
marrone brown
martedì (*m.*) Tuesday
marzo March
matematica math

mattina morning
mattone (*m.*) brick
medico doctor
mela apple
melo apple tree
meno less, minus
mentre while
menù (*m.*) menu
mercoledì (*m.*) Wednesday
meridionale southern
mese (*m.*) month
metro meter
mettere to put
mettersi to put on, wear, set about, begin to
mezzanotte (*f.*) midnight
mezzo half
mezzogiorno noon
mica not really/quite
migliore better
milione million
mille thousand
minestra soup
minore smaller, minor
mio my
molto much, a lot
momento moment
monaco monk
motocicletta (**moto**) motorcycle
musica music
musicista (*m.*/*f.*) musician
mutande (*f.*, *pl.*) underwear

N

nascere (**essere**) to be born
Natale (*m.*) Christmas
navigare to navigate, **navigare in Internet** to surf the Internet
nazione (*f.*) nation
né neither, nor
neanche not even
negozio store
nel caso che in the event that
nel frattempo in the meantime
nemmeno not even
neppure not even
nero black
nessuno none, no one
niente nothing
nipote (*m.*/*f.*) grandson/granddaughter, nephew/niece
no no
noi we, us
nome (*m.*) name
non not
non... affatto not at all
nonna grandmother
nonno grandfather
nono ninth

nonostante che despite
nostro our
notte (*f.*) night
novembre November
nulla nothing
nuora daughter-in-law
nuovo new

O

o or
occhiali (*m., pl.*) (eye)glasses
occhio eye
occidentale western
oggi today
oggigiorno nowadays
ogni each, every
opinione (*f.*) opinion
ora hour, time (of day)
orientale eastern
ormai by now
orologio watch
orzo barley
ottavo eighth
ottobre October

P

pace (*f.*) peace
padre (*m.*) father
pagare to pay
paio pair
pane (*m.*) bread
pantaloni (*m., pl.*) pants
papà (*m.*) dad
parecchio several, quite a few
parete (*f.*) wall (partition)
parlare to speak
partire (**essere**) to leave, depart
partita game, match
Pasqua Easter
pasta pasta
patata potato
patente (*f.*) driver's license
pazienza patience
peggiore worse
penna pen
pensare to think
pepe (*m.*) pepper
per for, through
per caso by chance
per favore please
pera pear
perché why, because
perdere to lose
pero pear tree
persona person
pesante heavy
pesca peach

pesce (*m.*) fish
pesco peach tree
piacere (**essere**) to like, be pleasing to
pianeta planet
pianista (*m./f.*) pianist
pianoforte (*m.*) piano
piatto dish
piccolo small, little
piede (*m.*) foot
piovere to rain
pittore (*m.*) / **pittrice** (*f.*) painter
più more, plus, no longer
piuttosto rather
plurale plural
poco little, few
poi after, then
pomeriggio afternoon
pomodoro tomato
popolare popular
porco pig
porta door
portare to bring
portatile (*m.*) laptop
possibile possible
potere to be able to
povero poor
preciso precise
preferire (*type 2*) to prefer
prendere to take
preoccuparsi to worry
prepararsi to prepare oneself
presto early
prima first, before
prima che before
primo first
probabile probable
problema (*m.*) problem
professore (*m.*) / **professoressa** (*f.*) professor
programma (*m.*) program
proprio own, really
prossimo next
psicologo (*m.*) / **psicologa** (*f.*) psychologist
pulire (*type 2*) to clean
purché provided that
purtroppo unfortunately

Q

qua right over here
qualche some
qualcuno someone
quale which
qualsiasi whichever, any
qualunque whichever, any
quando when
quanto how much
quarto fourth
quarto quarter

quasi almost
qui here
quinto fifth

R

radio (*f.*) radio
ragazza girl
ragazzo boy
ragioniere (*m.*) / **ragioniera** (*f.*) accountant (bookkeeper)
ragù (*m.*) meat sauce
raro rare
regione (*f.*) region
regolare regular
ricco rich
rientrare (essere) to get back, return home
riga straight ruler
riso rice
rispondere to answer
ristorante (*m.*) restaurant
ristretto short/strong coffee
riunione (*f.*) meeting
rivista magazine
romanzo novel
rosa pink
rosso red

S

sabato Saturday
sale (*m.*) salt
salire (**essere**) to go up
salotto living room
salvagente (*m.*) life jacket
sapere to know
sbaglio mistake
scarpa shoe
scatola box
scegliere to choose, select
scendere to descend
sciarpa scarf
scienza science
scorso last
scrivere to write
scultore (*m.*) / **scultrice** (*f.*) sculptor
scuola school
se if
sebbene although
secondo second; according to
sedia chair
sembrare (**essere**) to seem
semplice simple
sempre always
sentire to feel, hear
sentirsi to feel
senza without
sera evening
sesto sixth
sete (*f.*) thirst

settembre September
settentrionale northern
settimana week
settimo seventh
sì yes
siciliano Sicilian
sicuro sure
signora lady, woman, Mrs., Ms.
signore (*m.*) gentleman, sir, Mr.
signorina young lady, Miss
simpatico nice, charming
sindaco (*m./f.*) mayor
sinistra left
sistema (*m.*) system
soldi (*m., pl.*) money
solo only
sopra over, on top
soprano soprano
sorella sister
sotto under, below
spagnolo Spanish
speciale special
sperare to hope
spesso often
spia spy
sport (*m.*) sport
sposarsi to marry, get married
stamani this morning
stanco tired
stanza room
stare (**essere**) to stay
stare zitto to be quiet
stasera tonight, this evening
stella star
stesso the same
stivale (*m.*) boot
storia history
studente (*m.*) / **studentessa** (*f.*) student
studiare to study
su on
subito right away
succo di frutta fruit juice
Suo (*pol., sing.*) your
suo his, her, its
suocera mother-in-law
suocero father-in-law
suonare to play (an instrument)
svegliarsi to wake up

T

tanto much, a lot
tardi late
tassì (*m.*) taxi
tavola table
tazza cup
tè (*m.*) tea
tedesco German

telefonare to phone
televisione (*f.*) television
tempo time (abstract), weather
tenere to keep, hold
tennis (*m.*) tennis
teologo theologian
teorema (*m.*) theorem
terzo third
tesi (*f.*) thesis
testa head
tornare (**essere**) to return
torta cake
tra between, among
tram (*m.*) streetcar, trolley
triste sad
troppo too much
tu (*fam., sing.*) you
tuo (*fam., sing.*) your
tutto all

U

ultimo last
università (*f.*) university
uomo man
uscire (**essere**) to go out
utile useful
uva grapes

V

va bene OK
vacanza vacation
vaglia (*m.*) money order
valigia suitcase

vecchio old
vedere to see
veloce fast
vendere to sell
venerdì (*m.*) Friday
venire (**essere**) to come
verde green
vergognarsi to be ashamed, be embarrassed
verità truth
vero true
vestirsi to get dressed
vestito dress, suit
vicino near(by)
vincere to win
viola violet, purple
violento violent
virgola comma
virtù (*f.*) virtue
visitare to visit
vivere (**essere**) to live
voi (*fam., pl.*) you
volentieri gladly
volere to want
volta time (occurrence)
vostro (*fam., pl.*) your

Z

zabaione (*m.*) egg custard
zaino backpack
zero zero
zia aunt
zio uncle
zucchero sugar

English-Italian glossary

A

a lot molto
according to secondo
accountant ragioniere (*m.*) / ragioniera (*f.*)
actor/actress attore (*m.*) / attrice (*f.*)
address indirizzo
after dopo, poi
afternoon pomeriggio
again ancora, di nuovo
ago fa
all tutto
almost quasi
already già
also anche
although benché, sebbene
always sempre
American americano
among fra, tra
analysis analisi (*f.*)
and e
answer rispondere
anthropologist antropologo (*m.*) / antropologa (*f.*)
any qualsiasi, qualunque
apple mela
apple tree melo
April aprile
architect architetto (*m./f.*)
arm braccio
arrive arrivare (essere)
as come, così
as a matter of fact anzi
as if come se
ask chiedere
at a, in
attach allegare
August agosto
aunt zia
author autore (*m.*) / autrice (*f.*)
automobile automobile (*f.*)

B

backpack zaino
bad cattivo, male
bank banca
bankbook libretto
barely appena
barley orzo
bathroom bagno
be essere (essere)
be able to potere
be ashamed vergognarsi
be born nascere (essere)
be called chiamarsi
be embarrassed vergognarsi
be familiar with conoscere
be named chiamarsi
be necessary bisognare
be quiet stare zitto
be there esserci
bean fagiolo
beautiful bello
because perché
become diventare (essere)
become angry arrabbiarsi
become bored annoiarsi
bedroom camera
before prima
begin cominciare
believe credere
below sotto
benevolent benevolo
better migliore
between fra, tra
big grande
bigger maggiore
bill conto
biologist biologo
biology biologia
black nero
blond biondo

blue azzurro
body corpo
book libro
boot stivale (*m.*)
bottle bottiglia
box scatola
boy ragazzo
bread pane (*m.*)
brick mattone (*m.*)
bring portare
brother fratello
brother-in-law cognato
brown marrone
bus autobus (*m.*)
business transaction affare (*m.*)
but ma
buy comprare
by di, da
by chance per caso
by now ormai
bye ciao

C

cake torta
call chiamare
capital of a region capoluogo
cappuccino cappuccino
car macchina
car horn clacson (*m.*)
carrot carota
cat gatto
cell phone cellulare (*m.*)
centimeter centimetro
central centrale
certain certo
chair sedia
charming simpatico
chemistry chimica
cherry ciliegia
cherry tree ciliegio
child bambino
choose scegliere
Christmas Natale (*m.*)
city città (*f.*)
clean pulire (*type 2*)
close chiudere
coat cappotto
coffee caffè (*m.*)
coffee with milk caffellatte (*m.*)
cold freddo
come venire (essere)
comma virgola
common comune
complain lamentarsi
computer computer (*m.*)
cost costare (essere)
cousin cugino (*m.*) / cugina (*f.*)

crisis crisi (*f.*)
cup tazza

D

dad babbo, papà (*m.*)
dark blue blu
date data
daughter figlia
daughter-in-law nuora
day giorno
dear caro
December dicembre
decide decidere
dentist dentista (*m./f.*)
descend scendere
desire desiderare
despite nonostante che
diagram diagramma (*m.*)
difficult difficile
dish piatto
do fare
doctor dottore (*m.*) / dottoressa (*f.*), medico
dog cane (*m.*)
dollar dollaro
donkey asino
door porta
double doppio
doubt dubitare
downtown centro
dozen dozzina
draftsperson geometra (*m./f.*)
drama dramma (*m.*)
dress vestito
drink bere
drinking toast brindisi (*m.*)
drive guidare
driver's license patente (*f.*)
dumpling gnocco

E

each ogni
early presto
Easter Pasqua
eastern orientale
easy facile
eat mangiare
egg custard zabaione (*m.*)
eighth ottavo
elegant elegante
elephant elefante (*m.*) / elefantessa (*f.*)
e-mail mail (*f.*)
English inglese (*m./f.*)
enjoy oneself divertirsi
enormous enorme
enough abbastanza, assai
enter entrare (essere)
espresso coffee espresso

euro euro (*inv.*)
evening sera
ever mai
every ogni
exam esame (*m.*)
expensive costoso
eye occhio
eyeglasses occhiali (*m., pl.*)

F

face faccia
fall cadere (essere)
far lontano
fast veloce
fat grasso
father padre (*m.*)
father-in-law suocero
favor favore (*m.*)
February febbraio
feel sentirsi
few poco
fifth quinto
fig fico
fig tree fico
finger dito
finish finire (*type 2*)
first primo
fish pesce (*m.*)
foot piede (*m.*)
for per
forget dimenticarsi
fork forchetta
fourth quarto
French francese (*m./f.*)
Friday venerdì (*m.*)
friend amico (*m.*) / amica (*f.*)
from da
fruit frutta
fruit juice succo di frutta

G

game partita, gioco
gentleman signore (*m.*)
geography geografia
German tedesco
get back rientrare (essere)
get better guarire (*type 2*)
get dressed vestirsi
get up alzarsi
girl ragazza
give dare
gladly volentieri
glass bicchiere (*m.*)
glasses (eye) occhiali (*m., pl.*)
go andare (essere)
go away andare via
go out uscire (essere)

go up salire (essere)
good buono; (**at something**) bravo
Good afternoon! Buon pomeriggio!
Good day! Buongiorno! Buona giornata!
Good evening! Buonasera!
Good morning! Buongiorno!
Good night! Buonanotte!
granddaughter nipote (*f.*)
grandfather nonno
grandmother nonna
grandson nipote (*m.*)
grapes uva
gray grigio
great grande
greater maggiore
Greek greco
green verde
guard guardia

H

hair (on the head) capelli (*m., pl.*)
half mezzo
hand mano (*f.*)
handsome bello
happy felice
have avere
have to dovere
he lui, egli
head testa
head of a department caporeparto
headache mal di testa
heal guarire (*type 2*)
hear sentire
heavy pesante
her suo
here qui
here (it is) ecco
hi ciao
his suo
history storia
hold tenere
homework assignment compito
hope sperare
hot caldo
hour ora
house casa
how come
how much quanto
hunger fame (*f.*)
hypothesis ipotesi (*f.*)

I

I io
ice cream gelato
if se
imagine immaginare
important importante

in in
in a hurry in fretta
in the event that nel caso che
in the meantime nel frattempo
indicate indicare
instead invece
intelligent intelligente
interesting interessante
invent inventare
island isola
it esso
Italian italiano
its suo

J

jacket giacca
January gennaio
July luglio
June giugno
just appena

K

keep tenere
key chiave (*f.*)
kiss (*verb*) baciare
kiss (*noun*) bacio
kitchen cucina
knee ginocchio
knife coltello
know conoscere
know sapere

L

lady signora
lake lago
language lingua
laptop portatile (*m.*)
large grande
last (*verb*) durare (essere)
last scorso, ultimo
late tardi
lawyer avvocato
learn imparare
leave partire (essere)
left sinistra
lemon limone (*m.*)
lemon tree limone (*m.*)
lemonade limonata
less meno
lie bugia
life jacket salvagente (*m.*)
light leggero
like come
like (*verb*) piacere (essere)
lion leone (*m.*)/leonessa (*f.*)
lip labbro
listen ascoltare

little poco
little book libricino
live vivere (essere)
living room salotto
long lungo
look at guardare
look for cercare
lose perdere

M

magazine rivista
major maggiore
make fare
man uomo
mandarin mandarino
mandarin tree mandarino
March marzo
marry / get married sposarsi
math matematica
May maggio
maybe forse
mayor sindaco (*m./f.*)
meat carne (*f.*)
meat sauce ragù (*m.*)
meet incontrare
meeting riunione (*f.*)
menu menù (*m.*)
meter metro
midnight mezzanotte (*f.*)
milk latte (*m.*)
million milione
minor minore
minus meno
Miss signorina
mistake sbaglio
mom mamma
moment momento
Monday lunedì (*m.*)
money soldi (*m., pl.*)
money order vaglia (*m.*)
monk monaco
month mese (*m.*)
more più
morning mattina
mother madre (*f.*)
mother-in-law suocera
motorcycle motocicletta (la moto)
movie film (*m.*)
movie theater cinematografo (il cinema)
Mr. signore (*m.*)
Mrs., Ms. signora
much molto, tanto
music musica
musician musicista (*m./f.*)
mustache baffi (*m., pl.*)
my mio

N

name nome (*m.*)
nation nazione (*f.*)
navigate navigare
near(by) vicino
necktie cravatta
neither né
nephew nipote (*m.*)
never mai
new nuovo
newspaper giornale (*m.*)
next prossimo
nice simpatico
niece nipote (*f.*)
night notte (*f.*)
ninth nono
no no
no longer più
no one nessuno
none nessuno
noon mezzogiorno
nor né
northern settentrionale
not non
not at all affatto
not even neanche, nemmeno, neppure
not really/quite mica
nothing niente, nulla
novel romanzo
November novembre
now adesso
nowadays oggigiorno
nurse infermiere (*m.*) / infermiera (*f.*)

O

October ottobre
of di
often spesso
OK va bene
old vecchio
on su
on the dot in punto
on top sopra
only solo
open aprire
opera libretto libretto
opinion opinione (*f.*)
or o
orange (*noun*) arancia
orange (*adjective*) arancione
orange drink aranciata
orange tree arancio
other altro
our nostro
over sopra
over there là
ox bue (*m.*)

P

painter pittore (*m.*) / pittrice (*f.*)
pair paio
pants pantaloni (*m., pl.*)
parent genitore (*m.*)
party festa
pasta pasta
patience pazienza
pay pagare
peace pace (*f.*)
peach pesca
peach tree pesco
pear pera
pear tree pero
pen penna
people gente (*f.*)
pepper pepe (*m.*)
person persona
pharmacist farmacista (*m./f.*)
pharmacy farmacia
phone telefonare
photograph fotografia (la foto)
physics fisica
pianist pianista (*m./f.*)
piano pianoforte (*m.*)
pig porco
pink rosa
place luogo
planet pianeta
play (a sport) giocare, **(an instrument)** suonare
please per favore
plural plurale
plus più
poor povero
popular popolare
possible possibile
postage stamp francobollo
potato patata
precise preciso
prefer preferire (*type 2*)
prepare oneself prepararsi
probable probabile
problem problema (*m.*)
professor professore (*m.*) / professoressa (*f.*)
program programma (*m.*)
provided that purché
psychologist psicologo (*m.*) / psicologa (*f.*)
purple viola
purse borsa
put mettere
put on mettersi

Q

quarter quarto
quite assai

R

radio radio (*f.*)
railroad ferrovia
rain piovere
rainbow arcobaleno
raincoat impermeabile (*m.*)
rare raro
rather piuttosto
read leggere
really proprio
red rosso
region regione (*f.*)
regular regolare
restaurant ristorante (*m.*)
return tornare (essere)
rice riso
rich ricco
right (direction) destra; **(correctness)** giusto
right away subito
right over here qua
room stanza
rooster gallo
rope cordone (*m.*)
run into incontrare

S

sad triste
safe (for valuables) cassaforte (*f.*)
salad insalata
salt sale (*m.*)
same stesso
Saturday sabato
say dire
scarf sciarpa
school scuola
science scienza
scissors forbici (*f., pl.*)
screwdriver cacciavite (*m.*)
script copione (*m.*)
sculptor scultore (*m.*) / scultrice (*f.*)
second secondo
see vedere
seem sembrare (essere)
select scegliere
sell vendere
send mandare
September settembre
seventh settimo
several alcuni (*m.*) / alcune (*f.*)
she lei, ella
shirt camicia
shoe scarpa
short basso
Sicilian siciliano
simple semplice
sing cantare
singer cantante (*m./f.*)

sister sorella
sister-in-law cognata
sixth sesto
skinny magro
skirt gonna
sky blue celeste
sleep dormire
slow lento
small piccolo
smaller minore
so così
so that affinché
soccer calcio
soft drink bibita
some alcuni (*m.*) / alcune (*f.*), qualche
someone qualcuno
son figlio
son-in-law genero
soprano soprano
sore throat mal di gola
soup minestra
southern meridionale
Spanish spagnolo
speak parlare
special speciale
spoon cucchiaio
sport sport (*m.*)
spy spia
star stella
stay stare (essere)
still ancora
stomachache mal di stomaco
store negozio
straight ruler riga
streetcar tram (*m.*)
string bean fagiolino
student studente (*m.*) / studentessa (*f.*)
study studiare
sugar zucchero
suit vestito
suitcase valigia
Sunday domenica
sure sicuro
surf the Internet navigare in Internet
surname cognome (*m.*)
sweet dolce
system sistema (*m.*)

T

table tavola
take prendere
tall alto
task compito
taxi tassì (*m.*)
tea tè (*m.*)
teaspoon cucchiaino
television televisione (*f.*)

tell dire
tennis tennis (*m.*)
tenth decimo
thank you grazie
that che
their loro
then allora, poi
theologian teologo
theorem teorema (*m.*)
there lì
thesis tesi (*f.*)
they loro
thing cosa
think pensare
third terzo
thirst sete (*f.*)
this morning stamani
thousand mille
through per
Thursday giovedì (*m.*)
ticket biglietto
time (**of day**) ora, (**abstract**) tempo, (**occurrence**) volta
tired stanco
to a, in
today oggi
together insieme
tomato pomodoro
tomorrow domani
tonight stasera
too anche
too much troppo
toothache mal di denti
tree albero
trolley car tram (*m.*)
true vero
truth verità
Tuesday martedì (*m.*)

U

ugly brutto
uncle zio
under sotto
understand capire (*type 2*)
underwear mutande (*f., pl.*)
unfortunately purtroppo
university università (*f.*)
university graduate dottore (*m.*) / dottoressa (*f.*)
unless a meno che
until now finora
useful utile
usually di solito

V

vacation vacanza
violent violento
violet viola

virtue virtù (*f.*)
visit visitare

W

wait (**for**) aspettare
waiter/waitress cameriere (*m.*) / cameriera (*f.*)
wake up svegliarsi
wall (**partition**) parete (*f.*)
want volere
wash oneself lavarsi
watch (*verb*) guardare
watch (*noun*) orologio
water acqua
we noi
wear mettersi
weather tempo
Wednesday mercoledì (*m.*)
week settimana
well bene
western occidentale
what che
when quando
where dove
wherever dovunque
which che, cui
whichever qualsiasi, qualunque
while mentre
white bianco
who che, chi
whoever chi, chiunque
why perché
win vincere
window finestra
with con
without senza
woman donna
work lavorare
worry preoccuparsi
worse peggiore
write scrivere

Y

year anno
yellow giallo
yes sì
yesterday ieri
yet ancora
you tu (*fam., sing.*), Lei (*pol., sing.*), voi (*fam., pl.*) Loro (*pol., pl.*)
young giovane
young lady signorina
your tuo (*fam., sing.*), Suo (*pol., sing.*), vostro (*fam., pl.*), Loro (*pol., pl.*)
youth gioventù (*f.*)

Z

zero zero

Answer key

1·1 **A.** 1. zii 2. ragazzo 3. libri 4. gatto 5. figli 6. zia 7. ragazze 8. penna
9. figlie 10. casa 11. cani 12. cellulare 13. padri 14. parete 15. madri
16. nazione 17. notti 18. cosa 19. case 20. anno 21. giorni 22. vestito
23. cravatte 24. donna 25. gonne 26. macchina 27. chiavi 28. cognome
29. giornali 30. nome 31. copioni 32. riunione 33. cordoni 34. mattone

B. 1. A suo nipote piace la matematica. 2. L'amore conquista tutto. 3. Quella donna
ha chiamato mia nipote. 4. Marco è un caro amico. 5. La mia amica vive in
periferia. 6. I miei amici hanno comprato un televisore plasma. 7. L'italiano è una
lingua facile. 8. Lui è italiano, ma lei è americana. 9. Dov'è quella regione?
10. A che ora c'è la riunione?

C. 1. Quei due uomini sono italiani. 2. La gente parla troppo. 3. Sara è siciliana.
4. Alessandro parla francese.

1·2 **A.** 1. americano, americana 2. italiano, italiana 3. amico, amica 4. soprano, soprano
5. guardia, guardia 6. stella, stella 7. spia, spia 8. persona, persona 9. inglese,
inglese 10. francese, francese 11. cantante, cantante 12. infermiere, infermiera

B. 1. il nipote 2. gli americani 3. le italiane 4. la nipote 5. i camerieri 6. le
cameriere 7. il signore 8. la signora

1·3 **A.** 1. luoghi 2. tedeschi 3. antropologi 4. greci 5. amici 6. giochi 7. biologi
8. laghi 9. monaci 10. fichi 11. sindaci 12. porci 13. righe 14. greche
15. banche 16. camicie

B. 1. bacio 2. occhio 3. zio 4. orologio 5. farmacia 6. bugia 7. faccia
8. valigia

1·4 **A.** 1. (lo) zucchero 2. (gli) occhiali 3. (i) baffi 4. (il) latte 5. (l') uva

B. 1. (il) sale e (il) pepe 2. (la) carne, (il) pane e (il) riso 3. (la) fame e (la) sete
4. (l') acqua 5. le acque del mare 6. (i) pantaloni e (le) mutande 7. (le) forbici e
(gli) occhiali

1·5 **A.** 1. Paola 2. Franco 3. Alessandra 4. Giovanni 5. nipote 6. signore
7. professoressa 8. dottore 9. geometra 10. ragioniere 11. la dottoressa Totti
12. il professor Nardini 13. architetto 14. avvocato

B. 1. Luca, Andrea e Nicola sono amici. 2. Amo (il) Natale e (la) Pasqua in Italia.
3. Il signor Rossi è un amico della famiglia. 4. «Salve, signor Rossi.» 5. La signora
Rossi è un'amica della famiglia. 6. «Buongiorno, signora Rossi.»

C.

	Common	Proper	Count	Mass	Masc.	Fem.	Sing.	Pl.
1.	X	—	X	—	X	—	X	—
2.	—	X	—	—	—	X	X	—
3.	X	—	X	—	X	—	—	X
4.	X	—	X	—	—	X	—	X
5.	—	X	—	—	X	—	X	—
6.	X	—	X	—	—	X	X	—
7.	X	—	—	X	X	—	X	—
8.	X	—	X	—	—	X	—	X

D. 1. La signora Binni è italiana.   2. Maria e Paola sono due donne.   3. Le ragazze sono francesi.   4. Il professor Jones è americano.   5. Pasquale è mio zio.

1·6   1. Trento è il capoluogo del Trentino-Alto Adige.   2. La Sardegna, l'Umbria e la Valle d'Aosta sono regioni.   3. Venezia è il capoluogo del Veneto. / Torino è il capoluogo del Piemonte.   4. Firenze e Aosta sono capoluoghi.   5. La Basilicata è una regione.

2·1
A. 1. pianista   2. dentista   3. farmacista   4. musicista

B. 1. attrice   2. scultore   3. autrice   4. pittore   5. farmacista   6. dottore   7. leonessa   8. professore   9. elefantessa   10. avvocato   11. studentessa

C. 1. ciliegia   2. pero   3. mela   4. arancio   5. pesca   6. limone   7. mandarino   8. fico

2·2
A. 1. ipotesi   2. tesi   3. programmi   4. problemi   5. sistemi

B. 1. brindisi   2. crisi   3. diagramma   4. teorema   5. dramma   6. analisi

2·3
A.

	Masculine	Feminine
1. città	—	X
2. lunedì	X	—
3. papà	X	—
4. tè	X	—
5. menù	X	—
6. ragù	X	—
7. caffè	X	—
8. gioventù	—	X
9. virtù	—	X
10. università	—	X
11. tassì	X	—
12. tram	X	—
13. autobus	X	—

B. 1. caffè   2. città   3. foto   4. cinema   5. moto   6. computer   7. vaglia   8. mail   9. dita   10. braccio   11. paia   12. ginocchio   13. i bracci della croce   14. il labbro della ferita   15. buoi   16. radio   17. mani   18. pianeta   19. clacson   20. sport

2·4
A. 1. asinello, asinone   2. ragazzina (ragazzetta), ragazzona   3. libricino, librone   4. manina, manona

B. 1. un braccione   2. un corpaccio   3. una manetta   4. un problemino   5. un problemone   6. un problemaccio   7. un affaraccio   8. un affarone   9. Mariuccia

2·5
A. 1. arcobaleni   2. salvagente   3. ferrovie   4. cassaforte   5. pianoforti

B. 1. il caporeparto   2. il cacciavite   3. il francobollo   4. il pianoforte   5. il capoluogo

C. 1. a   2. b   3. a   4. b   5. a   6. a   7. b   8. a

D. 1. pianista, pianisti, pianista, pianiste   2. farmacista, farmacisti, farmacista, farmaciste   3. attore, attori, attrice, attrici   4. scultore, scultori, scultrice, scultrici   5. elefante, elefanti, elefantessa, elefantesse   6. studente, studenti, studentessa, studentesse

E. 1. caffè   2. città   3. foto   4. sport   5. tennis   6. autobus   7. dita   8. paia

2·6   1. b   2. a   3. a   4. b   5. a

3·1
A. 1. un americano   2. un'americana   3. uno studente   4. una zia   5. una studentessa   6. un'ora   7. uno gnocco   8. un portatile   9. una tesi   10. un brindisi   11. un problema   12. un programma   13. un caffè   14. una foto   15. un computer   16. una mano   17. una radio   18. un pianoforte   19. un'isola   20. una porta   21. uno psicologo   22. una psicologa   23. un orologio

B. 1. una cara amica   2. un piccolo zio   3. una brava figlia   4. un bravo cantante   5. una grande professoressa   6. un bravo signore   7. una brava musicista   8. un grande scultore

3·2 **A.** 1. il vestito, i vestiti   2. la studentessa, le studentesse   3. lo psicologo, gli psicologi   4. la psicologa, le psicologhe   5. la tesi, le tesi   6. il tedesco, i tedeschi   7. lo sport, gli sport   8. il problema, i problemi   9. l'orologio, gli orologi   10. l'ora, le ore   11. l'amico, gli amici   12. l'amica, le amiche   13. lo zio, gli zii   14. la zia, le zie   15. il bambino, i bambini   16. la bambina, le bambine   17. lo gnocco, gli gnocchi   18. lo studente, gli studenti

B. 1. gli zii   2. il vaglia   3. le valige   4. la virtù   5. gli uomini   6. il tè   7. gli gnocchi   8. il sistema   9. gli scultori   10. il programma   11. le radio   12. l'università   13. le paia   14. l'orologio   15. i musicisti   16. l'infermiera

3·3 **A.** 1. Mia madre aveva mal di denti ieri.   2. Anch'io ho mal di gola.   3. Che bella musica!   4. Mio padre ha mal di testa o mal di stomaco.   5. Che bella macchina!   6. In questa classe conosco solo uno studente e una studentessa.   7. Lui è una persona simpatica; e anche lei è una persona simpatica.   8. Io studio sempre un'ora ogni giorno.

B. 1. (Io) ho solo una zia e uno zio.   2. (Io) ho comprato una macchina / un'automobile.   3. Che bella casa! / Che casa bella!   4. Che grande film!

3·4 **A.** 1. L'acqua è necessaria per vivere.   2. Il caffè è buono.   3. Gli italiani sono simpatici.   4. La pazienza è la virtù più importante.   5. Anche gli americani sono simpatici.   6. Mi piacciono le lingue e la storia.   7. La Sicilia è una bella regione.   8. L'anno prossimo vado in Piemonte.   9. Forse vado nell'Italia settentrionale.   10. Mia zia vive a Roma.   11. Lei si mette sempre la giacca per andare in centro.   12. Il venerdì, io gioco sempre a tennis.   13. La domenica vado regolarmente in chiesa.   14. Il martedì o il mercoledì guardo la televisione.   15. Il giovedì o il sabato vado in centro.   16. Come si chiama la professoressa d'italiano?   17. Come sta, professoressa Bianchi?   18. Mi fa male la testa.

B. 1. (Io) bevo solo (il) tè.   2. (Io) amo gli spaghetti.   3. (Io) ho solo uno zio e una zia in Italia.   4. Lui vive nell'Italia meridionale.   5. Lei vive negli Stati Uniti orientali.   6. Io invece vivo negli Stati Uniti occidentali.   7. Mi piacciono la biologia, la chimica, la scienza, la geografia, la matematica e la fisica.   8. Lei è molto brava in musica e nelle lingue.   9. Il mese scorso ho comprato la/una macchina.   10. L'anno prossimo vado in Italia.   11. La settimana prossima vado in centro.   12. Lui vive a sinistra e lei a destra.

C. 1. il ragazzo   2. un anno   3. la settimana   4. un mese   5. il caffè   6. uno psicologo

D. 1. i ragazzi   2. gli spagnoli   3. le scienze   4. le giacche   5. gli amici   6. le amiche   7. i cellulari   8. le virtù

E. 1. Che bel film!   2. Ho mal di stomaco.   3. Loro hanno un cane e un gatto.   4. Sono la zia e lo zio dall'Italia.   5. Io amo la carne.   6. Gli italiani sanno vivere.   7. Loro vanno spesso in Italia.   8. La Francia è un bel paese.   9. Oggi vado in centro con lo zio.   10. Il venerdì vanno spesso al cinema.   11. Conosci il professor Martini?   12. Mio fratello ama la matematica.   13. Lei è andata al cinema la settimana scorsa.   14. Loro vivono a destra.

F. 1. f   2. e   3. a   4. g   5. b   6. c   7. d

3·5 1. il   2. X; X   3. X   4. il   5. X

4·1 **A.** 1. la bambina ricca   2. i ragazzi alti   3. la casa grande   4. le case grandi   5. gli uomini stanchi   6. le donne povere   7. la bambina bella   8. i cantanti brutti   9. le cantanti magre   10. la giacca rossa   11. le giacche blu   12. le sciarpe verdi   13. le sciarpe viola   14. la camicia bianca   15. le camicie marrone   16. gli zaini celesti   17. le gonne grige   18. i vestiti rosa   19. l'impermeabile azzurro   20. gli impermeabili gialli   21. i cappotti arancione   22. la camicia e la sciarpa bianche   23. la gonna e il cappotto rossi

B. 1. gli zii vecchi   2. la studentessa intelligente   3. le valige grandi   4. la città piccola   5. gli uomini ricchi   6. la donna stanca   7. i ragazzi simpatici   8. la cantante simpatica   9. i vestiti lunghi   10. la sciarpa lunga

C. 1. la macchina vecchia   2. gli uomini bassi   3. le donne ricche   4. il cane piccolo   5. i cantanti magri   6. i professori brutti   7. le ragazze ricche   8. il vestito bianco

4·2 **A.** 1. Lui è un simpatico studente.   2. È uno zaino nuovo.   3. Ho comprato un nuovo orologio.   4. Marco e Maria sono simpatici amici.   5. Lei è una ricca amica.

B. 1. a   2. b   3. a   4. b   5. a   6. b   7. b   8. a

4·3　**A.** 1. buono zio　2. buona zia　3. buon amico　4. buon'amica　5. buon padre　6. buoni ragazzi　7. buone amiche　8. bello zaino　9. bel libro　10. bell'orologio　11. begli zaini　12. bei libri　13. begli orologi　14. bella donna　15. belle donne　16. bell'attrice　17. belle attrici

B. 1. uno zaino bello　2. degli scultori grandi　3. un caffè buono　4. dei ragionieri buoni　5. un uomo bello　6. un portatile buono　7. dei programmi belli　8. uno psicologo buono　9. una psicologa buona　10. un problema grande　11. una pesca buona　12. delle autrici grandi　13. un orologio buono　14. un musicista grande　15. una donna bella　16. un affare buono

C. 1. San Marco　2. Sant'Isabella　3. San Bernardo　4. San Francesco　5. Sant'Agnese　6. Sant'Alessio

4·4　**A.** 1. a. Giovanni è così alto come Maria. / Giovanni è tanto alto quanto Maria. b. Giovanni è così intelligente come Maria. / Giovanni è tanto intelligente quanto Maria. c. Giovanni è così simpatico come Maria. / Giovanni è tanto simpatico quanto Maria. d. Giovanni è così felice come Maria. / Giovanni è tanto felice quanto Maria.　2. a. Il signor Sabatini è più felice degli studenti. b. Il signor Sabatini è più ricco degli studenti. c. Il signor Sabatini è più simpatico degli studenti. d. Il signor Sabatini è più stanco degli studenti.　3. a. La signora Sabatini è meno felice degli studenti. b. La signora Sabatini è meno ricca degli studenti. c. La signora Sabatini è meno simpatica degli studenti. d. La signora Sabatini è meno stanca degli studenti.　4. a. Le giacche sono più costose/care dei cappotti. b. Le giacche sono più lunghe dei cappotti. c. Le giacche sono più belle dei cappotti. d. Le giacche sono più nuove dei cappotti.　5. a. Gli impermeabili sono meno costosi/cari dei vestiti. b. Gli impermeabili sono più lunghi dei vestiti. c. Gli impermeabili sono meno belli dei vestiti. d. Gli impermeabili sono più vecchi dei vestiti.

B. 1. Lui è il professore più bravo dell'università.　2. Lei è la più intelligente di tutti.　3. Giovanni è più bravo che intelligente.　4. Giovanni è più bravo di Pasquale.　5. Gli studenti sono più simpatici che intelligenti.　6. Maria è più intelligente di quello che crede.

C. 1. migliori　2. maggiore　3. peggiore　4. minori　5. maggiori　6. ricchissimo　7. rossissimi　8. facilissimo/facilissima　9. bellissime　10. simpaticissimi　11. simpaticissime　12. buonissima

D. 1. la donna intelligente　2. l'amico elegante　3. la zia alta　4. il bello studente　5. la sorella simpaticissima　6. il buon amico　7. la ragazza francese　8. un bravissimo professore　9. una buona zia　10. un bel ragazzo　11. una bell'amica　12. San Mario

E. 1. b　2. b　3. b　4. a　5. b　6. a

4·5　1. Fa caldo e/ed è piovoso.　2. Fa sempre freddo qui e/ed è sempre nuvoloso.　3. Il tempo è bello oggi. / Fa bel tempo oggi. È sereno e fa fresco.　4. È piovoso / Piove oggi. Il tempo è cattivo. / Fa cattivo tempo.

5·1　**A.** 1. Anch'io voglio andare in Italia.　2. Devi chiamare tu, non io!　3. Non è possibile che siano stati loro.　4. Mio fratello guarda sempre la TV. Lui guarda sempre programmi interessanti.　5. Mia sorella legge molto. Lei vuole diventare professoressa d'università.　6. Anche noi siamo andati in centro ieri.　7. Siete proprio voi?　8. Galileo era un grande scienziato. Egli era toscano.　9. Elsa Morante è una grande scrittrice. Ella è molto famosa.　10. Maria, vai anche tu alla festa?　11. Signora Marchi, va anche Lei al cinema?　12. Signore e signori, anche voi/Loro siete/sono felici?

B. 1. Anche essi sono (dei) problemi importanti.　2. Anche esse sono (delle) tesi interessanti.　3. Noi andremo in Italia quest'anno.　4. Loro sono italiani.　5. Loro sono italiane.

5·2　**A.** 1. a. Giovanni mi chiama ogni sera. b. Giovanni mi ha dato la sua penna.　2. a. La sua amica ti ha telefonato, non è vero? b. Lui vuole che io ti chiami stasera.　3. a. Professoressa, La chiamo domani, va bene? b. Professoressa, Le do il mio compito domani, va bene?　4. a. Conosci Marco? Mia sorella gli telefona spesso. b. Sì, io lo conosco molto bene.　5. a. Ieri ho visto Maria e le ho dato il tuo indirizzo. b. Anche tu hai visto Maria, no? No, ma forse la chiamo stasera.　6. a. Marco e Maria, quando ci venite a visitare? b. Signor Verdi e signora Verdi, quando ci telefonerete?　7. a. Claudia e Franca, vi devo dire qualcosa. b. Claudia e Franca, non vi ho dato niente ieri.　8. a. Conosci quegli studenti? No, non li conosco. b. Scrivi mai a quegli studenti? No, non gli scrivo mai.　9. a. Conosci quelle studentesse? No, non le conosco. b. Scrivi mai a quelle studentesse? No, non gli scrivo mai.

B. 1. Marco la guarda sempre ogni sera.　2. Anche lei lo preferisce.　3. Li mangeremo volentieri in quel ristorante.　4. Anche Maria le vuole.　5. Le compreremo domani.　6. Loro li compreranno in centro.　7. Anch'io lo prendo, va bene?　8. La vuoi anche tu?

5·3 **A.** 1. a. Claudia chiama solo me ogni sera, non la sua amica. b. Giovanni ha dato la sua penna a me, non al suo amico.   2. a. Claudia ha telefonato a te, non è vero? b. Lui vuole che io chiami anche te stasera.   3. a. Dottor Marchi, chiamo Lei, non l'altro medico, domani, va bene? b. Professoressa Verdi, do il mio compito a Lei domani, va bene?   4. a. Conosci il professor Giusti? Mia sorella telefona solo a lui per studiare per gli esami. b. Sì, io conosco proprio lui molto bene.   5. a. Ieri ho visto la tua amica e ho dato il tuo indirizzo anche a lei. b. Anche tu hai visto Paola, no? No, ma forse esco con lei stasera.   6. a. Marco e Maria, quando uscirete con noi? b. Signor Verdi e signora Verdi, quando telefonerete a noi?   7. a. Marco e Maria, parlerò di voi alla professoressa. b. Claudia e Franca, non ho dato niente a voi ieri.   8. a. Conosci quegli studenti? Sì, e domani parlerò di loro al professore. b. Scrivi mai a quegli studenti? No, non scrivo mai a loro.   9. a. Conosci quelle studentesse? Sì, e domani parlerò di loro al professore. b. Scrivi mai a quelle studentesse? No, non scrivo mai a loro.

B. 1. Marco darà il tuo/Suo indirizzo a me, non a lui!   2. Ieri (io) ho scritto a te, e solo a te!   3. Maria viene con noi, non con loro, al cinema domani.   4. Il professore / La professoressa parla sempre di voi, non di noi!   5. Maria, l'ho fatto per te!   6. Signora Verdi, l'ho fatto per Lei!

5·4 **A.** 1. Sì, ne comprerò.   2. Mio fratello ne comprerà domani.   3. Ne devo guardare due stasera.   4. Di solito ne leggo molte ogni settimana.   5. Anche lei ne ha parlato.   6. Ci andiamo domani.   7. Mia sorella ci vive da molti anni.   8. Loro ne arrivano tra poco.

B. 1. Mio fratello mangia assai/molto/tanto.   2. Dorme molto tua sorella?   3. Ieri abbiamo mangiato troppo.   4. Solo alcuni vanno in Italia quest'anno. Ma molti sono andati l'anno scorso. [The masculine plural forms are the appropriate ones for the pronouns when the gender is unmarked.]   5. Di quelle donne, molte sono italiane e alcune sono americane.

C. 1. a 2. b 3. a 4. a 5. a 6. b 7. b

D. 1. Claudia lo darà a me domani.   2. Io le darò a te dopo.   3. Io le ho dato le scarpe.   4. Li voglio anch'io.   5. Lui li chiama spesso.   6. Lui ne vuole.   7. Non la voglio.   8. Ne prendo due.   9. Marco ci andrà domani.   10. Lei ne comprerà molte per la festa.   11. Ne prendo quattro di solito.

5·5 1. Gina, ti chiamo domani, va bene?   2. Professore, Le ho dato il regalo per Natale.   3. Gina e Claudia, partite anche voi domani?   4. Signore, chi è Lei?   5. Professoressa, ho dato quella cosa a Lei ieri.

6·1 **A.** 1. Mio fratello l'ha (lo ha) comprato ieri.   2. Gli abbiamo dato quello zaino.   3. Loro li hanno presi ieri.   4. Gli ho dato quegli stivali ieri.   5. Mia sorella l'ha (la ha) comprata ieri.   6. Mia madre le ha dato quella borsa.   7. Le abbiamo viste in centro.   8. Gli abbiamo dato quelle scarpe ieri.   9. Ne ho mangiate tre.   10. Ne abbiamo comprate molte in centro ieri.

B. 1. Sì, l'ho (lo ho) preso.   2. Sì, le ho comprate.   3. Sì, l'ho (la ho) vista.   4. Sì, li ho chiamati.   5. Sì, ne ho mangiate.

6·2 **A.** 1. Mia sorella me l'ha (lo ha) comprato ieri.   2. Gliel'ho (Glielo ho) dato ieri.   3. Loro te li hanno presi ieri.   4. Glieli ho dati ieri.   5. Nostra madre ce l'ha (la ha) comprata qualche anno fa.   6. Mia madre gliel'ha (gliela ha) data.   7. Ve le abbiamo comprate in centro.   8. Gliele abbiamo date ieri.   9. Gliene ho date tre.   10. Gliene abbiamo comprate molte in centro ieri.

B. 1. Sì, ve l'ho preso.   2. Sì, gliele ho comprate.   3. Sì, me le hai date.   4. Sì, gliele ho dette.   5. Sì, te ne ho prese.

6·3 **A.** 1. Prima di berla, voglio mangiare.   2. Vedendoli, li ho chiamati.   3. Eccole.   4. Eccoteli.   5. Non voglio mangiarli. / Non li voglio mangiare.   6. Potremo andarci tra poco. / Ci potremo andare tra poco.   7. Vogliamo scrivergliene molte. / Gliene vogliamo scrivere molte.   8. Giovanni, bevilo!   9. Alessandro dammela!   10. Maria, faglielo!   11. Signora Marchi, me la dica!   12. Franco, dimmela!

B. 1. Giovanni, da' la penna a me! / Giovanni, dammi la penna! Non darla a lei! / Non dargliela! / Non la dare a lei! / Non gliela dare!   2. Dottor/Dottoressa Verdi, gli dica la verità! Ma non la dica a loro! / Ma non gliela dica!   3. Mamma, fa' quel compito per me! / Mamma, fammi quel compito! Ma non farlo per lui! / Ma, non lo fare per lui! / Ma non farglielo! / Ma non glielo fare!   4. Marco, fammi un favore! Ma non farlo a loro! / Ma non lo fare a loro! / Ma non glielo fare! / Ma non farglielo!   5. Maria, va' in centro con noi! Non andarci con lui! / Non ci andare con lui!   6. Signora Verdi, vada in centro con noi! Non ci vada con lei!

C. 1. Marco me lo darà domani.   2. Io te le ho date ieri.   3. Loro gliele hanno date.   4. Prima di mangiarli, voglio mangiare l'antipasto.   5. Eccoli.   6. Lui le ha comprate ieri.   7. Non voglio mangiarla. / Non la voglio mangiare.   8. Claudia, mangiale!   9. Giovanni, dammene due!   10. Mio fratello ci è andato ieri.   11. Lei ne ha comprate molte ieri.   12. Ce ne sono quattro nello zaino.

D. 1. Bruno me lo ha comprato. Bruno mi ha comprato quegli orologi. Bruno me li ha comprati.   2. Marco, mangiala! Marco, mangia quelle mele! Marco, mangiale!   3. Paola ve lo darà domani. Paola vi darà quei libri domani. Paola ve li darà domani.   4. Anche tu me l'hai (la hai) comprata nello stesso negozio, vero? Anche tu mi hai comprato quelle camicie nello stesso negozio, vero? Anche tu me le hai comprate nello stesso negozio, vero?   5. Lui l'ha (lo ha) bevuto volentieri. Lui ha bevuto quei caffè volentieri. Lui li ha bevuti volentieri.

6·4 1. Gina, non me la dare!   2. Luca, non andarci!   3. Ti posso dare questo libro?   4. Voglio chiamarti subito.

7·1 **A.** 1. questi affari   2. queste attrici   3. questi biologi   4. queste bugie   5. questi camerieri   6. queste cameriere

B. 1. questo diagramma   2. questo dito   3. questo francese   4. questa francese   5. questo giornale

7·2 **A.** 1. quegli architetti   2. quelle autrici   3. quelle braccia   4. quelle cameriere   5. quegli zaini   6. quelle ipotesi   7. quelle macchine   8. quei simpatici bambini   9. quei bei ragazzi   10. quelle belle ragazze

B. 1. quel programma   2. quel problema   3. quell'inglese   4. quell'inglese   5. quel nome   6. quella notte   7. quell'occhio   8. quel paio   9. quello spagnolo simpatico   10. quel teorema e quella tesi

7·3 **A.** 1. quello   2. quelle   3. quello   4. quelli   5. quello   6. quelli   7. quelli   8. quelli   9. quelle   10. questa   11. questa   12. queste   13. questo   14. questo   15. questi   16. questi

B. 1. No, quello.   2. No, quelli.   3. No, quella.   4. No, quelle.   5. No, quello.   6. No, quelli.   7. No, quello.   8. No, quella.

7·4 **A.** 1. No, quell'orologio lì.   2. No, quegli impermeabili lì.   3. No, quella camicia là.   4. No, quelle sciarpe là.   5. No, quel libro lì.   6. No, quegli zaini là.

B. 1. Ecco la penna.   2. Sì, c'è (un'americano qui). / No, non c'è (un'americano qui).   3. Sì, è uno studente d'italiano. / No, non è uno studente d'italiano.   4. Ecco quelle persone.   5. Sì, ci sono (persone italiane lì). / No, non ci sono (persone italiane lì).   6. Sì, sono amici. / No, non sono amici.

C. 1. quel ragazzo   2. questa nuova macchina   3. quello qui/qua   4. questi studenti lì   5. quelle amiche simpatiche   6. questi simpatici psicologi   7. quegli gnocchi là   8. queste paia di pantaloni

D. 1. Io, invece, voglio quell'impermeabile.   2. Io, invece, voglio quei libri.   3. Io, invece, voglio quella camicia.   4. Io, invece, voglio quelle giacche.   5. Io, invece, voglio quello zaino.   6. Io, invece, voglio quegli orologi.   7. Io, invece, voglio quelle foto.

E. 1. Giovanni e Maria non ci sono. / Giovanni e Maria non sono qui.   2. Dove sono quelle camicie? Ecco le camicie.   3. Che cosa è? / Che cos'è? È una macchina nuova. / È una nuova macchina.   4. Dove sono gli studenti? Ecco gli studenti.   5. Sono qua? No, sono là.

7·5 1. Ecco perché (lui) non l'ha fatto.   2. Ecco, questa è la verità.   3. Ecco tutto. Non c'è altro da dire.   4. Eccoci (qui) finalmente.

8·1 **A.** 1. la mia bibita, la tua bibita, la nostra bibita, la loro bibita   2. il mio cappuccino, il tuo cappuccino, il nostro cappuccino, il loro cappuccino   3. i miei bicchieri, i tuoi bicchieri, i nostri bicchieri, i loro bicchieri   4. le mie braccia, le tue braccia, le nostre braccia, le loro braccia   5. il mio cappotto, il tuo cappotto, il nostro cappotto, il loro cappotto   6. la mia cravatta, la tua cravatta, la nostra cravatta, la loro cravatta   7. le mie dita, le tue dita, le nostre dita, le loro dita   8. i miei diagrammi, i tuoi diagrammi, i nostri diagrammi, i loro diagrammi

B. 1. No, è il loro espresso.   2. No, sono i suoi figli.   3. No, sono le sue figlie.   4. No, è il loro giornale.   5. No, è la tua professoressa.   6. No, sono i suoi amici.   7. No, sono le mie chiavi.

8·2 **A.** 1. Sì, è la sua macchina.   2. Sì, è il suo caffè.   3. Sì, è il suo caffè.   4. Sì, sono i suoi amici.   5. Sì, sono i suoi amici.   6. Sì, sono le sue amiche.   7. Sì, sono le sue amiche.   8. Sì, è la sua foto.   9. Sì, sono le sue foto.

B. 1. Maria, è il tuo caffè? 2. Signora Rossi, è il Suo caffè? 3. Gino, è il tuo cappuccino? 4. Signor Bruni, è il Suo cappuccino? 5. Claudia, sono le tue amiche? 6. Signorina Verdi, sono le Sue amiche? 7. Giovanni, sono le tue forbici? 8. Professor Marchi, sono le Sue forbici? 9. Maria e Claudia, è il vostro caffè? 10. Signora Rossi e signorina Verdi, è il Loro caffè? 11. Gino e Marco, è il vostro cappuccino? 12. Signor Bruni e dottor Rossini, è il Loro cappuccino? 13. Claudia e Maria, sono le vostre amiche? 14. Signorina Verdi e dottoressa Dini, sono le Loro amiche? 15. Giovanni e Claudia, sono le vostre forbici? 16. Professor Marchi e dottoressa Bruni, sono le Loro forbici?

8·3 **A.** 1. a. Marco è mio cugino. b. Marco è il suo fratello minore / più piccolo / più giovane. c. Marco è tuo padre. d. Marco è il nostro zio italiano. e. Marco è il loro amico. 2. a. Maria è mia cugina. b. Maria è la sua sorella maggiore / più grande / più vecchia. c. Maria è tua madre. d. Maria è vostra zia. e. Maria è la loro amica. 3. a. Il signor Verdi e la signora Verdi sono mio nonno e mia nonna. b. Il signor Verdi e la signora Verdi sono il suo zio e la sua zia italiani. c. Il signor Verdi e la signora Verdi sono tuo suocero e tua suocera. d. Il signor Verdi e la signora Verdi sono vostro genero e vostra nuora. e. Il signor Verdi e la signora Verdi sono il loro cognato e la loro cognata italiani.

B. 1. i miei cugini 2. le mie nonne 3. i tuoi fratelli 4. le tue sorelle 5. i suoi zii 6. le sue zie 7. i nostri generi 8. le nostre suocere 9. i vostri cognati 10. le vostre cognate 11. i loro fratelli 12. le loro sorelle

8·4 **A.** 1. Sì, è la mia. 2. Sì, è la loro. 3. Sì, sei il nostro. 4. Sì, sono la sua. 5. Sì, è il suo. 6. Sì, è il loro. 7. Sì, sono i miei. 8. Sì, sono le nostre.

B. 1. È la mia. 2. È il suo. 3. È la sua. 4. È il nostro. 5. Sono i loro. 6. Sono le mie. 7. Sono i suoi. 8. Sono le sue.

C. 1. i miei orologi 2. la nostra amica 3. le mie camicie 4. il nostro libro 5. i tuoi cani 6. la vostra amica 7. le tue macchine 8. il vostro amico 9. i suoi gatti 10. la sua amica 11. i loro amici 12. la loro casa

D. 1. Lui è mio fratello. 2. Lei è la nostra sorella maggiore. 3. Quel ragazzo è il loro figlio. 4. Lei è la sua figlia più grande. 5. Signora Marchi, come si chiama Sua figlia? 6. Signora e signor Marchi, come si chiama il Loro figlio? 7. Lui è un mio amico, tra molti amici. 8. Anche lei è una mia amica, tra molte amiche. 9. Questo libro è mio. Dov'è il tuo?

8·5 1. (Lei) è mia sorella, non la mia amante! 2. Ecco il mio ragazzo e tuo fratello. 3. (Lei) è la mia ragazza, non ancora la mia fidanzata. 4. Mia sorella è anche la mia amica.

9·1 **A.** 1. dei coltelli 2. uno sbaglio 3. delle forchette 4. un salotto 5. degli zii 6. una cucina 7. degli psicologi 8. un bagno 9. delle camere 10. una bottiglia 11. delle sedie 12. una tavola 13. dei bicchieri 14. un cucchiaio 15. dei cucchiaini 16. una forchetta 17. dei coltelli 18. uno gnocco 19. delle automobili 20. un amico

B. 1. Sono delle automobili italiane. 2. Sono delle nuove sedie. / Sono delle sedie nuove. 3. Sono dei bravi psicologi. / Sono degli psicologi bravi. 4. Sono dei vecchi amici. / Sono degli amici vecchi. 5. Sono delle vecchie amiche. / Sono delle amiche vecchie. 6. Sono dei bagni grandi. 7. Sono delle camere piccole. 8. Sono dei bei salotti. / Sono dei salotti belli. 9. Sono delle belle cucine. / Sono delle cucine belle.

9·2 **A.** 1. alcuni coltelli 2. alcune sedie 3. alcuni gnocchi 4. alcune automobili 5. alcuni cucchiai 6. alcuni amici

B. 1. qualche cucchiaino 2. qualche tavola 3. qualche zaino 4. qualche automobile 5. qualche bicchiere 6. qualche sbaglio

C. 1. Alcuni amici nostri sono italiani. 2. Qualche amico nostro è italiano. 3. Alcune ragazze sono americane. 4. Qualche ragazza è americana.

9·3 **A.** 1. un po' d'insalata 2. dell'uva 3. un po' di pesce 4. della carne 5. un po' di minestra 6. del riso 7. un po' di zucchero 8. dell'orzo 9. un po' di pasta 10. dell'acqua

B. 1. Voglio del pesce e dei fagioli. 2. Voglio dell'insalata e delle carote. 3. Voglio della pasta e dei fagiolini. 4. Voglio della carne e delle mele. 5. Voglio del caffè e dello zucchero. 6. Voglio dell'uva e delle patate.

9·4

A. 1. Mario non mangia patate. 2. Io non voglio fagiolini. 3. Il ragazzo non prende carne. 4. La ragazza non vuole zucchero. 5. Anch'io non voglio biglietti. 6. Maria non prende pomodori.

B. 1. nessuna carota 2. nessun fagiolino 3. nessun cucchiaio 4. nessuna patata 5. nessuno zaino 6. nessun'arancia

9·5

A. 1. l'ultima donna 2. pochi studenti 3. tutta la minestra 4. parecchi bambini 5. una certa signora 6. qualsiasi città 7. qualunque ristorante 8. abbastanza soldi 9. assai studenti 10. ogni settimana

B. 1. Ho bisogno di poche patate. 2. Ho bisogno di tutti i fagioli. 3. Ho bisogno di tante carote. 4. Ho bisogno di molti fagiolini. 5. Ho bisogno di poche mele. 6. Ho bisogno di tutta la minestra. 7. Ho bisogno di tanta pasta. 8. Ho bisogno di molti cucchiai.

C. 1. dei bambini, alcuni bambini, qualche bambino 2. delle patate, alcune patate, qualche patata 3. dei fagioli, alcuni fagioli, qualche fagiolo 4. delle mele, alcune mele, qualche mela 5. degli zaini, alcuni zaini, qualche zaino 6. delle forchette, alcune forchette, qualche forchetta

D. 1. b 2. b 3. b 4. b 5. a 6. a

9·6

1. Amo / Mi piace l'uva. 2. (Lei) mi ha mandato/inviato delle/alcune comunicazioni/informazioni ieri. 3. Questo chicco è azzurro! 4. (Lui) mi manda/invia sempre poche informazioni.

10·1

A. 1. a. (io) arrivo, (tu) arrivi, (lui/lei) arriva, (Lei) arriva, (noi) arriviamo, (voi) arrivate, (loro) arrivano, (Loro) arrivano b. (io) cerco, (tu) cerchi, (lui/lei) cerca, (Lei) cerca, (noi) cerchiamo, (voi) cercate, (loro) cercano, (Loro) cercano c. (io) comincio, (tu) cominci, (lui/lei) comincia, (Lei) comincia, (noi) cominciamo, (voi) cominciate, (loro) cominciano, (Loro) cominciano d. (io) mangio, (tu) mangi, (lui/lei) mangia, (Lei) mangia, (noi) mangiamo, (voi) mangiate, (loro) mangiano, (Loro) mangiano e. (io) pago, (tu) paghi, (lui/lei) paga, (Lei) paga, (noi) paghiamo, (voi) pagate, (loro) pagano, (Loro) pagano 2. a. (io) chiedo, (tu) chiedi, (lui/lei) chiede, (Lei) chiede, (noi) chiediamo, (voi) chiedete, (loro) chiedono, (Loro) chiedono b. (io) rispondo, (tu) rispondi, (lui/lei) risponde, (Lei) risponde, (noi) rispondiamo, (voi) rispondete, (loro) rispondono, (Loro) rispondono c. (io) vendo, (tu) vendi, (lui/lei) vende, (Lei) vende, (noi) vendiamo, (voi) vendete, (loro) vendono, (Loro) vendono d. (io) leggo, (tu) leggi, (lui/lei) legge, (Lei) legge, (noi) leggiamo, (voi) leggete, (loro) leggono, (Loro) leggono e. (io) chiudo, (tu) chiudi, (lui/lei) chiude, (Lei) chiude, (noi) chiudiamo, (voi) chiudete, (loro) chiudono, (Loro) chiudono 3. a. (io) apro, (tu) apri, (lui/lei) apre, (Lei) apre, (noi) apriamo, (voi) aprite, (loro) aprono, (Loro) aprono b. (io) dormo, (tu) dormi, (lui/lei) dorme, (Lei) dorme, (noi) dormiamo, (voi) dormite, (loro) dormono, (Loro) dormono c. (io) parto, (tu) parti, (lui/lei) parte, (Lei) parte, (noi) partiamo, (voi) partite, (loro) partono, (Loro) partono 4. a. (io) capisco, (tu) capisci, (lui/lei) capisce, (Lei) capisce, (noi) capiamo, (voi) capite, (loro) capiscono, (Loro) capiscono b. (io) finisco, (tu) finisci, (lui/lei) finisce, (Lei) finisce, (noi) finiamo, (voi) finite, (loro) finiscono, (Loro) finiscono c. (io) preferisco, (tu) preferisci, (lui/lei) preferisce, (Lei) preferisce, (noi) preferiamo, (voi) preferite, (loro) preferiscono, (Loro) preferiscono

B. 1. Neanche io capisco la lezione. 2. Anche noi partiamo domani. 3. Anche tu giochi a calcio da molti anni. 4. Neanche voi aspettate mai. 5. Anche Luigi telefona spesso a mia sorella. 6. Anche le mie amiche giocano sempre a tennis.

C. 1. Signor Verdi, capisce la lezione? 2. Sara, cerchi qualcosa? 3. Signori, partono domani? 4. Ragazze, cominciate a studiare la matematica?

10·2

A. 1. (io) voglio, (tu) vuoi, (lui/lei) vuole, (noi) vogliamo, (voi) volete, (loro) vogliono 2. (io) vengo, (tu) vieni, (lui/lei) viene, (noi) veniamo, (voi) venite, (loro) vengono 3. (io) esco, (tu) esci, (lui/lei) esce, (noi) usciamo, (voi) uscite, (loro) escono 4. (io) tengo, (tu) tieni, (lui/lei) tiene, (noi) teniamo, (voi) tenete, (loro) tengono 5. (io) sto, (tu) stai, (lui/lei) sta, (noi) stiamo, (voi) state, (loro) stanno 6. (io) so, (tu) sai, (lui/lei) sa, (noi) sappiamo, (voi) sapete, (loro) sanno 7. (io) posso, (tu) puoi, (lui/lei) può, (noi) possiamo, (voi) potete, (loro) possono 8. (io) faccio, (tu) fai, (lui/lei) fa, (noi) facciamo, (voi) fate, (loro) fanno 9. (io) sono, (tu) sei, (lui/lei) è, (noi) siamo, (voi) siete, (loro) sono 10. (io) devo, (tu) devi, (lui/lei) deve, (noi) dobbiamo, (voi) dovete, (loro) devono 11. (io) dico, (tu) dici, (lui/lei) dice, (noi) diciamo, (voi) dite, (loro) dicono 12. (io) do, (tu) dai, (lui/lei) dà, (noi) diamo, (voi) date, (loro) danno 13. (io) bevo, (tu) bevi, (lui/lei) beve, (noi) beviamo, (voi) bevete, (loro) bevono 14. (io) ho, (tu) hai, (lui/lei) ha, (noi) abbiamo, (voi) avete, (loro) hanno 15. (io) vado, (tu) vai, (lui/lei) va, (noi) andiamo, (voi) andate, (loro) vanno

B. 1. Marco: Ciao, Maria, come stai?

2. Maria: Ciao, Marco, io sto molto bene. E tu?

3. Marco: Io sto così, così. Anzi, sto male.

4. Maria: Perché?

5. Marco: Sto male quando fa cattivo o brutto tempo. Ho freddo!

6. Maria: Domani, per fortuna, dovrebbe fare bel tempo.

7. Marco: Meno male! E allora spero di avere caldo!

C. 1. Signor Rossi, dove va?   2. Maria, come stai?   3. Signorina Verdi, cosa vuole?   4. Giovanni, quando vieni alla festa?   5. Signor Verdi e signora Verdi, quando escono stasera?

10·3   **A.** 1. a. (io) telefoni, (tu) telefoni, (lui/lei; Lei) telefoni, (noi) telefoniamo, (voi) telefoniate, (loro; Loro) telefonino b. (io) cerchi, (tu) cerchi, (lui/lei; Lei) cerchi, (noi) cerchiamo, (voi) cerchiate, (loro; Loro) cerchino c. (io) cominci, (tu) cominci, (lui/lei; Lei) cominci, (noi) cominciamo, (voi) cominciate, (loro; Loro) comincino d. (io) mangi, (tu) mangi, (lui/lei; Lei) mangi, (noi) mangiamo, (voi) mangiate, (loro; Loro) mangino e. (io) paghi, (tu) paghi, (lui/lei; Lei) paghi, (noi) paghiamo, (voi) paghiate, (loro; Loro) paghino   2. a. (io) scriva, (tu) scriva, (lui/lei; Lei) scriva, (noi) scriviamo, (voi) scriviate, (loro; Loro) scrivano b. (io) legga, (tu) legga, (lui/lei; Lei) legga, (noi) leggiamo, (voi) leggiate, (loro; Loro) leggano   3. a. (io) apra, (tu) apra, (lui/lei; Lei) apra, (noi) apriamo, (voi) apriate, (loro; Loro) aprano b. (io) parta, (tu) parta, (lui/lei; Lei) parta, (noi) partiamo, (voi) partiate, (loro; Loro) partano   4. a. (io) capisca, (tu) capisca, (lui/lei; Lei) capisca, (noi) capiamo, (voi) capiate, (loro; Loro) capiscano b. (io) preferisca, (tu) preferisca, (lui/lei; Lei) preferisca, (noi) preferiamo, (voi) preferiate, (loro; Loro) preferiscano

B. 1. Penso che Mario dorma fino a tardi.   2. Lui crede che tu finisca alle sei?   3. Sappiamo che voi scrivete un'e-mail.   4. Sara sa che tu capisci tutto.   5. La professoressa Marchi dice che noi studiamo molto.   6. Sembra che lui studi molto. [There is no need to repeat the -i ending in this case.]   7. Marco spera che io paghi il conto.   8. Loro vogliono che lui cominci a studiare.

10·4   **A.** 1. a. voglia b. venga c. esca   2. a. tenga b. stia c. sappia   3. a. possa b. faccia c. sia   4. a. dobbiamo b. diciamo c. diamo   5. a. beviate b. abbiate c. andiate   6. a. siano b. facciano c. diano

B. 1. Penso che sia vero.   2. Crediamo che domani faccia caldo.   3. Sembra che Sara stia bene.   4. Dubito che Alessandro dia i soldi a sua sorella.   5. Speriamo che lui possa venire alla festa.   6. Sembra che loro devano (debbano) studiare di più.   7. Penso che Marco voglia uscire.   8. Crediamo che lui dica sempre la verità.

10·5   **A.** 1. È probabile che domani non faccia caldo.   2. Bisogna che tu dica la verità.   3. Lui è la persona più elegante che ci sia.   4. Vengo anch'io alla festa, a meno che non ci sia la tua amica.   5. Devi studiare di più, affinché tu possa parlare italiano meglio.   6. Benché faccia brutto tempo, esco lo stesso.   7. Dovunque tu vada, vengo anch'io.   8. Nel caso che venga tuo cugino alla festa, io sto a casa.   9. Nonostante che tu dica questo, io non ci credo.   10. Prima che loro escano, devono studiare.   11. Faccio quello che dici, purché sia facile.   12. Sebbene lui voglia uscire stasera, io devo stare a casa a studiare.   13. Faccio tutto, senza che tu dica niente.   14. Che faccia brutto tempo!

B. 1. Lei crede che io possa uscire stasera (questa sera).   2. Noi crediamo che lui parli italiano bene.   3. Lui pensa di scrivere bene.   4. Loro credono di parlare italiano bene.

C. 1. b   2. b   3. b   4. b   5. b   6. a   7. a   8. b   9. b   10. b   11. a or b   12. b   13. b   14. b

D. 1. Maria, studi l'italiano?   2. Signora Verdi, studia la matematica?   3. Penso che Maria esca stasera.   4. Benché/Sebbene faccia freddo, esco lo stesso.

10·6   1. It is necessary that he always tell the truth.   2. I hope that he always tells the truth.   3. It's crucial that she do this.   4. I doubt that she does this often.

11·1

A. 1. a. (io) ho cercato, (tu) hai cercato, (lui/lei; Lei) ha cercato, (noi) abbiamo cercato, (voi) avete cercato, (loro; Loro) hanno cercato b. (io) sono andato (-a), (tu) sei andato (-a), (lui/lei; Lei) è andato (-a), (noi) siamo andati (-e), (voi) siete andati (-e), (loro; Loro) sono andati (-e) 2. a. (io) ho conosciuto, (tu) hai conosciuto, (lui/lei; Lei) ha conosciuto, (noi) abbiamo conosciuto, (voi) avete conosciuto, (loro; Loro) hanno conosciuto b. (io) ho voluto, (tu) hai voluto, (lui/lei; Lei) ha voluto, (noi) abbiamo voluto, (voi) avete voluto, (loro; Loro) hanno voluto 3. a. (io) ho capito, (tu) hai capito, (lui/lei; Lei) ha capito, (noi) abbiamo capito, (voi) avete capito, (loro; Loro) hanno capito b. (io) sono uscito (-a), (tu) sei uscito (-a), (lui/lei; Lei) è uscito (-a), (noi) siamo usciti (-e), (voi) siete usciti (-e), (loro; Loro) sono usciti (-e)

B. 1. Anch'io non ho capito la lezione. / Neanche/Nemmeno/Neppure io ho capito la lezione. 2. Anche noi siamo già partiti. 3. Anche tu hai già studiato la lezione. 4. Anche voi siete appena usciti. 5. Anche Luigi ha telefonato prima a mia sorella. 6. Anche le mie amiche sono andate in Italia un anno fa.

C. 1. Signor Verdi, ha capito la lezione? 2. Sara, hai pagato il conto? 3. Signori, sono usciti ieri sera? 4. Ragazze, avete cominciato a studiare la matematica?

11·2

A. 1. Io ho aperto la finestra. 2. Tu hai bevuto l'espresso. 3. Marco ha chiesto qualcosa. 4. Quando hanno chiuso? 5. A chi ha dato la rivista tuo fratello? 6. Voi non avete deciso, vero? 7. Anche loro hanno detto la verità. 8. Loro sono stati (-e) in Italia. 9. Che tempo ha fatto? 10. Che cosa hai letto? 11. Dove hai messo quel libro? 12. Chi ha perso spesso? 13. Cosa avete preso voi? 14. Quale hai scelto, Maria? 15. A che ora sono scesi (-e)? 16. A chi avete scritto? 17. Io sono stato (-a) in casa. 18. Ho visto i miei amici. 19. A che ora sono venute le ragazze?

B. 1. Tu scegli la borsa adesso. Penso che tu scelga la borsa adesso. Tu hai già scelto la borsa. 2. Tu scrivi l'e-mail adesso. Penso che tu scriva l'e-mail adesso. Tu hai già scritto l'e-mail. 3. Loro scelgono lo zaino adesso. Penso che loro scelgano lo zaino adesso. Loro hanno già scelto lo zaino. 4. Lei viene adesso. Penso che lei venga adesso. Lei è già venuta. 5. Lui viene adesso. Penso che lui venga adesso. Lui è già venuto. 6. Loro dicono la verità adesso. Penso che loro dicano la verità adesso. Loro hanno già detto la verità. 7. Voi non fate niente adesso. Penso che voi non facciate niente adesso. Voi non avete già fatto niente.

11·3

A. 1. Mio fratello crede che io abbia appena scritto quell'e-mail. 2. Tutti pensano che io sia già stato in Italia. 3. Credo che anche tu non abbia capito, no? / Credo che neanche/nemmeno/neppure tu abbia capito, no? 4. È probabile che quella donna abbia finito di lavorare presto. 5. Dubito che quella donna sia uscita al cinema con gli amici. 6. Non è possibile che Marco abbia visto la sua professoressa in centro ieri. 7. Immagino che quell'uomo sia uscito al cinema con gli amici. 8. Lui dubita che noi abbiamo già letto quel libro. 9. Non credo che tu sia stato a Roma due anni fa, vero? 10. Lei non crede che noi siamo andati al cinema ieri sera. 11. Dubito che voi siate tornati tardi ieri sera. 12. È probabile che voi non abbiate mai studiato l'italiano, vero? 13. Penso che i miei amici abbiano preso un caffellatte. 14. Credo che i tuoi amici siano venuti tardi alla festa. 15. Dubito che le nostre amiche abbiano detto la verità. 16. Non è possibile che quelle camicie siano costate così tanto.

B. 1. Siamo andati al cinema lo stesso, sebbene abbia fatto brutto tempo. 2. Mio fratello è venuto alla festa, nonostante abbia piovuto. 3. Marco e Maria sono usciti lo stesso ieri sera, benché abbiano lavorato fino a tardi. 4. Io ho scritto quell'e-mail, sebbene non abbia avuto tanto tempo.

11·4

A. 1. a. mangiai b. dovei (dovetti) c. capii 2. a. andasti b. potesti c. preferisti 3. a. cominciò b. vendé (vendette) c. finì 4. a. arrivammo b. dovemmo c. partimmo 5. a. portaste b. poteste c. usciste 6. a. comprarono b. venderono (vendettero) c. dormirono

B. 1. Io mangiai il risotto alla milanese molti anni fa. 2. Tu andasti in Italia molti anni fa. 3. Mia sorella vendé (vendette) la macchina molti anni fa. 4. Mio fratello dové (dovette) fare quella cosa molti anni fa. 5. Noi finimmo di studiare molti anni fa. 6. Anche voi mangiaste il risotto molti anni fa. 7. Loro tornarono molti anni fa.

11·5 **A.** 1. (io) volli, (tu) volesti, (lui/lei; Lei) volle, (noi) volemmo, (voi) voleste, (loro; Loro) vollero

2. (io) venni, (tu) venisti, (lui/lei; Lei) venne, (noi) venimmo, (voi) veniste, (loro; Loro) vennero

3. (io) vidi, (tu) vedesti, (lui/lei; Lei) vide, (noi) vedemmo, (voi) vedeste, (loro; Loro) videro

4. (io) stetti, (tu) stesti, (lui/lei; Lei) stette, (noi) stemmo, (voi) steste, (loro; Loro) stettero

5. (io) scrissi, (tu) scrivesti, (lui/lei; Lei) scrisse, (noi) scrivemmo, (voi) scriveste, (loro; Loro) scrissero

6. (io) scesi, (tu) scendesti, (lui/lei; Lei) scese, (noi) scendemmo, (voi) scendeste, (loro; Loro) scesero

7. (io) scelsi, (tu) scegliesti, (lui/lei; Lei) scelse, (noi) scegliemmo, (voi) sceglieste, (loro; Loro) scelsero

8. (io) seppi, (tu) sapesti, (lui/lei; Lei) seppe, (noi) sapemmo, (voi) sapeste, (loro; Loro) seppero

9. (io) presi, (tu) prendesti, (lui/lei; Lei) prese, (noi) prendemmo, (voi) prendeste, (loro; Loro) presero

10. (io) persi, (tu) perdesti, (lui/lei; Lei) perse, (noi) perdemmo, (voi) perdeste, (loro; Loro) persero

11. (io) nacqui, (tu) nascesti, (lui/lei; Lei) nacque, (noi) nascemmo, (voi) nasceste, (loro; Loro) nacquero

12. (io) misi, (tu) mettesti, (lui/lei; Lei) mise, (noi) mettemmo, (voi) metteste, (loro; Loro) misero

13. (io) lessi, (tu) leggesti, (lui/lei; Lei) lesse, (noi) leggemmo, (voi) leggeste, (loro; Loro) lessero

14. (io) feci, (tu) facesti, (lui/lei; Lei) fece, (noi) facemmo, (voi) faceste, (loro; Loro) fecero

15. (io) fui, (tu) fosti, (lui/lei; Lei) fu, (noi) fummo, (voi) foste, (loro; Loro) furono

16. (io) dissi, (tu) dicesti, (lui/lei; Lei) disse, (noi) dicemmo, (voi) diceste, (loro; Loro) dissero

17. (io) decisi, (tu) decidesti, (lui/lei; Lei) decise, (noi) decidemmo, (voi) decideste, (loro; Loro) decisero

18. (io) diedi, (tu) desti, (lui/lei; Lei) diede, (noi) demmo, (voi) deste, (loro; Loro) diedero

19. (io) conobbi, (tu) conoscesti, (lui/lei; Lei) conobbe, (noi) conoscemmo, (voi) conosceste, (loro; Loro) conobbero

20. (io) chiusi, (tu) chiudesti, (lui/lei; Lei) chiuse, (noi) chiudemmo, (voi) chiudeste, (loro; Loro) chiusero

21. (io) chiesi, (tu) chiedesti, (lui/lei; Lei) chiese, (noi) chiedemmo, (voi) chiedeste, (loro; Loro) chiesero

22. (io) caddi, (tu) cadesti, (lui/lei; Lei) cadde, (noi) cademmo, (voi) cadeste, (loro; Loro) caddero

23. (io) bevvi (bevetti), (tu) bevesti, (lui/lei; Lei) bevve (bevette), (noi) bevemmo, (voi) beveste, (loro; Loro) bevvero (bevettero)

24. (io) ebbi, (tu) avesti, (lui/lei; Lei) ebbe, (noi) avemmo, (voi) aveste, (loro; Loro) ebbero

B. 1. Galileo inventò il telescopio.   2. Colombo venne nel Nuovo Mondo nel 1492.   3. Leonardo Fibonacci fu un grande matematico.   4. Leonardo Da Vinci fece molte scoperte.   5. Il compositore Giuseppe Verdi nacque nel 1813.   6. Alessandro Manzoni scrisse *I promessi sposi*.

C. 1. Dopo avere mangiato, siamo andati al cinema.   2. Dopo avere comprato quella macchina, abbiamo venduto l'altra macchina nostra.   3. Dopo essere andate in Italia, le mie amiche cominciarono (hanno cominciato) a parlare italiano molto bene.

D. 1. (tu) hai cantato, abbia cantato, cantasti   2. (io) ho mangiato, abbia mangiato, mangiai   3. (lui) ha pagato, abbia pagato, pagò   4. (noi) abbiamo venduto, abbiamo venduto, vendemmo   5. (voi) avete letto, abbiate letto, leggeste   6. (loro) hanno scritto, abbiano scritto, scrissero   7. (lei) è nata, sia nata, nacque [Don't forget the agreement between past participle and subject when the verb is conjugated with essere.]   8. (io) ho capito, abbia capito, capii   9. (tu) hai finito, abbia finito, finisti   10. (lui) è venuto, sia venuto, venne   11. (loro) hanno detto, abbiano detto, dissero   12. (voi) avete dato, abbiate dato, deste   13. (noi) abbiamo fatto, abbiamo fatto, facemmo   14. (io) ho chiesto, abbia chiesto, chiesi   15. (lui) è stato, sia stato, fu

E. 1. Marco ha venduto la sua macchina ieri.   2. Maria è andata al cinema ieri.   3. Maria ha comprato le scarpe nuove ieri.   4. I miei amici sono andati in Italia la settimana scorsa.   5. Anche le sue amiche sono andate in Italia qualche giorno fa.   6. Loro hanno visto quel film già.   7. Voi avete già mangiato, non è vero?   8. Noi tutti siamo andati al cinema ieri.   9. Signor Verdi, quando è uscito ieri Lei?   10. Signora Verdi, quando è uscita ieri Lei?

F. 1. Penso che il film sia durato tre ore.   2. Quanto è costata la carne?   3. Benché/Sebbene mia sorella abbia venduto la sua macchina, lei ha una moto.   4. Ieri abbiamo parlato al signor Verdi.   5. Penso che (lui) abbia dormito troppo ieri.   6. Benché/Sebbene (io) abbia mangiato già, voglio mangiare di nuovo (ancora).   7. Nostro nonno venne / è venuto negli Stati Uniti nel 1994.

11·6   1. Michelangelo scolpì il David(e).   2. Giuseppe Verdi compose/scrisse molte belle opere.   3. (Il) Petrarca scrisse delle belle poesie.   4. Pavarotti fu/era un grande tenore.

12·1 **A.** 1. (io) cantavo   2. (io) stavo   3. (io) facevo   4. (lui) cominciava   5. (lui) era   6. (lui) diceva   7. (io) leggevo   8. (noi) davamo   9. (noi) bevevamo   10. (io) capivo   11. (tu) guardavi   12. (io) bevevo   13. (tu) dormivi   14. (tu) vedevi   15. (tu) eri   16. (lei) aveva   17. (noi) davamo   18. (lui) faceva   19. (voi) eravate   20. (voi) uscivate   21. (lei) diceva   22. (noi) sapevamo   23. (voi) potevate   24. (noi) pagavamo   25. (voi) mangiavate   26. (loro) arrivavano   27. (loro) avevano   28. (loro) venivano   29. (lei) preferiva   30. (noi) capivamo

B. 1. b   2. b   3. b   4. a   5. b   6. a   7. b   8. b

12·2 **A.** 1. (io) cantassi   2. (io) facessi   3. (io) stessi   4. (lui) fosse   5. (lui) cominciasse   6. (lui) leggesse   7. (io) dicessi   8. (noi) bevessimo   9. (noi) dessimo   10. (io) guardassi   11. (tu) capissi   12. (io) bevessi   13. (tu) dormissi   14. (tu) vedessi   15. (tu) fossi   16. (lei) avesse   17. (noi) dessimo   18. (lui) facesse   19. (voi) foste   20. (voi) usciste   21. (lei) dicesse   22. (noi) sapessimo   23. (voi) poteste   24. (noi) pagassimo   25. (voi) mangiaste   26. (loro) arrivassero   27. (loro) venissero   28. (loro) avessero   29. (lei) preferisse   30. (noi) capissimo

B. 1. È possibile che da bambina mia madre suonasse il pianoforte.   2. Credo che da giovane mio padre avesse i capelli lunghi.   3. Pensavamo che mentre lui dormiva, tu guardassi la TV.   4. Sembra che di solito lui studiasse il sabato.   5. Credevamo che mentre tu studiavi, lui giocasse a calcio.   6. È possibile che da bambini i nostri amici andassero spesso in Italia.   7. Credo che da bambina lei non volesse mangiare la pasta.   8. Lui pensa che alcuni anni fa io andassi spesso al cinema.

12·3 **A.** 1. avevo mangiato, avessi mangiato   2. avevo venduto, avessi venduto   3. ero partita, fossi partita   4. avevo avuto, avessi avuto   5. eri andato, fossi andato   6. avevi venduto, avessi venduto   7. eri uscito, fossi uscito   8. avevi fatto, avessi fatto   9. era arrivato, fosse arrivato   10. aveva potuto, avesse potuto   11. aveva preferito, avesse preferito   12. era stata, fosse stata   13. avevamo pagato, avessimo pagato   14. avevamo dovuto, avessimo dovuto   15. avevamo dormito, avessimo dormito   16. avevamo detto, avessimo detto   17. avevate cantato, aveste cantato   18. avevate potuto, aveste potuto   19. eravate partiti, foste partiti   20. avevate dato, aveste dato   21. avevano cominciato, avessero cominciato   22. avevano dovuto, avessero dovuto   23. avevano capito, avessero capito   24. erano nati, fossero nati

B. 1. b   2. a   3. b   4. b   5. a   6. b   7. b

C. 1. io fossi arrivato   2. io vendessi   3. io avessi preferito   4. io andassi   5. io avessi avuto   6. tu mangiassi   7. tu avessi messo   8. tu mettessi   9. tu bevessi   10. tu fossi caduto   11. lui cominciasse   12. lei avesse chiesto   13. lui avesse capito   14. Lei desse   15. lei fosse   16. noi pagassimo   17. noi avessimo chiuso   18. noi avessimo finito   19. noi facessimo   20. noi potessimo   21. voi cercaste   22. voi metteste   23. voi aveste preferito   24. voi sapeste   25. voi aveste tenuto   26. loro mangiassero   27. loro avessero chiesto   28. loro fossero andati   29. loro vedessero   30. loro venissero

D. 1. a or c   2. b or c   3. c   4. a or c   5. a or b or c   6. a   7. a or b or c   8. b or c   9. b or c   10. b or c

12·4   1. a   2. b   3. a   4. b

13·1 **A.** 1. andare, andando, essendo andati (-e)   2. fare, facendo, avendo fatto   3. stare (essere), stando (essendo), essendo stato (-a)   4. leggere, leggendo, avendo letto   5. dare, dando, avendo dato   6. dire, dicendo, avendo detto   7. venire, venendo, essendo venuto (-a)   8. bere, bevendo, avendo bevuto

B. 1. Guardando la TV (Mentre guardava la TV), diventò / è diventato stanco.   2. Avendo fatto tutto, è uscito.   3. Studiando l'italiano ieri sera, (lei) diventò / è diventata assai stanca.   4. Essendo andati (-e) in Italia, loro impararono / hanno imparato a parlare bene.

13·2 **A.** 1. io sto mangiando, *I am eating*   2. tu stai leggendo, *you (fam., sing.) are eating*   3. Lei sta finendo, *you (pol., sing.) are finishing*   4. noi stiamo guardando, *we are watching / looking at*   5. voi state vedendo, *you (fam., pl.) are seeing*   6. lui sta dicendo, *he is saying / telling*   7. lei sta facendo, *she is doing / making*   8. loro stanno imparando, *they are learning*   9. che io stia aspettando, *that I am waiting*   10. che tu stia scrivendo, *that you (fam., sing.) are writing*   11. che Lei stia bevendo, *that you (pol., sing.) are drinking*   12. che noi stiamo andando, *that we are going*   13. che voi stiate uscendo, *that you (fam., pl.) are going*   14. che loro stiano andando, *that they are going*   15. che lui stia facendo, *that he is doing / making*   16. che lei stia vedendo, *that she is seeing*

B. 1. Penso che Giovanni stia mangiando in questo momento.   2. Maria crede che voi stiate guardando un programma alla televisione adesso.   3. Sembra che mio fratello stia dormendo.   4. Lui crede che io stia scrivendo un'e-mail.   5. Lei pensa che i miei amici stiano uscendo.   6. Loro credono che noi stiamo bevendo un caffè.   7. Dubito che voi stiate leggendo quel romanzo in questo momento.   8. Sembra che lui stia suonando il pianoforte.

C. 1. Franco, che (cosa) stai bevendo? Stai bevendo un espresso?   2. Quale/Che programma stanno guardando in questo momento?   3. Signora Marchi, che (cosa) sta dicendo?   4. Marco e Maria stanno uscendo in questo momento.   5. Dov'è Alessandro? Sta dormendo.   6. Che (cosa) stanno bevendo? Penso che stiano bevendo un cappuccino.

13·3 **A.** 1. io stavo andando   2. tu stavi cominciando   3. noi stavamo scrivendo   4. loro stavano leggendo   5. voi stavate preferendo   6. lei stava dormendo   7. che io stessi cominciando   8. tu stavi bevendo   9. noi stavamo dando   10. loro stavano facendo   11. voi stavate dicendo   12. lui stava studiando   13. che tu stessi leggendo   14. che lei stesse uscendo   15. che lui stesse mangiando   16. che noi stessimo venendo   17. che voi steste uscendo

B. 1. a or b   2. a or b   3. a   4. a or b   5. a or b   6. b

C. 1. parlare, avere parlato, parlando, avendo parlato   2. arrivare, essere arrivato (-a), arrivando, essendo arrivato (-a)   3. cadere, essere caduto (-a), cadendo, essendo caduto (-a)   4. vendere, avere venduto, vendendo, avendo venduto   5. dormire, avere dormito, dormendo, avendo dormito   6. partire, esser(e) partito (-a), partendo, essendo partito (-a)   7. fare, avere fatto, facendo, avendo fatto   8. dire, avere detto, dicendo, avendo detto   9. bere, avere bevuto, bevendo, avendo bevuto   10. dare, avere dato, dando, avendo dato

D. 1. a   2. a   3. a or b   4. a   5. a or b

E. 1. b   2. a   3. b   4. a   5. a or b

13·4 1. pesante, *heavy*   2. pendente, *pendant*   3. eccitante, *exciting*   4. insegnante, *teacher*

14·1 **A.** 1. (io) manderò, (tu) manderai, (lui/lei) manderà, (noi) manderemo, (voi) manderete, (loro) manderanno

2. (io) indicherò, (tu) indicherai, (lui/lei) indicherà, (noi) indicheremo, (voi) indicherete, (loro) indicheranno

3. (io) navigherò, (tu) navigherai, (lui/lei) navigherà, (noi) navigheremo, (voi) navigherete, (loro) navigheranno

4. (io) bacerò, (tu) bacerai, (lui/lei) bacerà, (noi) baceremo, (voi) bacerete, (loro) baceranno

5. (io) leggerò, (tu) leggerai, (lui/lei) leggerà, (noi) leggeremo, (voi) leggerete, (loro) leggeranno

6. (io) preferirò, (tu) preferirai, (lui/lei) preferirà, (noi) preferiremo, (voi) preferirete, (loro) preferiranno

7. (io) vorrò, (tu) vorrai, (lui/lei) vorrà, (noi) vorremo, (voi) vorrete, (loro) vorranno

8. (io) verrò, (tu) verrai, (lui/lei) verrà, (noi) verremo, (voi) verrete, (loro) verranno

9. (io) vedrò, (tu) vedrai, (lui/lei) vedrà, (noi) vedremo, (voi) vedrete, (loro) vedranno

10. (io) starò, (tu) starai, (lui/lei) starà, (noi) staremo, (voi) starete, (loro) staranno

11. (io) saprò, (tu) saprai, (lui/lei) saprà, (noi) sapremo, (voi) saprete, (loro) sapranno

12. (io) potrò, (tu) potrai, (lui/lei) potrà, (noi) potremo, (voi) potrete, (loro) potranno

13. (io) farò, (tu) farai, (lui/lei) farà, (noi) faremo, (voi) farete, (loro) faranno

14. (io) sarò, (tu) sarai, (lui/lei) sarà, (noi) saremo, (voi) sarete, (loro) saranno

15. (io) dovrò, (tu) dovrai, (lui/lei) dovrà, (noi) dovremo, (voi) dovrete, (loro) dovranno

16. (io) darò, (tu) darai, (lui/lei) darà, (noi) daremo, (voi) darete, (loro) daranno

17. (io) cadrò, (tu) cadrai, (lui/lei) cadrà, (noi) cadremo, (voi) cadrete, (loro) cadranno

18. (io) berrò, (tu) berrai, (lui/lei) berrà, (noi) berremo, (voi) berrete, (loro) berranno

19. (io) avrò, (tu) avrai, (lui/lei) avrà, (noi) avremo, (voi) avrete, (loro) avranno

20. (io) andrò, (tu) andrai, (lui/lei) andrà, (noi) andremo, (voi) andrete, (loro) andranno

B. 1. Manderò/Invierò un'e-mail a mia sorella domani.   2. (Lei) navigherà in/su Internet tra/fra poco.   3. (Loro) partiranno tra/fra una settimana.   4. Sai/Sa quanto costeranno/costano quelle scarpe? Costeranno 500 euro.   5. Chi sarà? A quest'ora sarà tuo fratello.

C. 1. Signor Dini, quando vedrà Sua figlia?   2. Signorina Marchi, dove andrà in vacanza?   3. Signor Verdi e signora Verdi, a che ora verranno alla festa?   4. Signora Rossini e signor Rossini, quando usciranno?

14·2

A. 1. (io) avrò imparato   2. (io) sarò uscita   3. (tu) avrai fatto   4. (tu) sarai venuto   5. (lui) avrà scritto   6. (lui) sarà andato   7. (lei) avrà letto   8. (lei) sarà tornata   9. (noi) avremo visto   10. (noi) saremo entrati   11. (voi) avrete chiamato   12. (voi) sarete stati   13. (loro) avranno bevuto   14. (loro) saranno rientrati   15. (io) avrò navigato

B. 1. Mangerò anche la carne, appena io avrò finito la pasta.   2. Sono sicura che lui sarà uscito già.   3. Claudia arriverà domani verso il tardo pomeriggio.   4. Quando andrete in Italia, tu e tua sorella?   5. È vero che verranno anche loro alla festa?   6. A quest'ora Sara sarà andata già a dormire.   7. Appena saranno arrivati/arriveranno, loro andranno al cinema insieme.   8. Quando loro avranno visto quel film, diranno che è un grande film.   9. Dopo che tu avrai mangiato questo dolce, sono sicuro che vorrai un altro dolce.   10. Quanto sarà costata / costerà quella macchina che poi non avete comprato?   11. A che ora ha chiamato la tua amica? Lei avrà chiamato alle cinque.

14·3

A. 1. io arriverei, sarei arrivato (-a)   2. io venderei, avrei venduto   3. io preferirei, avrei preferito   4. io andrei, sarei andato (-a)   5. io avrei, avrei avuto   6. tu mangeresti, avresti mangiato   7. tu metteresti, avresti messo   8. tu apriresti, avresti aperto   9. tu berresti, avresti bevuto   10. tu cadresti, saresti caduto (-a)   11. lui comincerebbe, avrebbe cominciato   12. lei chiederebbe, avrebbe chiesto   13. lui capirebbe, avrebbe capito   14. Lei darebbe, avrebbe dato   15. lei sarebbe, sarebbe stata   16. noi pagheremmo, avremmo pagato   17. noi chiuderemmo, avremmo chiuso   18. noi finiremmo, avremmo finito   19. noi faremmo, avremmo fatto   20. noi potremmo, avremmo potuto   21. voi cerchereste, avreste cercato   22. voi mettereste, avreste messo   23. voi preferireste, avreste preferito   24. voi sapreste, avreste saputo   25. voi terreste, avreste tenuto   26. loro mangerebbero, avrebbero mangiato   27. loro chiederebbero, avrebbero chiesto   28. loro preferirebbero, avrebbero preferito   29. loro vedrebbero, avrebbero visto   30. loro verrebbero, sarebbero venuti (-e)   31. voi verreste, sareste venuti (-e)   32. noi andremmo, saremmo andati (-e)

B. 1. (Io) vorrei mandare/inviare un'e-mail a mio fratello domani.   2. (Loro) sarebbero andati (-e) in Italia, ma non avevano abbastanza soldi.   3. (Loro) avrebbero comprato quella macchina, ma non sapevano guidare.   4. Potrei avere una tazza di caffè, per favore?   5. (Noi) saremmo andati (-e) al cinema ieri, ma dovevamo studiare.   6. Mi ha detto che sarebbe venuto.   7. Sapeva che (io) avrei capito.   8. Secondo Sara, (io) avrei dovuto studiare di più.   9. Nella loro opinione, (noi) avremmo dovuto vincere.   10. Potrei dire qualcosa?   11. Mi potresti dare la tua penna, per favore? / Mi potrebbe dare la Sua penna, per favore? Grazie!   12. Nella loro opinione, lui sarebbe una buona/brava persona.

14·4

A. 1. Se noi potessimo, compreremmo quella casa.   2. Se lui avesse soldi, andrebbe in Italia.   3. Se voi aveste più tempo, sono sicuro che andreste al cinema più spesso.   4. Se io vivessi in Italia, berrei solo il caffè espresso.   5. Se loro fossero stati in Italia, avrebbero visto tante belle cose.   6. Se tu avessi fatto i compiti ieri, oggi potresti / avresti potuto guardare la TV in pace.

B. 1. Se noi potessimo, compreremmo quella macchina.   2. Se io avessi soldi, andrei subito in Italia.   3. Se voi sapeste parlare italiano, sono sicuro che andreste in Italia.   4. Se io fossi stato (-a) in Italia, avrei visto molte belle cose.   5. Se loro avessero conosciuto un buon ristorante, saremmo andati lì ieri sera.   6. Magari non piovesse / avesse piovuto!

C. 1. io arrivo, arriverò, sarò arrivato (-a), arriverei, sarei arrivato (-a)   2. io vendo, venderò, avrò venduto, venderei, avrei venduto   3. io preferisco, preferirò, avrò preferito, preferirei, avrei preferito   4. io vado, andrò, sarò andato (-a), andrei, sarei andato (-a)   5. io ho, avrò, avrò avuto, avrei, avrei avuto   6. tu mangi, mangerai, avrai mangiato, mangeresti, avresti mangiato   7. tu metti, metterai, avrai messo, metteresti, avresti messo   8. tu apri, aprirai, avrai aperto, apriresti, avresti aperto   9. tu bevi, berrai, avrai bevuto, berresti, avresti bevuto   10. tu cadi, cadrai, sarai caduto (-a), cadresti, saresti caduto (-a)   11. lui comincia, comincerà, avrà cominciato, comincerebbe, avrebbe cominciato   12. lei chiede, chiederà, avrà chiesto, chiederebbe, avrebbe chiesto   13. lui capisce, capirà, avrà capito, capirebbe, avrebbe capito   14. Lei dà, darà, avrà dato, darebbe, avrebbe dato   15. lei è, sarà, sarà stata, sarebbe, sarebbe stata   16. noi paghiamo, pagheremo, avremo pagato, pagheremmo, avremmo pagato   17. noi chiudiamo, chiuderemo, avremo chiuso, chiuderemmo, avremmo chiuso   18. noi finiamo, finiremo, avremo finito, finiremmo, avremmo finito   19. noi facciamo, faremo, avremo fatto, faremmo, avremmo fatto   20. noi possiamo, potremo, avremo potuto, potremmo, avremmo potuto   21. voi cercate, cercherete, avrete cercato, cerchereste, avreste cercato   22. voi mettete, metterete, avrete messo, mettereste, avreste messo   23. voi preferite, preferirete, avrete preferito, preferireste, avreste preferito   24. voi sapete, saprete, avrete saputo, sapreste, avreste saputo   25. voi tenete, terrete, avrete tenuto, terreste, avreste tenuto   26. loro mangiano, mangeranno, avranno mangiato, mangerebbero, avrebbero mangiato   27. loro chiedono, chiederanno, avranno chiesto, chiederebbero, avrebbero chiesto   28. loro finiscono, finiranno, avranno finito, finirebbero, avrebbero finito   29. loro vedono, vedranno, avranno visto, vedrebbero, avrebbero visto   30. loro vengono, verranno, saranno venuti (-e), verrebbero, sarebbero venuti (-e)

D. 1. c or d   2. c or d   3. a   4. c   5. c   6. b   7. c   8. a   9. d   10. d

14·5 1. Potrei avere una tazza di caffè, per favore?   2 Mi potrebbe dire dov'è / dove si trova via Verdi?   3. Che (cosa) raccomanderesti?   4. Mi potresti aiutare?

15·1 **A.** 1. parla, parli, parliamo, parlate, parlino   2. indica, indichi, indichiamo, indicate, indichino   3. allega, alleghi, alleghiamo, allegate, alleghino   4. bacia, baci, baciamo, baciate, bacino   5. mangia, mangi, mangiamo, mangiate, mangino   6. leggi, legga, leggiamo, leggete, leggano   7. apri, apra, apriamo, aprite, aprano   8. pulisci, pulisca, puliamo, pulite, puliscano

B. 1. a. Giovanni, mangia la mela! b. Giovanni, chiama Maria! c. Giovanni, scrivi un'e-mail a tuo zio! d. Giovanni, apri la finestra! e. Giovanni, finisci di studiare!   2. a. Signora Verdi, aspetti l'autobus! b. Signora Verdi, cerchi il libro! c. Signora Verdi, metta la chiave nella (Sua) borsa! d. Signora Verdi, apra la porta! e. Signora Verdi, finisca il caffè!   3. a. Marco e Maria, cominciate a studiare! b. Marco e Maria, parlate italiano! c. Marco e Maria, chiudete la finestra! d. Marco e Maria, aprite la porta! e. Marco e Maria, pulite la casa!   4. a. Signor Rossini e signora Rossini, mangino la carne! b. Signor Rossini e signora Rossini, aspettino qui! c. Signor Rossini e signora Rossini, chiudano la finestra! d. Signor Rossini e signora Rossini, aprano la porta! e. Signor Rossini e signora Rossini, puliscano la casa!

C. 1. Signorina Bruni, ascolti la radio!   2. Marco, prendi questa tazza!   3. Professori, giochino a calcio!   4. Ragazzi e ragazze, leggete il giornale!

15·2 **A.** 1. a. Maria, non mangiare la torta! b. Maria, non pagare il conto!   2. a. Signora Marchi, non pulisca la casa! b. Signora Marchi, non chiuda la porta!   3. a. Ragazzi e ragazze, non aprite i vostri libri! b. Ragazzi e ragazze, non leggete quel romanzo!   4. a. Signore e signori, non paghino il conto! b. Signore e signori, non ascoltino la radio!

B. 1. a. Signore e signori, mangino la torta! b. Signore e signori, paghino il conto!   2. a. Ragazzi e ragazze, pulite la casa! b. Ragazzi e ragazze, chiudete la porta!   3. a. Signora Verdi, apra il Suo libro! b. Signora Verdi, legga quel romanzo!   4. a. Maria, finisci tutta la torta! b. Maria, ascolta la radio!

15·3 **A.** 1. (tu) vieni, (Lei) venga, (noi) veniamo, (voi) venite, (Loro) vengano   2. (tu) esci, (Lei) esca, (noi) usciamo, (voi) uscite, (Loro) escano   3. (tu) tieni, (Lei) tenga, (noi) teniamo, (voi) tenete, (Loro) tengano   4. (tu) sta', (Lei) stia, (noi) stiamo, (voi) state, (Loro) stiano   5. (tu) scegli, (Lei) scelga, (noi) scegliamo, (voi) scegliete, (Loro) scelgano   6. (tu) sappi, (Lei) sappia, (noi) sappiamo, (voi) sappiate, (Loro) sappiano   7. (tu) sali, (Lei) salga, (noi) saliamo, (voi) salite, (Loro) salgano   8. (tu) fa', (Lei) faccia, (noi) facciamo, (voi) fate, (Loro) facciano   9. (tu) sii, (Lei) sia, (noi) siamo, (voi) siate, (Loro) siano   10. (tu) di', (Lei) dica, (noi) diciamo, (voi) dite, (Loro) dicano   11. (tu) da', (Lei) dia, (noi) diamo, (voi) date, (Loro) diano   12. (tu) bevi, (Lei) beva, (noi) beviamo, (voi) bevete, (Loro) bevano   13. (tu) abbi, (Lei) abbia, (noi) abbiamo, (voi) abbiate, (Loro) abbiano   14. (tu) va', (Lei) vada, (noi) andiamo, (voi) andate, (Loro) vadano

B. 1. Claudia, non venire qui! 2. Signora Dini, faccia quella cosa! 3. Marco, non dire la verità! 4. Professore, vada via! 5. Franca, non stare zitta! 6. Paolo, va' via! 7. Professoressa, non stia qui! 8. Bruno, bevi quella bibita!

C. 1. Mangi la pizza! 2. Comincia a mangiare! 3. Aspetti qui! 4. Apri la porta! 5. Finisca la mela! 6. Cerca la chiave! 7. Paghi il conto! 8. Scrivi l'e-mail! 9. Chiuda la porta! 10. Dormi! 11. Aprano le porte! 12. Chiudete le porte! 13. Finiscano di studiare! 14. Abbi pazienza! 15. Vada a dormire!

D. 1. Non mangiare la pesca! 2. Guardi la televisione! 3. Non finiamo di mangiare! 4. Chiudi la porta! 5. Non bere tutta l'acqua! 6. Dica questo! 7. Non usciamo stasera!

E. 1. a. Claudia, mangia la mela! b. Claudia, non bere l'acqua! c. Claudia, chiudi la porta! d. Claudia, apri la finestra! 2. a. Claudia e Paolo, mangiate la mela! b. Claudia e Paolo, non bevete l'acqua! c. Claudia e Paolo, chiudete la porta! d. Claudia e Paolo, aprite la finestra! 3. a. Signora Verdi, mangi la mela! b. Signora Verdi, non beva l'acqua! c. Signora Verdi, chiuda la porta! d. Signora Verdi, apra la finestra! 4. a. Signora Verdi e signor Rossi, mangino la mela! b. Signora Verdi e signor Rossi, non bevano l'acqua! c. Signora Verdi e signor Rossi, chiudano la porta! d. Signora Verdi e signor Rossi, aprano la finestra!

15·4
1. Dottoressa Marchi, mi può dare / può darmi la ricetta? 2. Cameriere, mi può portare / può portarmi subito il caffè? 3. Signora, mi può dire / può dirmi tutto? 4. Professore, mi può aiutare / può aiutarmi?

16·1 **A.** 1. (tu) ti alzi, ti alzi, ti alzasti 2. (lei) si annoia, si annoi, si annoiò 3. (lui) si arrabbia, si arrabbi, si arrabbiò 4. (io) mi alzo, mi alzi, mi alzai 5. (noi) ci dimentichiamo, ci dimentichiamo, ci dimenticammo [Don't forget to maintain the hard **c** before -**i**.] 6. (voi) vi divertite, vi divertiate, vi divertiste 7. (io) mi lamento, mi lamenti, mi lamentai 8. (loro) si lavano, si lavino, si lavarono 9. (tu) ti metti, ti metta, ti mettesti 10. (lei) si preoccupa, si preoccupi, si preoccupò 11. (lui) si prepara, si prepari, si preparò 12. (noi) ci sentiamo, ci sentiamo, ci sentimmo 13. (voi) vi sposate, vi sposiate, vi sposaste 14. (loro) si svegliano, si sveglino, si svegliarono 15. (lui) si veste, si vesta, si vestì

B. 1. (tu) ti alzerai, ti alzeresti, ti stai alzando, ti stia alzando 2. (lei) si annoierà, si annoierebbe, si sta annoiando, si stia annoiando 3. (lui) si arrabbierà, si arrabbierebbe, si sta arrabbiando, si stia arrabbiando 4. (io) mi alzerò, mi alzerei, mi sto alzando, mi stia alzando 5. (noi) ci dimenticheremo, ci dimenticheremmo, ci stiamo dimenticando, ci stiamo dimenticando [Don't forget to maintain the hard **c** in the future and conditional.] 6. (voi) vi divertirete, vi divertireste, vi state divertendo, vi stiate divertendo 7. (io) mi lamenterò, mi lamenterei, mi sto lamentando, mi stia lamentando 8. (loro) si laveranno, si laverebbero, si stanno lavando, si stiano lavando 9. (tu) ti metterai, ti metteresti, ti stai mettendo, ti stia mettendo 10. (lei) si preoccuperà, si preoccuperebbe, si sta preoccupando, si stia preoccupando 11. (lui) si preparerà, si preparerebbe, si sta preparando, si stia preparando 12. (noi) ci sentiremo, ci sentiremmo, ci stiamo sentendo, ci stiamo sentendo 13. (voi) vi sposerete, vi sposereste, vi state sposando, vi stiate sposando 14. (loro) si sveglieranno, si sveglierebbero, si stanno svegliando, si stiano svegliando 15. (lui) si vestirà, si vestirebbe, si sta vestendo, si stia vestendo

C. 1. (tu) ti alzavi, ti alzassi, ti stavi alzando, ti stessi alzando 2. (lei) si annoiava, si annoiasse, si stava annoiando, si stesse annoiando 3. (lui) si arrabbiava, si arrabbiasse, si stava arrabbiando, si stesse arrabbiando 4. (io) mi alzavo, mi alzassi, mi stavo alzando, mi stessi alzando 5. (noi) ci dimenticavamo, ci dimenticassimo, ci stavamo dimenticando, ci stessimo dimenticando 6. (voi) vi divertivate, vi divertiste, vi stavate divertendo, vi steste divertendo 7. (io) mi lamentavo, mi lamentassi, mi stavo lamentando, mi stessi lamentando 8. (loro) si lavavano, si lavassero, si stavano lavando, si stessero lavando 9. (tu) ti mettevi, ti mettessi, ti stavi mettendo, ti stessi mettendo 10. (lei) si preoccupava, si preoccupasse, si stava preoccupando, si stesse preoccupando 11. (lui) si preparava, si preparasse, si stava preparando, si stesse preparando 12. (noi) ci sentivamo, ci sentissimo, ci stavamo sentendo, ci stessimo sentendo 13. (voi) vi sposavate, vi sposaste, vi stavate sposando, vi steste sposando 14. (loro) si svegliavano, si svegliassero, si stavano svegliando, si stessero svegliando 15. (lui) si vestiva, si vestisse, si stava vestendo, si stesse vestendo

D. 1. Ci parliamo spesso. 2. Si telefonano ogni giorno. 3. Non si vedono da un po' di tempo. 4. Non ci capiamo mai.

16·2 **A.** 1. (tu) ti sei alzato (-a), ti sia alzato (-a), ti sarai alzato (-a) 2. (lei) si è annoiata, si sia annoiata, si sarà annoiata 3. (lui) si è arrabbiato, si sia arrabbiato, si sarà arrabbiato 4. (io) mi sono alzato (-a), mi sia alzato (-a), mi sarò alzato (-a) 5. (noi) ci siamo dimenticati (-e), ci siamo dimenticati (-e), ci saremo dimenticati (-e) 6. (voi) vi siete divertiti (-e), vi siate divertiti (-e), vi sarete divertiti (-e) 7. (io) mi sono lamentato (-a), mi sia lamentato (-a), mi sarò lamentato (-a) 8. (loro) si sono lavati (-e), si siano lavati (-e), si saranno lavati (-e) 9. (tu) ti sei messo (-a), ti sia messo (-a), ti sarai messo (-a) 10. (lei) si è preoccupata, si sia preoccupata, si sarà preoccupata 11. (lui) si è preparato, si sia preparato, si sarà preparato 12. (noi) ci siamo sentiti (-e), ci siamo sentiti (-e), ci saremo sentiti (-e) 13. (voi) vi siete sposati (-e), vi siate sposati (-e), vi sarete sposati (-e) 14. (loro) si sono svegliati (-e), si siano svegliati (-e), si saranno svegliati (-e) 15. (lui) si è vestito, si sia vestito, si sarà vestito

B. 1. (tu) ti saresti alzato (-a), ti eri alzato (-a), ti fossi alzato (-a) 2. (lei) si sarebbe annoiata, si era annoiata, si fosse annoiata 3. (lui) si sarebbe arrabbiato, si era arrabbiato, si fosse arrabbiato 4. (io) mi sarei alzato (-a), mi ero alzato (-a), mi fossi alzato (-a) 5. (noi) ci saremmo dimenticati (-e), ci eravamo dimenticati (-e), ci fossimo dimenticati (-e) 6. (voi) vi sareste divertiti (-e), vi eravate divertiti (-e), vi foste divertiti (-e) 7. (io) mi sarei lamentato (-a), mi ero lamentato (-a), mi fossi lamentato (-a) 8. (loro) si sarebbero lavati (-e), si erano lavati (-e), si fossero lavati (-e) 9. (tu) ti saresti messo (-a), ti eri messo (-a), ti fossi messo (-a) 10. (lei) si sarebbe preoccupata, si era preoccupata, si fosse preoccupata 11. (lui) si sarebbe preparato, si era preparato, si fosse preparato 12. (noi) ci saremmo sentiti (-e), ci eravamo sentiti (-e), ci fossimo sentiti (-e) 13. (voi) vi sareste sposati (-e), vi eravate sposati (-e), vi foste sposati (-e) 14. (loro) si sarebbero svegliati (-e), si erano svegliati (-e), si fossero svegliati (-e) 15. (lui) si sarebbe vestito, si era vestito, si fosse vestito

C. 1. Io me la sono messa per la festa. 2. Tu te la sei già lavata vero? 3. Lui se le è lavate già. 4. Lei se li è lavati già. 5. Noi ce lo siamo messo, perché faceva freddo. 6. Voi ve lo siete dimenticato. 7. Loro se la sono messa.

16·3 **A.** 1. (tu) alzati, (Lei) si alzi, (noi) alziamoci, (voi) alzatevi, (Loro) si alzino 2. (tu) divertiti, (Lei) si diverta, (noi) divertiamoci, (voi) divertitevi, (Loro) si divertano 3. (tu) lavati, (Lei) si lavi, (noi) laviamoci, (voi) lavatevi, (Loro) si lavino 4. (tu) mettiti, (Lei) si metta, (noi) mettiamoci, (voi) mettetevi, (Loro) si mettano 5. (tu) preparati, (Lei) si prepari, (noi) prepariamoci, (voi) preparatevi, (Loro) si preparino 6. (tu) svegliati, (Lei) si svegli, (noi) svegliamoci, (voi) svegliatevi, (Loro) si sveglino 7. (tu) vestiti, (Lei) si vesta, (noi) vestiamoci, (voi) vestitevi, (Loro) si vestano

B. 1. a. Marco, lavati i capelli! b. Marco, non metterti / non ti mettere la nuova giacca! [Don't forget to use the infinitive as the **tu** form in the negative.] c. Marco, alzati presto! d. Marco, vestiti subito! e. Marco, divertiti alla festa! 2. a. Signora Verdi, si lavi i capelli! b. Signora Verdi, non si metta il nuovo vestito! c. Signora Verdi, si alzi presto! d. Signora Verdi, si vesta subito! e. Signora Verdi, si diverta in centro! 3. a. Marco e Maria, lavatevi i capelli! b. Marco e Maria, non vi mettete / non mettetevi le nuove scarpe! c. Marco e Maria, alzatevi presto! d. Marco e Maria, vestitevi subito! e. Marco e Maria, divertitevi alla festa! 4. a. Signor Rossi e signora Rossi, si preparino per uscire! b. Signor Rossi e signora Rossi, non si sveglino presto! c. Signor Rossi e signora Rossi, non si arrabbino! d. Signor Rossi e signora Rossi, non si dimentichino di chiamare! e. Signor Rossi e signora Rossi, si divertano alla festa!

C. 1. Signorina Bruni, si alzi presto! 2. Marco, non arrabbiarti / non ti arrabbiare! 3. Professori, si divertano! 4. Ragazzi e ragazze, preparatevi!

D. 1. Marco e Maria, mettetevi gli stivali! 2. Signor Marchi, non si alzi! 3. Sara, non alzarti / non ti alzare! 4. Signorina Verdi, non si preoccupi! 5. Alessandro, dimenticati!

E. 1. (Noi) ci alziamo presto ogni giorno. 2. Sembra che lui si diverta sempre in Italia. 3. (Lei) si sposerebbe, se incontrasse la persona giusta. 4. (Io) mi divertivo sempre da bambino (-a). 5. (Lei) si è alzata tardi ieri. 6. (Noi) non ci parliamo più. 7. (Loro) si telefonano spesso. 8. Franco e Claudia, non vi vedete da molti anni, non è vero?

16·4 1. (Io) mi sono vestito (-a) alcuni minuti fa / qualche minuto fa. 2. (Lei) non si era resa conto che (tu) eri qui. 3. (Lui) non si sveglia mai presto. 4. (Lei) si è alzata presto questa mattina / stamani.

17·1 **A.** 1. a. alla scuola b. alle città c. al ragazzo d. alla ragazza e. ai professori f. agli avvocati g. allo zio h. all'amico 2. a. della ragazza b. delle donne c. del professore d. della professoressa e. dei bambini f. degli uomini g. dello studente h. dell'amica 3. a. dalla scuola b. dalle città c. dal Giappone d. dalla Spagna e. dai medici f. dagli Stati Uniti g. dallo zio h. dall'Italia 4. a. nella città b. nelle città c. nel centro d. nella scuola e. nei ristoranti f. negli Stati Uniti g. nello sport h. nell'anno 5. a. sulla scuola b. sulle città c. sul ragazzo d. sulla ragazza e. sui professori f. sugli avvocati g. sullo zio h. sull'amico

B. 1. (Io) ho messo il coltello tra/fra il cucchiaio e la forchetta.   2. (Io) parlo con la (colla) signora Verdi questa sera (stasera).   3. (Lui) guida per la città.   4. (Io) ho messo la chiave sopra la scatola.   5. È sotto la scatola.   6. (Lui) è a casa.   7. (Io) vado nella macchina dei miei amici.

17·2 **A.** 1. I soldi sono nella scatola.   2. Ecco i cellulari degli amici miei.   3. Le scarpe sono sotto la / sulla tavola.   4. Domani mio zio andrà dal medico.   5. Arrivano alle dieci stasera.   6. Noi viaggeremo con Alitalia / con l'Alitalia / coll'Alitalia.   7. Il tappeto è tra/fra / sotto la sedia e la tavola.   8. Il gatto dorme sopra la / sulla tavola, non sotto.   9. Maria rimane a casa domani tutto il giorno.   10. Preferisco andare in macchina a scuola.   11. Andremo alla casa nuova di mio fratello.   12. Andremo nella macchina di mia sorella.

B. 1. (Io) vivo a Firenze.   2. (Loro) vivono negli Stati Uniti.   3. Ecco la nuova macchina di Sara.   4. Come si chiama la figlia del tuo professore / della tua professoressa?   5. (Loro) vanno dal medico domani?   6. (Io) vengo dall'Italia.   7. (Loro) vivono in Italia da sei anni.   8. Da bambino / Da bambina, (io) navigavo spesso (in) Internet.   9. (Lei) ama il suo vestito/abito da sera.

17·3 **A.** 1. certo   2. semplicemente   3. facile   4. popolarmente   5. benevolo   6. leggermente   7. enormemente   8. felice   9. precisamente   10. speciale   11. utilmente   12. vero   13. lentamente   14. elegante   15. regolarmente   16. triste   17. veramente   18. simpaticamente

B. 1. alto, altamente   2. felice, felicemente   3. lento, lentamente   4. leggero, leggermente   5. nuovo, nuovamente   6. raro, raramente

17·4 **A.** 1. a   2. a   3. a   4. a   5. b   6. a   7. b   8. b

B. 1. Prima questo e poi quello.   2. Ecco / Eccolo anche lui.   3. di nuovo / ancora domani   4. finora   5. fra poco / tra poco   6. in fretta   7. insieme   8. Va bene e male.   9. oggigiorno   10. nel frattempo   11. ormai   12. per caso   13. stamani non stasera   14. spesso   15. piuttosto

17·5 **A.** 1. velocemente, più velocemente, meno velocemente, il più velocemente   2. vicino, più vicino, meno vicino, il più vicino   3. regolarmente, più regolarmente, meno regolarmente, il più regolarmente   4. presto, più presto, meno presto, il più presto   5. spesso, più spesso, meno spesso, il più spesso   6. tardi, più tardi, meno tardi, il più tardi.

B. 1. a   2. b   3. a   4. b   5. a   6. b   7. a   8. b

C. 1. La borsa di Maria è bella.   2. Lui va all'università in macchina.   3. Questo è il cellulare del fratello di Sara.   4. Ci sono venti dollari nella scatola.   5. Arrivano dalla/in Francia lunedì.   6. L'ho messo tra/fra la porta e quella sedia.   7. Vivo a Napoli.   8. Vivono in Italia e precisamente nell'Italia settentrionle.   9. Domani vado dal medico.   10. Viviamo negli Stati Uniti da quarant'anni.

D. 1. Maria va in centro spesso/regolarmente/oggi/domani.   2. Questo film è veramente/proprio molto bello.   3. Noi andiamo spesso/raramente al cinema.   4. Marco l'ha fatto ancora/già una volta.   5. Lui vive vicino/lontano e lei lontano/vicino.   6. Sono quasi/già le venti.   7. Prima voglio mangiare e poi vado al cinema.   8. Sono già/appena usciti.

17·6 1. Ieri sono andato (-a) su Internet per due ore.   2. (Io) ho visto quel programma alla/in televisione ieri.   3. L'ho sentito alla radio.   4. L'ho letto sul giornale.

18·1 **A.** 1. È spagnolo Marco?   2. Maria è italiana?   3. Parla francese lui?   4. Tuo fratello va in Italia quest'anno?   5. Giocano a tennis i tuoi amici?

B. 1. Giovanni è italiano? / È italiano Giovanni?   2. Maria è francese? / È francese Maria?   3. I tuoi amici sono italiani? / Sono italiani i tuoi amici?   4. La tua amica va in Francia? / Va in Francia la tua amica?   5. I tuoi amici giocano a calcio? / Giocano a calcio i tuoi amici?   6. Ci sono i tuoi amici in questa classe? / In questa classe ci sono i tuoi amici?

C. 1. Prendi/Prende molto zucchero nel caffè, vero? / non è vero? / no?   2. Ti piace / Le piace quel programma, vero? / non è vero? / no?   3. Pensi/Pensa che l'italiano sia una bella lingua, vero? / non è vero? / no?   4. Tuo/Suo fratello è francese, vero? / non è vero? / no?

18·2 **A.** 1. Che è? / Che cosa è? / Cosa è?   2. Che sono? / Che cosa sono? / Cosa sono?   3. Chi è?   4. Di chi è la rivista? / Che cosa è?   5. A chi hai dato il libro? [If you have forgotten the present perfect tense, go to Unit 11]   6. Come stai? / Come sta?   7. Dove vivi? / Dove vive?   8. Perché non vai in centro? / Perché non va in centro?   9. Quali studenti sono loro? / Chi sono?   10. Quanta carne mangi/mangia oggi?   11. Quante carote mangia lei di solito?   12. Quando arrivano?   13. Com'è la mela?   14. Qual è? / Di chi è?

B. 1. Dove vanno quest'anno? Vanno in Italia. 2. Come si chiama tua sorella? Si chiama Sara. 3. Perché studia matematica tuo fratello? Perché lui è molto intelligente. 4. Che / Che cosa / Cosa fai stasera? Vado al cinema. 5. Quale caffè vuoi, questo o quello? Voglio quel caffè. 6. Chi è quella donna? È mia cugina. 7. Di chi è quel libro? È di mia mamma. 8. Quanto caffè vuoi? Poco. 9. Perché studi l'italiano? Perché voglio vivere in Italia. 10. Che / Che cos'è / Cos è? È una macchina nuova.

18·3 **A.** 1. Lui non mangia mai gli spaghetti. 2. Ieri non ho mangiato né la carne né le patate. 3. Marco non conosce nessuno in quella scuola. 4. Lui non vuole niente/nulla. 5. Quello non è affatto/mica vero.

B. 1. No, Marco non aspetta il suo amico. 2. No, non dorme Maria. 3. No, non conosco nessuno qui. 4. No, non vado mai in Italia. 5. No, non mi piace nulla/niente. 6. No, non studio più. 7. No, non mi piace neanche/nemmeno/neppure la pizza. 8. No, non voglio né (il) caffè né (il) tè. 9. No, non è affatto/mica vero.

18·4 **A.** 1. La professoressa risponde sempre alle domande. 2. Ogni sera telefono alla mia amica. 3. Ho chiesto quella cosa a Marco. 4. Cerco una nuova macchina. 5. Alessandro e Giovanni aspettano la loro sorella.

B. 1. Vado spesso in centro. 2. Mangio spesso la pasta. 3. Ogni sera ascolto la radio. 4. Chiamo spesso mia sorella. 5. Aspetto l'autobus.

18·5 **A.** 1. Quando Giacomo arriva, andremo al negozio. 2. Appena arriva la madre, ci metteremo a studiare. 3. Dopo che sei uscito, è arrivata Sandra. 4. Mentre tu studi, io leggo il giornale. 5. La persona che legge il giornale è una mia amica. 6. Le scarpe le quali hai comprato ieri sono molto belle. 7. La persona a cui hai dato il libro è un mio amico. 8. Chi va a Roma, si divertirà. 9. Ecco il ragazzo la cui sorella vuole essere medico.

B. 1. Sara sta studiando e/mentre suo fratello guarda la TV. 2. La ragazza che ha i capelli biondi parla italiano molto bene. 3. Paolo e Franca parlano italiano. 4. Mi piace il libro che Maria sta leggendo. 5. Non trovo lo zaino in cui/nel quale ho messo il tuo libro.

C. 1. Maria è italiana? / È italiana Maria? 2. Loro prendono lo zucchero (vero / non è vero / no)? 3. Marco parla italiano molto bene? / Parla italiano molto bene Marco? 4. Lui è andato al cinema ieri (vero / non è vero / no)?

D. 1. Che (cosa) leggi/legge? 2. Chi è? 3. Che (cosa) è? / Di chi è la penna? 4. Come si chiama il tuo / il Suo amico? 5. Dove vivono i tuoi / i Suoi amici? 6. Perché non vai/va alla festa? 7. Quale rivista ti piace / Le piace? 8. Quando vai/va a Roma? 9. Quanto zucchero prendi/prende?

E. 1. Marco studia e/mentre sua sorella guarda la TV. 2. Lui viene in autobus o a piedi. 3. Studio la matematica, ma mi piace l'italiano. 4. La persona che / la quale legge quella rivista è mia sorella. 5. Il ragazzo a cui ho dato il libro è mio fratello. 6. Non trovo la borsa in cui ho messo la mia chiave. 7. Ecco la rivista di cui ho parlato. 8. Chi va in Italia si divertirà. 9. Quello / Quel / Ciò che dici non è affatto vero. 10. Ecco l'uomo la cui sorella è medico. 11. Ecco la persona alla quale ho dato il mio portatile. 12. Ecco le persone delle quali ho parlato ieri.

18·6 1. Ci sei? 2. perché 3. quando 4. ti voglio tanto bene

19·1 **A.** 1. 2, 12, 22, 32, 42, 52, 62, 72, 82, 92 due, dodici, ventidue, trentadue, quarantadue, cinquantadue, sessantadue, settantadue, ottantadue, novantadue

2. 4, 14, 24, 34, 44, 54, 64, 74, 84, 94 quattro, quattordici, ventiquattro, trentaquattro, quarantaquattro, cinquantaquattro, sessantaquattro, settantaquattro, ottantaquattro, novantaquattro

3. 9, 19, 29, 39, 49, 59, 69, 79, 89, 99 nove, diciannove, ventinove, trentanove, quarantanove, cinquantanove, sessantanove, settantanove, ottantanove, novantanove

4. 8, 18, 28, 38, 48, 58, 68, 78, 88, 98 otto, diciotto, ventotto, trentotto, quarantotto, cinquantotto, sessantotto, settantotto, ottantotto, novantotto

5. 7, 17, 27, 37, 47, 57, 67, 77, 87, 97 sette, diciassette, ventisette, trentasette, quarantasette, cinquantasette, sessantasette, settantasette, ottantasette, novantasette

6. 1, 11, 21, 31, 41, 51, 61, 71, 81, 91 uno, undici, ventuno, trentuno, quarantuno, cinquantuno, sessantuno, settantuno, ottantuno, novantuno

7. 5, 15, 25, 35, 45, 55, 65, 75, 85, 95 cinque, quindici, venticinque, trentacinque, quarantacinque, cinquantacinque, sessantacinque, settantacinque, ottantacinque, novantacinque

8. 6, 16, 26, 36, 46, 56, 66, 76, 86, 96 sei, sedici, ventisei, trentasei, quarantasei, cinquantasei, sessantasei, settantasei, ottantasei, novantasei

9. 0, 10, 20, 30, 40, 50, 60, 70, 80, 90 zero, dieci, venti, trenta, quaranta, cinquanta, sessanta, settanta, ottanta, novanta

B. 1. settecento e un (settecentun) uomini   2. duecento novantuna donne   3. mille cinquecento sessantotto studenti   4. quarantacinque mila cinquecento cinquantatré cellulari   5. settecento ottantanove mila duecento settantotto dollari   6. due milioni quattrocento cinquantasei mila duecento trentatré euro   7. diciotto camerieri   8. otto milioni di euro   9. cento ventidue macchine   10. novecento novantun dollari   11. tre virgola cinquantaquattro centimetri   12. zero virgola cinquantasei metri

C. 1. un altro caffè, nessun caffè   2. un altro espresso, nessun espresso   3. un altro tè, nessun tè   4. un altro caffè ristretto, nessun caffè ristretto   5. un altro caffè lungo, nessun caffè lungo   6. un altro caffè corretto, nessun caffè corretto   7. un altro zabaione, nessuno zabaione   8. un'altra bibita, nessuna bibita   9. un altro bicchiere di vino, nessun bicchiere di vino   10. un altro bicchiere di latte, nessun bicchiere di latte   11. un altro caffellatte, nessun caffellatte   12. un altro cappuccino, nessun cappuccino   13. un'altra aranciata, nessun'aranciata   14. un'altra limonata, nessuna limonata   15. un altro succo di frutta, nessun succo di frutta

19·2

A. 1. Sono le quattordici e venti.   2. Sono le otto e trentacinque.   3. Sono le sedici e cinquanta.   4. Sono le nove e quattordici.   5. Sono le diciassette e dodici.   6. Sono le dieci e quarantadue.   7. È l'una e cinque della notte.   8. Sono le undici e ventotto.   9. Sono le diciannove e diciotto.   10. Sono le venti e ventinove.   11. Sono le ventidue e trenta.   12. Sono le ventitré e trentotto.

B. 1. Sono le sei e quindici di mattina / della mattina / del mattino. Sono le sei e un quarto della mattina / del mattino. Buongiorno!   2. Sono le sette e trenta di sera / della sera. Sono le sette e mezzo/mezza di sera / della sera. Buonasera!   3. Sono le nove e quarantacinque di mattina / della mattina / del mattino. Sono le nove e tre quarti di mattina / della mattina / del mattino. Sono le dieci meno un quarto di mattina / della mattina / del mattino. Buongiorno!   4. Sono le otto e trenta di sera / della sera. Sono le otto e mezzo/mezza di sera / della sera. Buonasera!   5. Sono le nove e cinquantotto di mattina / della mattina / del mattino. Sono le dieci meno due di mattina / della mattina / del mattino. Buongiorno!   6. Sono le dodici della notte. È mezzzanotte. Buonanotte!   7. Sono le dodici del pomeriggio. È mezzogiorno. Buon pomeriggio!   8. È l'una precisa del pomeriggio. È l'una in punto del pomeriggio. Buon pomeriggio!   9. Sono le otto precise di mattina / della mattina / del mattino. Buongiorno!

C. 1. Il tempo vola!   2. Faccio qualcosa sempre due o tre volte.   3. Che ora è? / Che ore sono?

19·3

A. 1. la prima volta e l'undicesima volta   2. la seconda volta e la ventiduesima volta   3. il terzo piano e il trentatreesimo piano   4. il quarto capitolo e il quarantaquattresimo giorno   5. la quinta bibita e il cinquantacinquesimo espresso   6. la sesta foto/fotografia e la sessantaseiesima settimana   7. il settimo bicchiere di latte e il settantasettesimo mese   8. l'ottavo cappuccino e l'ottantottesimo anno   9. la nona limonata e la novantanovesima volta   10. la decima studentessa e la centesima lezione   11. un diciottesimo e cinque settimi   12. due terzi e (la) metà di tutto   13. mezzo litro

B. 1. Papa Giovanni Ventitreesimo (23º)   2. Lei è la prima (1ª) della classe.   3. Lui è l'ottavo (8º) in fila.

19·4

A. 1. È il ventitré gennaio.   2. È il quattordici febbraio.   3. È il sette marzo.   4. È il quattro aprile.   5. È il tre maggio.   6. È il trenta giugno.   7. È il trentun luglio.   8. È il primo agosto.   9. È l'otto settembre.   10. È il ventisette ottobre.   11. È il diciotto novembre.   12. È il venticinque dicembre.

B. 1. È il ventuno dicembre 2014.   2. Sono nato (-a) il...   3. Voglio il doppio. / Voglio un caffè doppio.   4. C'è una dozzina di studenti in classe   5. Due più otto fa dieci.   6. Otto meno tre fa cinque.   7. Quattro per ventidue fa ottantotto.   8. Venti diviso per quattro fa cinque.   9. Ho ventidue/ trentatré/... anni.

C. 1. sette, settimo   2. dodici, dodicesimo   3. diciassette, diciassettesimo   4. diciotto, diciottesimo   5. diciannove, diciannovesimo   6. ventiquattro, ventiquattresimo   7. trentuno, trentunesimo   8. quarantatré, quarantatreesimo   9. cinquantotto, cinquantottesimo   10. trecentonovantotto, trecentonovantottesimo   11. duemila dodici, duemila dodicesimo   12. trentaquattro mila cinquecento novantanove, trentaquattro mila cinquecento novantanovesimo

D. 1. quattro mila euro   2. cinque milioni di dollari   3. ventuna ragazze   4. Ho trentuno/trentun anni.   5. nessuno zio   6. nessuna zia   7. un altro ragazzo   8. un'altra ragazza   9. mezzo litro   10. Sedici diviso per quattro fa quattro.   11. È lunedì, il dodici luglio.   12. Sono nato/nata il ventitré giugno.   13. Che giorno è?

19·6   1. Sono le diciotto e venti.   2. Vengo alle ventidue e quindici stasera, va bene?   3. Di solito, usciamo alle venti per andare a mangiare.   4. Arriveranno alle ventiquattro.

20·1   **A.** 1. a   2. b   3. b   4. b   5. a   6. b   7. b

B. 1. Ci piace quel libro. / A noi piace quel libro.   2. Ma non ci piacciono quegli altri libri.   3. Lui le piace. / Lui piace a lei.   4. E lei gli piace. / E lei piace a lui.   5. Io piaccio a Maria.   6. (Loro) non mi sono piaciuti.   7. Noi non gli siamo piaciuti. / Noi non siamo piaciuti a lui.   8. Quella musica piace a lui, non a lei.

20·2   **A.** 1. La pizza non è stata mangiata da mia sorella ieri.   2. Solo mio fratello mangia gli spaghetti.   3. Le patate sono mangiate sempre da Alessandro a cena.   4. Tutti leggono quel libro.   5. La macchina giapponese sarà comprata da quella donna.   6. Il mio amico scrisse quell'e-mail tempo fa.   7. Quella giacca è stata comprata da Maria.   8. I miei genitori hanno comprato quella casa.   9. Quella lezione sarà studiata dagli studenti per domani.

B. 1. La lezione è cominciata alle nove.   2. I negozi sono aperti a quest'ora.   3. Si beve quel caffè solo in Italia. / Quel caffè è bevuto solo in Italia.   4. Si mangiano quelle patate solo in Italia. / Quelle patate sono mangiate solo in Italia.   5. Si è vista quella cosa solo in Italia.   6. Si è felici in Italia.   7. Ci si diverte sempre in Italia.

20·3   **A.** 1. a   2. b   3. a   4. b   5. a   6. b   7. b   8. b

B. 1. Maria fa lavare i piatti a sua sorella.   2. Maria li fa lavare a lei. / Maria glieli fa lavare.   3. Lo potrei fare, ma non lo farò.   4. (Loro) cominciano a parlare italiano bene.   5. Marco, devi imparare a usare Internet.   6. (Loro) finiscono sempre di lavorare alle sei.   7. (Noi) cercheremo di rientrare / tornare a casa presto.   8. Hanno sempre voluto / Sono sempre voluti andare in Italia.

C. 1. a   2. b   3. a   4. b   5. a   6. b   7. a   8. b

D. 1. Avrei potuto farlo prima. / Lo avrei potuto fare prima.   2. Vorrei farlo / Lo vorrei fare, ma non posso.   3. Avrei voluto farlo. / Lo avrei voluto fare.   4. Dovrei farlo. / Lo dovrei fare.   5. Avrei dovuto farlo. / Lo avrei dovuto fare.   6. Mia sorella mi ha fatto lavare i piatti.   7. (Io) volevo uscire stasera, ma non posso perché devo studiare.   8. Si possono fare molte cose interessanti in Italia.

20·4   1. I like John, and you don't.   2. The students like the professor a lot.   3. I am sure that my friends will like you.   4. I think that she likes only that type of novel.